WRITING ESSAYS ABOUT LITERATURE
Third Edition

A Guide and Style Sheet

WRITING ESSAYS ABOUT LITERATURE

Third Edition

A Guide and Style Sheet

KELLEY GRIFFITH, JR.
University of North Carolina at Greensboro

HBJ

Harcourt Brace Jovanovich, Publishers

San Diego   New York   Chicago   Austin   Washington, D.C.
London   Sydney   Tokyo   Toronto

Copyrights and Acknowledgments

The author wishes to acknowledge the following publishers and copyright holders for permission to reprint material in this book.

HARCOURT BRACE JOVANOVICH, INC. For excerpts from *The Oedipus Rex of Sophocles: An English Version*, by Dudley Fitts and Robert Fitzgerald. Reprinted by permission of Harcourt Brace Jovanovich, Inc.; copyright 1949 by Harcourt Brace Jovanovich, Inc.; copyright 1977 by Cornelia Fitts and Robert Fitzgerald. And for excerpts from *The Misanthrope* by Molière. Reprinted by permission of Harcourt Brace Jovanovich, Inc.; translated and copyright © 1954, 1955 by Richard Wilbur.

HARVARD UNIVERSITY PRESS For excerpts from the poem "Because I Could Not Stop for Death," by Emily Dickinson. Reprinted by permission of the publishers and the Trustees of Amherst College from *The Poems of Emily Dickinson*, edited by Thomas H. Johnson, Cambridge, Mass.: The Belknap Press of Harvard University Press, copyright 1951, © 1955, 1979, 1983 by The President and Fellows of Harvard College.

THE NEW YORK TIMES For the essay "In Defense of Sentimentality," by John Irving. Copyright © 1979 by the New York Times Company. Reprinted by permission.

ISBN: 0-15-597863-2

Library of Congress Catalog Card Number: 89-84376

Printed in the United States of America

For Gareth and Bronwen

PREFACE

I wrote this book in response to needs that constantly arose in my literature courses. When I assigned out-of-class essays, students would respond with perplexity and even panic: "What should I look for?" "What do you want?" "How long should the essay be?" "Do we have to use footnotes?" Some students had never written essays about literature, at least not for a long time. They felt lost and did not know where to begin. After trying to cope with such responses, I realized I wanted a book that would not only offer my students the assistance they needed but would cover most of the aspects of writing about literature. That book would introduce students to the study of literature, define key terms, explain details of usage, and include whole essays that would serve as illustrations of good student writing.

Although *Writing Essays About Literature: A Guide and Style Sheet* has evolved over its three editions, it still tries to accomplish these purposes. It does so in three general ways. First, it provides guidance in reading literature. Reading well, it stands to reason, is essential to writing well. But reading is also an end in itself, and this book provides an introduction to literature that should make the reading experience rich and fulfilling. The largest section of the book—chapters 3 through 8—discusses the three major genres—fiction, drama, and poetry—and offers ways to analyze individual works. It provides questions and exercises for reviewing and thinking about works. It suggests criteria for evaluating the quality of works. And its reading lists and discussion of critical approaches invite students to expand their studies beyond the scope of this book.

Second, the book offers comprehensive guidance for writing about literature. The organization of the book reflects the four stages of the writing process: prewriting, drafting, revising, and editing. The first part of the book deals with the prewriting or invention stage of the process. Chapter 1 establishes a rationale for writing about literature: Essays about literature are arguments; their purpose is to persuade. Chapter 2 explains strategies for sparking thought processes and for evaluating the quality of topics. Chapters 3 through 8 present methods of generating ideas about individual works that could serve as essay topics and theses. These chapters define the elements of literature, but equally important, they provide devices—questions and "thinking-on-paper" exercises—that should help students use these definitions to develop their own ideas. Chapter 9 covers the next stage of the writing process, drafting. This chapter explains how students can use reasoning and organization as means to move from early to final drafts of the essay.

Third, the book serves as a style sheet for the third and fourth stages of the writing process, revising and editing. Chapter 11 offers general advice about revising, provides rules for quotations and other matters of usage common to essays about literature, and gives guidelines for the appearance and format of the essay. The chapter on documentation (chapter 10) explains what research papers are, how to find information and opinion, how to incorporate them into essays, and how to document sources using MLA style. The book concludes with a chapter on taking essay tests and a chapter containing six student essays—two each on a short story, a poem, and a play. All of these essays illustrate good principles of literary analysis and serve as good examples of student writing.

New in this Third Edition are more suggestions for generating ideas and topics (chapter 2), the "thinking-on-paper" exercises relating to the elements of literature (chapters 4, 5, and 6), more bibliographies "for further reading," an expanded chapter on critical approaches, including post-World War II literary theory (chapter 7), and a new chapter on reasoning and organization (chapter 9).

The book is not meant to be an all-inclusive treatment of the study of literature; rather, it explains succinctly how to go about the rewarding task of thinking about and discussing literature. The work can be used in many ways. Instructors can use it as a textbook in introductory courses or as a supplement in more advanced courses. Students can use it on their own as an introduction to the study of literature, as a guide to writing essays about literature, and as a reference manual.

I am grateful to many people for their help. I am indebted to the writers whose works I have consulted. I thank my colleagues Walter Beale and William Tucker for reading and criticizing this work in its initial stages and for making suggestions for improving it once it was published. My colleague Marilyn Tyler provided thought-provoking reactions to the first draft of the chapter on reasoning and organization in this edition. During the revision of the first edition, I incorporated the valuable comments of Laurence Perrine; Frank Garratt, Tacoma Community College; George Gleason, Southwest Missouri State University; John Hanes, Duquesne University; Jacqueline Hartwich, Bellevue Community College; and Irving Howe, Hunter College. Reviewers for the Second Edition also provided insightful suggestions: Suzanne O. Edwards, The Citadel; James H. Iddings, University of Nevada, Las

Vegas; Peggy H. Phillips, Valencia Community College; Edward Pixley, State University of New York at Oneonta; and Dexter Westrum, Ottawa University. Reviewers for the Third Edition were especially helpful in suggesting ways to emphasize the writing process: Jeff Bagato, Virginia Polytechnic Institute; John Hanes, Duquesne University; and Helen O'Grady, University of Wyoming. I thank my editor Bill McLane for his sympathetic support of this project and for his intelligent guidance of it over the years.

And I am deeply grateful to my family for the encouragement they always give me.

CONTENTS

1

The Essay About Literature

L IKE ALL ART, literature gives pleasure. It has a certain magic that transports us from the "real" world to a seemingly more remote and enjoyable place. We can experience this quality without thinking about it. But literature also poses intellectual challenges that do demand thought. For most readers, grappling with these challenges enhances the pleasure of literature. By studying literature, we "see" more of it to appreciate. And we often learn that, far from being remote from life, good literature pleases by reflecting and giving order to life and by redefining our own place in the real world.

ESSAYS ABOUT LITERATURE ARE USUALLY ARGUMENTS

Essays about literature are written works that take up the intellectual challenges posed by literature. They raise and try to answer fascinating and challenging questions: How does the work reflect its time? How does it reflect the author's life and thought? What does it mean? What are its techniques? Is it good art? Has it had an impact on society? What human problems does it portray? What implications does it have for our own time? But you will write better essays if you recognize another quality of essays about literature: They are almost always arguments. An *argument* is an essay that has three main qualities. It persuades an audience of the validity of your ideas. It uses facts, reasoning, and sometimes testimony (the commentary of people other than yourself) to explain and support your ideas. And it has a *thesis*, one overall point that ties together all the specific claims in the essay.

There are two reasons why essays about literature are usually arguments. The first emerges from the relationship between the work and its reader. Good literature is complex. It communicates on many levels of meaning and by many methods. A single work may exist as a system of sounds, of symbols, of ideas, of images, of analogies, of actions, of psychological portrayals, of moods, of grammatical structures—all of which are separate entities, yet all of which interrelate. Furthermore, good literature also invites the reader to participate in creating the work. A work is not complete until it is read. The author leaves "gaps" in the work for readers to fill with the imagination. The completed work—the work that is read—is something more than the words on the page. It is a collaboration between text and reader. As a result, perceptions of a work vary from age to age, reader to reader, even reading to reading. This variability of perception occurs because no single reading, however careful, can take in all the elements of a work, or synthesize them into all their structural relationships, or include all the vantage points from which even one reader might experience a work.

Consequently, no single view of a work, whether your own or someone else's, can be the all-encompassing or final view. Cultures change, people change, and as a result, perception changes. It is a common experience for people as children to enjoy works—*Huckleberry Finn, Gulliver's Travels,* "Rip Van Winkle," *Alice in Wonderland*—and as adults to enjoy them again, but for very different reasons and with entirely new understandings of them. This does not mean that all interpretations of a work are equally valid. Interpretations of literature are subject to the same rules of human thought—accurate observation, sound reasoning, systematic procedure, thoroughness of treatment—as any other interpretive discourse. But no single interpretation can encompass the whole work.

Because literature is complex and can be perceived variously, essays about literature are usually arguments. You, the writer of the essay, cannot take for granted that your reading of the work is the same as your reader's. Your reader may have missed the very facts in the work you have found most compelling or most "obvious." Your reader may have a totally different understanding of the work from you. If, therefore, you want your reader to grasp your reading or accept it as valid, you must explain and persuade. You must write an argument.

A second reason that essays about literature are usually arguments lies in the relationship between the writer of the essay and the audience of the essay. When you write essays of any kind, you establish a relationship with an audience—your readers. The subject matter of your essay strongly influences the nature of this relationship. Literature is a subject matter that creates certain expectations in your audience. Because literature is a complex product of the imagination, readers of essays about literature expect you to interpret it—to explain, to clarify, to analyze, to give the meaning of it. And interpretation demands argumentation. Consider, by way of comparison, two kinds of essay that differ from argument: the subjective essay and the informational essay. Do they meet an audience's expectations when the subject matter is literature?

In the *subjective essay*, writers retell their own experiences and especially their own emotional reactions to them. The first person pronoun, "I," is omnipresent because the subject matter is really the "I" and the feelings of the "I." People read subjective essays because they are interested in the person writing, in his or her unique point of view, or in the way the person writes, not because they believe the writer is consistently, profoundly, precisely, or objectively developing a given topic. When literature is the topic of the subjective essay, comments about it remain vague and inexact: "In my senior year, I absolutely absorbed *The Great Gatsby*"; "I never could get the hang of Shakespeare's sonnets"; "Hawthorne bores me"; "Last night's production of *Waiting for Godot* left me speechless"; "Caddy's plight in *The Sound and the Fury* never fails to move me deeply"; "Eliot's poetry strikes me as being dryly witty"; "Tolstoy is for me the greatest novelist"; "Shelley's poetry is too abstract." In brief, the subjective essay fails to meet the expectations of an audience interested in literature because the writer says nothing meaningful about it. The audience may learn about the writer but little if anything about the literature.

The *informational essay* is more revealing about literature than the subjective essay but is nonetheless limited in what it can deliver to an audience. As its name suggests, the informational essay exists to present information. Perhaps the best examples of the informational essay are the nonfiction articles in popular magazines like *McCall's* and *Popular Mechanics* or in more literary magazines like the *New York Times Magazine* and *Atlantic Monthly*. These essays may have a unifying idea that looks like a "thesis," but in fact the idea is simply a handy way of framing the facts the article wants to present. The facts are there not to support a line of reasoning or a thesis but because the writer thinks they might be interesting.

Informational essays about literature do exist, and you might have occasion to write one yourself. If so, ask yourself if your audience already knows the information you plan to present or if the audience wants to know it. You could, for example, write an essay showing that the Russian writer Anton Chekhov based the events and characters of his story "The Lady with the Pet Dog" on his own life. But having done that, what have you accomplished? How would you respond to a reader who says, "So what? I wanted to understand Chekhov's story better, and all I am getting from this paper is facts about Chekhov's life"? A limitation of purely informational essays is that they do not *use* the facts they present. There may be times when a reader might be interested in facts about authors, the locals they depict in their works, and the details of how and when their works were written and published. The magazine *National Geographic*, for example, often runs glossy features on authors: Dickens's London, The Brontës' Yorkshire, Twain's Mississippi River, Scott's Scotland, Wordsworth's Lake Country. Presumably the readers of these articles might want to go to these places, or to use the text and photographs to imagine themselves there, or perhaps even to visualize the places described in the works. But usually readers want information about authors and their works in order to understand the works better. This is one feature that informational essays in their purest form do not provide.

The subjective essay and the informational essay rarely exist in "their purest form." If the subjective essay did nothing but express vague emotional reactions or if the informational essay did nothing but present one dry fact after another, each would probably be unreadable or at least extremely boring. Rather, both kinds of essay typically contain some elements of argumentation, just as many argumentative essays contain some elements of the informational and the subjective essays. Our point here is that whatever an essay about literature might contain of the subjective and the informational, it is predominately argumentative. It backs up its key claims, including those of an emotional origin, with reasoning, and it uses most of its facts to develop that reasoning. It does these things because literature requires interpretation and because readers of essays about literature want and expect interpretation.

A LITERARY CONTROVERSY

The people who make a profession of writing essays about literature are called literary critics, and the product of their writing is literary criticism. Literary criticism is not "criticism" in the sense that it searches out and exposes the bad qualities of something. Rather, it analyzes literature. Its purpose is to explain works of literature to interested readers. When you write essays about literature, you are writing literary criticism.

The following essay was written by a professional writer, the novelist John Irving, and it illustrates the argumentative nature of essays about literature. This essay deals with a well-known literary controversy—the appropriateness of the ending of Charles Dickens's novel *Great Expectations* (1861). There would probably be no controversy had Dickens not written two endings rather than one. He wrote the second ending after his friend Edward Bulwer Lytton urged him to provide a "happy ending" that would unite Pip, the protagonist, and Estella, the beautiful but perverse object of Pip's affections. Just before publication, Dickens suppressed the first ending, in which Pip says goodbye forever to Estella, and substituted the second, in which Pip and Estella look toward a future together. Until the twentieth century, the second ending had been printed in all editions of the novel and had stirred no controversy, but in 1937 George Bernard Shaw published a new edition of the novel and included the first ending instead of the second. He claimed in his preface that the first was the better ending. Since then, many critics have agreed with Shaw. Most recent editions print both endings, so readers can decide for themselves.

John Irving addresses this controversy and another one that he sees related to it: Dickens's sentimentality. Many twentieth-century critics have downgraded Dickens's work because of its sometimes extravagant sentimentality. Irving published the essay in the *New York Times Book Review* shortly before Christmas, a time of widespread indulgence in sentimentality. And he begins by discussing Dickens's most famous work, *A Christmas Carol*. But Irving means for the essay to speak for all times of the year, not just Christmas.

IN DEFENSE OF SENTIMENTALITY

JOHN IRVING

Well over a century ago, Dickens gave his first public reading of *A Christmas Carol*—it was just two days after Christmas, and 2,000 people gave the author their rapt attention (and frequent applause). The reading took three hours, though in later years Dickens would prune *A Christmas Carol* to a two-hour performance; he liked it well enough that first time, however, to repeat the reading three days later—to an audience of 2,500, almost exclusively composed of working people, for whom he had requested that the auditorium be reserved. He thought they were his best audience. "They lost nothing, misinterpreted nothing, followed everything closely, laughed and cried," Dickens said, "and [they] animated me to the extent that I felt as if we were all bodily going up into the clouds together."

I wish I could have been there. I try to imagine it, every Christmas, when I watch the new and old television versions of *A Christmas Carol;* some are better than others, and in some I can imagine Dickens himself—who loved to act—taking the part of Scrooge, or playing the Ghost of Christmas Past. Dickens might have enjoyed the mesmerizing popularity of television, though he surely would have detested the lifelessness of television's language; it was at his insistence that the price of *A Christmas Carol* was held to five shillings—so that it might reach a wider audience.

In his biography of Charles Dickens, Edgar Johnson writes, "*A Christmas Carol* is a serio-comic parable of social redemption, and Scrooge's conversion is the conversion for which Dickens hopes among mankind." Indeed, it is the hopefulness of that inspired dream of a book (Tiny Tim is spared, and Scrooge sees the error of his ways) that makes *A Christmas Carol* ever-appropriate for Christmas. "Against Scrooge and the orthodox economists," Mr. Johnson writes, "Dickens insists that no way of life is sound or rewarding that leaves out men's need of loving and of being loved."

And, in the spirit of Christmas, who could fault *A Christmas Carol?* "Who can listen," Thackeray said, "to objections regarding such a book as this? It seems to me a national benefit, and to every man or woman who reads it a personal kindness." It is surprising, however, how many readers reserve Dickens—and hopefulness in general—for Christmas; it seems that what we applaud in Dickens—his kindness, his generosity, his belief in our dignity—is also what we condemn him for (under another name) in the off-Christmas season.

The other name is sentimentality—and, to the modern reader, too often when a writer risks being sentimental, the writer is already guilty. But as a writer it is cowardly to so fear sentimentality that one avoids it altogether. It is typical—and forgivable—among student writers to avoid being mush-minded by simply refusing to write about people, or by refusing to subject characters to emotional extremes. A short story about a four-course meal from the point of view of a fork will never be sentimental; it may never matter very much to us, either. A fear of contamination by soap opera haunts the educated writer—and reader—though we both forget that in the hands of a clod, *Madame Bovary* would have been perfect material for daytime television and a contemporary treatment of *The Brothers Karamazov* could be stuck with a campus setting. Dickens took Christmas risks all the year round.

"I must make the most I can out of the book," he said, before beginning *Great Expectations*—"I think [it's] a good name?" he said. Good, indeed, and a title many writers wish were free for them to use, a title many wonderful novels could have had: *The Great Gatsby, To the Lighthouse, The Mayor of Casterbridge, The Sun Also Rises, Moby Dick*—all great expectations, of course.

Yet the hopefulness that makes everyone love *A Christmas Carol* draws fire when Dickens employs it in his best novel; when Christmas is over, Dickens's original ending to *Great Expectations,* that Pip and his impossible love, Estella, should stay apart, is thought to be the proper (and certainly the modern) conclusion—from which Dickens eventually shied away; for such a change of heart and mind, he is accused of selling out. After an early manhood of shallow goals, Pip is meant finally to see the falseness of his values—and of Estella—and he emerges as a sadder though a wiser fellow. Many have expressed how Dickens stretches credulity too far when he leads us to suppose—in his revised ending—that Estella and Pip could be happy ever after; or that anyone can. Of his new ending—where Pip and Estella are reconciled—Dickens himself remarked to a friend: "I have put in a very pretty piece of writing, and I have no doubt the story will be more acceptable through the alteration." That Estella would make Pip—or anyone—a rotten wife is not the point; they are linked: Happily or unhappily, they belong together.

Biographically, it is difficult to resist the association of Pip's trapped worship of Estella with Dickens's own sad adoration of the young actress, Ellen Ternan. Although the suggestion that Dickens revise the original ending came from his friend Bulwer Lytton, who wished the book to end on a happier note, Edgar Johnson wisely points out that "the changed ending reflected a desperate hope that Dickens could not banish from within his own heart." That hope is no last-minute alteration, tacked-on, but simply the culmination of a hope that abides throughout the novel: that Estella might change; after all, Pip changes. The book isn't called *Great Expectations* for nothing. It is not, I think, meant to be an entirely bitter title.

In fact, it is the first ending that is out of character—for Dickens, and for the novel. Pip, upon meeting Estella (after two years of hearing only rumors of her), remarks with a pinched heart: "I was very glad afterwards to have had the interview; for in her face, and in her voice, and in her touch, she gave me the assurance that suffering had been stronger than Miss Havisham's teaching, and had given her a heart to understand what my heart used to be." Although that tone—of self-congratulation and self-pity— is more modern than Dickens's romantic revision, I fail to see how we or our literature would be better for it.

The revised ending reads: "I took her hand in mine, and we went out of the ruined place; and, as the morning mists had risen long ago when I first left the forge, so the evening mists were rising now, and in all the broad expanse of tranquil light they showed me, I saw no shadow of another parting from her." A very pretty piece of writing, as Dickens noted, but eternally open—still ambiguous (Pip's hopes have been dashed before)—and far more the mirror of the quality of trust in the novel as a whole. It is that hopeful ending that sings with all the rich contradiction we should love Dickens for; it both underlines and undermines everything before it. Pip is basically good, basically gullible; he starts out being human, he learns by error, he keeps on being human. That touching illogic seems not only generous but true.

"When people say that Dickens exaggerates," George Santayana writes, "it seems to me that they can have no eyes and no ears. They probably have only *notions* of what things and people are; they accept them conventionally, at their diplomatic value." And to those who contend that no one was ever so sentimental, or that there was no one ever like Wemmick or Jaggers or Bentley Drummle, to name a few, Santayana says: "The polite world is lying; there *are* such people; we are such people ourselves in our true moments, in our veritable impulses; but we are careful to stifle and hide those moments from ourselves and from the world; to purse and pucker ourselves into the mask of conventional personality; and so simpering, we profess that it is very coarse and inartistic of Dickens to undo our life's work for us in an instant, and remind us of what we are." Santayana is also brilliant at defending Dickens's stylistic excesses: "He mimics things to the full; he dilates and exhausts and repeats; he wallows," Santayana admits, though he adds, "this faculty, which renders him a consummate comedian, is just what alienated him from a later generation in which people of taste were aesthetes and virtuous people were higher snobs; they wanted a mincing art, and he gave them copious improvisation, they wanted analysis and development, and he gave them absolute comedy."

Christmas—or any other demonstration of giving—is no time for "a mincing art"; we should learn that there is really no good time for such cramped elitism. "God bless us every one!" cried Tiny Tim. But this Christmas, since we're so familiar with *A Christmas Carol*—in its several versions—we might well read *Great Expectations;* it is a book many of us read last when we were in school, when we were too young to appreciate it. For its Christmas spirit—its open-hearted and forgiving qualities, and its feast of language—it is the best of novels by a writer of no mincing art.

And when we writers—in our own work—escape the slur of sentimentality, we should ask ourselves if what we are doing matters.

Irving's essay has characteristics of both the subjective and the informational essay. As you would expect in a subjective essay, Irving frequently uses "I," and he expresses some opinions that seem personal, emotional, and vague. He calls *A Christmas Carol* a "dream of a book." He says that neither we nor our literature are "better" for the first ending of *Great Expectations.* He urges us to read *Great Expectations* because it is a "feast of language." And as you would expect in an informational essay, Irving presents information that is interesting for itself and that does not seem at first glance germane to any points he is making. This is especially true of the opening paragraph, which he uses as an attention grabber. Furthermore, there is an informal quality to the essay, imparted partly by Irving's familiar tone and his somewhat rambling organization.

Nonetheless, Irving's essay is an argument. It is an argument because he has a thesis (or something like one), he develops a line of reasoning, and he uses facts, including those that at first seem irrelevant, to support his claims. He even brings in testimony from several "experts" to strengthen the credibility of his positions: Edgar Johnson (Dickens's biographer), William Makepeace Thackeray (a great novelist and a contemporary of Dickens), and George Santayana (a twentieth-century American philosopher). Irving does not neatly lay out his argument so that its logical structure is immediately clear; but if you were to outline his line of thought, the outline would look something like this:

1. Question: Is sentimentality, which twentieth-century people so distrust, a bad quality—not just in literature but in life? (Irving does not state this question, but it lies behind the main point of the essay.)

2. Answer: No, sentimentality is not bad, because it expresses love, hope, trust, and a concern for people. (This is Irving's thesis; it answers the above question.)

3. An example of the practice and goodness of sentimentality is the life and work of Charles Dickens.

4. Two works in particular illustrate Dickens's sentimentality: *A Christmas Carol* and *Great Expectations*.

5. *A Christmas Carol* is sentimental because it involves us emotionally with people who love or need love. (To support this point, Irving draws facts not only from the novel but from Dickens's life—the facts at the beginning of the essay about how much Dickens enjoyed the emotional reactions of the working-class audience at his second reading.)

6. *Great Expectations* is sentimental because it is about hope and trust. The second ending, which reflects hope and trust, is thus better than the first, which does not. (Here again, Irving combines facts from the novel with facts about Dickens's life—Dickens's desperate hope that he and his mistress Ellen Ternan would live happily together—to support this point.)

7. In conclusion, the "sentimental" consists of a number of important qualities, all of which we can see at work in the spirit of Christmas and in the work of Charles Dickens: caring about and loving people, trusting in people and fate, hoping for the best that people can become. In our age, intellectuals have suppressed an open and emotional expression of these qualities. But if we do not admit the sentimental into our art and lives, our art may not matter and we may not matter.

Irving's essay illustrates a final point concerning essays about literature: They are usually dialogues between writer and reader. As *writers* of an argument we need to anticipate the reservations, objections, and questions readers may have about our ideas. Irving does this constantly when he explains how "modern readers"—including the readers of his essay—might react to Dickens's work. As *readers* of an argument we can do something we cannot do with the subjective or informational essay: We can argue back. Neither the subjective nor the informational essay assumes a dialogue between writer and reader—at least, not an extensive dialogue—but the argument always does. What can you say in response to a subjective statement of opinion except "Oh, that's nice" or "My, how opinionated you are"? How can you respond to statements of fact except "Yes, your facts are correct" or "No, they aren't." But in an argument you can reply to the *ideas* of the writer: Do you agree with Irving? Do you accept his definition of *sentimentality*? Do you agree with his claim that there is a modern distaste for the sentimental? Do you agree with his insinuation that intellectuality and emotionalism are mutually exclusive? Are there qualities of hope, trust, love, and concern that we ought to distrust? Are Dickens and the Christmas season the best sources for a definition of sentimentality?

In other words, Irving's essay is not the end of the matter. You can write a response to him, and he or someone else can write a response to you, and so on and so forth until everyone agrees or drops the topic. All argumentative essays assume there is an audience out there that may challenge and question all you say. But the writer *wants* an intelligent and critical response. You do not write arguments to browbeat an audience into accepting your ideas. Otherwise you would write purely emotional persuasion, like advertisements, or propaganda, which demands only one response: Don't think, just believe. Rather, you write arguments because you care about the free exchange of ideas. You care about what other people think. You care about the quest for truth. And you care about your subject matter.

2

How to Choose a Topic

W HAT CAN I write about?" Probably the hardest part of writing an essay, whether about literature or anything else, is answering this question. Choosing a good topic is a creative act, and like most creative acts, certain qualities of thought and circumstance must be present for it to occur. Although no set of guidelines can provide a foolproof formula for generating topics, this chapter contains suggestions that should at least get you started.

STEPS IN CHOOSING A TOPIC

1. Read the Work Well

The first thing you must do is read the work well. You might think that this is easy, that all you have to do is read one word after another they way you read anything. But beyond the purely mechanical act of reading, there are tricks to doing it well.

The greatest difficulty some people face when they read is that they cannot "get into" the work. They find it boring or strange, so that even though they are conscientious about reading, nothing much sinks in. Surely everyone has this experience at some time or another. Missing from the experience is an imaginative involvement with the work. Some kinds of literature easily grip the imagination—popular literature like detective novels and thrillers, for example. When this happens, you transfer yourself imaginatively into the world of the work and block out the real world. You lose yourself in the work. One reason for this is that literature is always concrete and experiential. The author may want to make certain abstract points, but he or she does so by representing a concrete world you can experience vicariously. If no barriers keep you from grasping that concrete world and if you find it attractive, then you slip into it and forget everything else.

But barriers sometimes do exist that prevent such an imaginative transference to works of literature. The work may be old, so that the language or conventions of the work seem strange. The work may be in a form that requires more study than usual. Poetry, for example, is a concentrated and elliptical form. The work may be written by authors who are experimenting with new forms. A work may contain complex or unfamiliar ideas. A good beginning toward getting past these barriers is simply to admit that they exist and identify the ones that seem to apply to your situation. Do not be embarrassed to make such an admission; you are probably not alone. The next step is to do something about eliminating the barriers. Here are some suggestions:

1. Set aside enough time to do the reading, find a place free from distractions, and concentrate on what you read.

2. Read the work at least twice. This is easy to do for short poems, but time may limit your doing it for long works. If you are pressed for time, one strategy is to skim the work to get your bearings and then to reread it carefully. Don't bog down. Skim the parts that seem interminable. Once you have finished reading, you may see how the parts you skimmed are important and find them more interesting the second time around. The most practical strategy is probably to read carefully the first time, underlining key passages as you go, then skim it the second time, paying careful attention to notes taken from class and to your underlinings. You might want to combine these two strategies, reading carefully most of the first time through but skimming when you are in danger of bogging down.

Read poems more than once. If you find yourself mystified by a poem after the first time through, read it again. The more times you read a poem carefully, the more it should become clear to you.

3. Try to project yourself consciously into the situation created by the work. Don't assume that you can automatically make an imaginative transference to all literature. Instead, assume that you must bring to the work something like the same mind-set and knowledge the author took for granted in the original audience. To achieve the status of "ideal intended audience" is probably impossible, especially for older works. But you can go a long way toward attaining this end by locating the

"key" to the work. The key is the knowledge you lack to make the imaginative transference the intended audience could make automatically. Try to recover some of that knowledge.

You may be able to recognize the key simply by studying the work carefully and treating it as a puzzle you need to solve. Poems with complex verbal relationships are often solvable in this way. But sometimes the key lies *outside* the work—in historical and biographical circumstances, in facts about the form of the work, and in explanations of the author's philosophical ideas. For example, it is difficult to understand the poetry of William Butler Yeats without knowing facts both about historical events in Ireland during his lifetime and about people he knew. Similarly, it is helpful to know something about stream-of-consciousness techniques when you read James Joyce's *Ulysses*, Virginia Woolf's *Mrs. Dalloway*, T. S. Eliot's "The Love Song of J. Alfred Prufrock," and William Faulkner's *The Sound and the Fury*. It is advantageous to know something about existentialist philosophy when you read Albert Camus's *The Stranger* and *The Plague* or Jean Paul Sartre's *No Exit*. It helps to know something about the theories underlying American Romanticism when you read Ralph Waldo Emerson's essays. It is much easier to project yourself into Geoffrey Chaucer's literary world if you know something about medieval Christianity, symbolism, and cosmology, and if you have a basic understanding of Middle English.

Your instructor, of course, should help provide such keys; but if you are on your own, you need to seek out secondary sources. Writers and works, especially those that are notoriously difficult, usually have been written about extensively. Begin with introductory treatments of them. If you must cope with Faulkner's *The Sound and the Fury*, for example, try Edmond Volpe's *A Reader's Guide to William Faulkner* (New York: Farrar 1964), which offers chapters on Faulkner himself, on his techniques, and on each of his major works. The sections on *The Sound and the Fury* give brief plot summaries, genealogical tables, and even specific notations on where the time shifts occur in the stream-of-consciousness sections of the novel. For some people, strange and difficult works like *The Sound and the Fury* are fun to read just because they are strange and difficult. These readers find fresh approaches and intellectual puzzles challenging and may not want or need outside help. But for most readers, works like Volpe's save time and provide more immediate access to the work.

4. Project yourself into the work. Your imaginative participation in many works is unconscious and automatic, but some works may

require conscious participation. This means that you must add personal information to the work that will make it meaningful to you. Perhaps the best way to do this is to find parallels in your own life—what you know about, the kind of person you are—to the ideas and situations in the work. In effect you are asking, "What would my life be like in these circumstances? How would I be affected by the ideas undergirding the work?"

If your task is to read Puritan American literature, for example, imagine how you would think and feel had you lived then—about your family responsibilities, the wilderness surrounding you, the harsh physical circumstances of your existence, the loved ones left behind in England, your religious goals, your sexuality, your war against disease, the hostile Indians hidden in the forests. What would your outlook be if you believed that the Devil might pop out from behind a tree at any moment and tempt you to attend a witch's meeting? How would you feel about your community if large groups of people were backsliding from the fervent goals of the first settlers? What would your psychological state be if you thought *you* were one of the backsliders? What mental conflicts would you undergo if your experience conflicted with the dogma of your religion? Would you want to hide certain feelings and deeds from your Puritan peers? Answering such questions should help you recapture the literary worlds of Anne Bradstreet, Edward Taylor, Mary Rowlandson, and Jonathan Edwards. These writers' circumstances, beliefs, and assumptions about their original audiences are so remote from us that we have to make a *conscious* imaginative effort to read their work with sympathy and understanding.

5. As you read longer works, like novels, plays, and narrative poems, try to grasp the ideas the author is developing. A work of literature is always *about* something. This "aboutness" is the work's ideas. By identifying ideas, you help yourself understand relationships among details and parts of the work. Some critics argue that recognizing the ideas in a work helps you *notice* important details. This act of interpretation is essential for getting a sense of the whole work once you have finished reading it, but you can begin formulating theories about the work's meaning as you read. Your hypotheses will help you pay attention and will propel you from section to section. Don't worry if you revise your interpretations as you go along. You cannot get a complete understanding of the work's ideas until you have finished it, but part of the suspense and thus the interest of reading a work is to notice the interplay of ideas and to see which ones will predominate in the end.

If reading a work, then, seems boring or frustrating, it may be because you are missing its ideas. You can raise your level of interest by consciously asking questions about the work's meaning as you read, especially after each major section of the work—after each chapter in a novel, for example. What is the author trying to say about social structures, ethical dilemmas, love, the nature of art, problems of communication, and so forth? What comments does the author make about the work's meaning? What ideas are implicit in the work's details? What attitudes toward life do the major characters seem to represent? Does one set of values conflict with another? Do characters change their ideas? Does the author address issues prevalent at the time of writing? How might readers at the time of publication have responded to the author's subject matter and ideas? How do you respond to them? Do they seem archaic and naïve or fresh and relevant?

The characters in a work are a particularly good place to look for the ideas represented in a work. A novel about a strike in a steel manufacturing city in the late nineteenth century, for example, might have a number of conflicting ideas, each represented by a different character. The owner of the steel mill might represent unrestrained capitalism. The leader of the strike might represent the peaceful use of existing legal and political systems to solve social problems. A fanatical member of the union might represent the belief in violence as a catalyst for change. A priest might represent meditation and religous faith as the proper response to suffering. And different workers might represent other responses to the plight of the oppressed. The number of ideas in a work are often limited only by the number of characters the author can put in. As you read, you begin to wonder which of these ideas will win out and which ones the author seems to sympathize with. So to help yourself read intelligently and with interest, *think* about what these ideas might be.

2. Identify Your Audience

After reading the work at least once with care, your next step toward choosing a topic is to think about the essay you want to write. The most logical place to begin is with your audience. An essay is a communication. With whom do you communicate? What do they want from you? What effect do you want to have on them?

When you write essays for college courses, you have two and possibly three audiences. One is the instructor. The effect you want to have on the instructor (one assumes) is to make him or her think well of your essay and give it a good grade. Be aware, then, of the instructor's criteria for judging student essays. If the instructor is like most, he or she will want a well-crafted essay—clear statement of thesis, logical and coherent organization, fluent and correct prose style, convincingly supported claims, and so forth. But the instructor will probably base his or her judgment on a more general criterion: how well your essay communicates to a general audience, an audience larger than just the instructor.

Several advantages result from writing for a general audience rather than for just your instructor. First, you practice skills of communication useful once you leave college. Your writing in the "real world" will usually be for groups of people, not just one person. A second advantage is that by meeting the needs of a general audience, you will almost certainly meet the requirements of your instructor. In fact, you will probably write a better essay if you write for a general audience than for just your instructor. The reason is that you won't take for granted—that is, leave out—the facts and reasoning that *both* a general audience and your instructor need to understand and to be convinced by you. When writing solely for the instructor, students often think, "The instructor already knows this, so I won't put it in." In fact, the instructor *does* want you to put it in. The instructor cannot read your mind. He or she must see how you arrived at the claims you make.

Who, then, makes up your reading audience? Two groups who probably will *not* are, first, experts on your subject and, second, people intellectually incapable of grasping your reasoning (children, for example). You could write for both of these audiences. But if you wrote for an audience of experts, you would have to be an expert yourself and, furthermore, have something to tell them that they do not already know. Most college students do not have enough time to master subjects that thoroughly. This, by the way, is another reason for not writing solely for your instructor. The instructor is an "expert" who, fortunately, rarely expects students to meet an expert's demands. On the other hand, if you wrote for the mentally immature, your essay would be too simpleminded for college courses.

Instead, write for an audience consisting of people who are intelligent, who have read or can read the work you want to discuss, and who want to understand it better. Assume that this audience consists of people who are your equals; they form a community of which you are a part, to whom you can talk with equal authority. They share your interests and eagerly await your comments. If it will help, visualize people you know—classmates, boyfriends, girlfriends, relatives, students at other campuses, people anywhere who enjoy literature—as belonging to this audience. When you write, imagine yourself in dialogue with them, saying things that would interest them, responding to their questions and comments. Project an image of yourself as the conscientious searcher for truth. Let your audience know that you are doing everything capable, within the limits of your time and ability, to answer the questions you have raised.

A third audience is yourself. Writing essays is one way of satisfying your own intellectual needs and desires. Writing is not simply the end product of thinking; it is a *way* of thinking. Some theorists argue that not until you write out your ideas can you be sure you have thought them through carefully. The process of writing essays, for example, underscores the need to use sound logic, to include all the steps in your reasoning, to state ideas precisely in order to produce arguments that will withstand the scrutiny of objective and intelligent people. It is easy *not* to do these things when you are just thinking to yourself or speaking to other people. Francis Bacon's maxim calls attention to this result of writing: "Reading maketh a full man, conference a ready man, and writing an exact man."

But perhaps the most important effect on you of the writing process is its ability to draw forth your ideas. One kind of essay about literature is the essay examination (discussed in chapter 12). You may find essay examinations burdensom and even traumatic; but in writing them students often discover ideas they never knew they had. That is, the writing process mates the students' knowledge of literature with the instructor's questions to give birth to new ideas. Essays about literature, then, can be journeys of self-discovery in which you happen upon new intellectual vistas as you write. In this sense, you are part of your audience. You share your readers' curiosity and their desire to have puzzling questions answered. You write to convince them; but you write also to discover and clarify your own ideas and to convince yourself of their validity.

3. Raise a Key Question About the Work

Identifying your audience provides a rationale for the final step, choosing the topic itself. Your audience is interested in the work you wish to discuss; they want to understand it better. As we said in chapter 1, you could write an informational essay to satisfy this desire—*if* you felt your audience wanted to know this information and could use it to understand the work better. But more than likely, you will write an argument—an interpretation you explain and defend with facts and reasoning. But what will you interpret—everything in the work or just some part of it? You probably do not have time or space to interpret everything, so you will have to limit yourself to a part of the work. But which part?

The answer: Write about any aspect of the work that you think presents a problem of interpretation to your reader. The topic of your paper, then, is a "problem"; your paper explains the problems and offers a solution to it. Put another way, your topic is based on a question; your paper identifies that question and provides an answer to it. This is *always* true of argumentative essays. You might announce your topic as something like "Hamlet's Indecision" or "Macbeth's Hunger for Power," but your audience will ask, "Well, what *about* Hamlet's indecision or Macbeth's hunger for power?" The audience knows that lying behind topics like these are questions—Why does Hamlet hesitate to act? What propels Macbeth to seek power and to keep on seeking it?— and that the reason for raising such topics is to answer the questions lying behind them. You do not *have* to state your topic in the form of a question, but good topics always *imply* questions of interpretation. Otherwise you would have no reason to write papers on them; you would have nothing to say.

4. Choose a "Good" Topic

What makes a topic good? One way to judge the quality of an essay topic is to ask yourself how easily an average reader could answer the question that lies behind it. A useful guideline is that a topic is "good" if most readers could *not* answer the question after reading the work once. That is, readers could not answer it convincingly, either for themselves or for others, without reviewing and studying the work. The topic must be genuinely thought-provoking.

A second consideration is the meaningfulness of the topic. In order for a topic to be good, it should be worth considering. Admittedly, there is a subjective judgment called for here. Some members of your audience may think a question worth answering; others may not. But this is a judgment you can train yourself to make. A topic is good if you think most members of your audience would learn from a discussion of it. It should help you, when making this decision, to imagine yourself as part of your audience. Generally, what intrigues you should intrigue them. Common sense should tell you that one of the *least* intriguing questions is, What happened in the work? True, the events and details of works are sometimes hard to understand and need clarification (in William Faulkner's or T. S. Eliot's writings, for example), but usually readers can understand a work's details after reading it one time. There is no need to provide information your audience already knows.

A third way to assess the quality of a topic is to ask if it is focused narrowly enough for the confines of your essay. Most of the essays you write for college literature classes will run from three to ten typewritten pages (900 to 3,000 words). Your topic is good if you can deal with it thoroughly within those limits. For example, "comedy in *Romeo and Juliet*" would be too broad for an essay topic; "the nurse as comic figure" would be more specific and manageable. "Love in *Romeo and Juliet*" would be too broad; "Juliet's mature love versus Romeo's adolescent love" would be better. "Values in *Romeo and Juliet*"—too broad; "Shakespeare's attitude toward suicide"—better. "Juliet as character"—too broad; "Juliet's change from child to young woman"—better.

Charlotte Brontë's novel *Jane Eyre* provides an example of an essay topic that meets all three criteria. Brontë grew up absorbing the superstitions of the English north country. These superstitions included beliefs in fairies, elves, and demons, and one does not have to read far into *Jane Eyre* before encountering references to them. Jane, the narrator and main character, says that as a child she looked for elves in vain "under mushrooms and beneath the ground-ivy" and concluded that "they were all gone out of England to some savage country where the woods were wilder and thicker, and the population more scant." After her first encounter with Mr. Rochester, he accuses her of being a fairy who "bewitched" his horse and caused it to fall. Her reply is that the fairies "all forsook England a hundred years ago." Throughout her relationship, he calls her "elf," "fairy," "dream," "changeling," "sprite." After she returns at the end of the novel, he reverts to his epithets, once again calling her "fairy," "ghost," "changeling," "fairy-born and human-bred."

A topic for an essay about *Jane Eyre*, then, might be its use of fairy lore. (The title of the essay might be "Charlotte Brontë's Use of Fairy Lore in *Jane Eyre*.") The question underlying the topic would be, What significance does this lore have in the novel? The purpose of the essay would be, first, to raise this question; second, to show that the fairy lore actually does exist in the novel; and third, to provide an answer to the question. This answer would be the "thesis" of the essay. The topic is meaningful because fairy lore is prominent in the work and is consistently associated with the main character; the topic promises to teach the reader a great deal about the novel. Furthermore, the topic is complex enough so that a reader could not answer its implicit question fully and convincingly without rereading and studying the novel. And the topic is specific enough to be dealt with thoroughly in an essay of about 1,200 to 1,500 words. The topic, in short, is "good." For other examples of good topics as well as how they are developed, see the sample essay in chapter 13.

5. Use Search Strategies to Generate Good Topics

For some people, finding good topics is easy and automatic. A student might be reading *Jane Eyre* and just happen to notice the references to fairies, and think, "Hey, that would be interesting to write about." For others, however, discovering good topics is difficult and frustrating, capable of inducing a severe case of writer's block. One writer can experience both situations. You might find that one work suggests all kinds of topics, whereas another leaves you at a total loss. If you ever find yourself in the latter situation, try a search strategy.

A *search strategy* is a procedure for locating and examining important aspects of a work. It is a self-teaching device that helps you think and learn about the work. As you examine the work, you become aware of areas you can raise questions about, questions that may lead to good topics. Some search strategies allow you to examine works of literature more thoroughly than others. Some have been used for decades; others are fairly new; you may be able to invent still others on your own. Here is a list and brief discussion of several of them.

Analysis Analysis allows a thorough and systematic investigation of works of literature. So useful is this strategy that the next four chapters are devoted to it.

Traditional patterns of thinking Generations of communicators have recognized that certain ways of thinking—patterns of thought—are helpful tools for examining subjects and developing ideas about them. In his *Rhetoric*, perhaps the greatest of all books about writing, Aristotle called these patterns *topoi*, which means "places." Aristotle seems to have meant that these patterns are "places" to look when you need to find ideas. Several of the traditional patterns are especially useful—at times inevitable—for generating ideas about literature and for providing methods of explaining it. The patterns are definition, structural analysis, process analysis, comparison, and cause-and-effect analysis.

Because these *topoi* are ways not only of locating topics but of developing essays about them, they are discussed in chapter 9 (on style and organization).

Comments by critics   A fruitful source of topics is comments by literary critics. Critics write about individual works, about an author's entire work, about the nature of literature itself, and about many other things as well. Your purpose would be to make a critic's whole approach or an isolated comment by a critic the starting point of your essay. Chapter 7 outlines several well-known critical approaches to literature, but consider for the moment how a student might use the following observation about narrative made by Terry Eagleton in *Literary Theory: An Introduction* (Minneapolis: U of Minnesota P, 1983):

> Watching his grandson playing in his pram one day, Freud observed him throwing a toy out of the pram and exclaiming *fort!* (gone away), then hauling it in again on a string to the cry of *da!* (here). This, the famous *fort-da* game, Freud interpreted in *Beyond the Pleasure Principle* (1920) as the infant's symbolic mastery of its mother's absence; but it can also be read as the first glimmerings of narrative. *Fort-da* is perhaps the shortest story we can imagine: an object is lost, and then recovered. But even the most complex narratives can be read as variants on this model: the pattern of classical narrative is that an original settlement is disrupted and ultimately restored. (185)

Here, Eagleton states a quality in narrative that many people have probably not thought about consciously: that there is a lost-and-found pattern and variations on it in many narratives. Examples abound: Homer's *The Odyssey*, Milton's *Paradise Lost*, Melville's *Moby-Dick*, Coleridge's *The Rime of the Ancient Mariner*, Keats's "La Belle Dame Sans Merci," Shakespeare's *King Lear*, Jane Austen's *Pride and Prejudice*.

You could make Eagleton's comment the basis for an essay about a particular narrative—a novel, a short story, a poem, or a play. You would try to explain how the pattern or a variation on it operates in your narrative. You would begin your essay by explaining Eagleton's idea, giving proper credit to him. (For when and how to give credit in your essays, see chapter 10.) Then you would try to answer questions such as these: What has been lost? How was it lost? How are the protagonists trying to recover it? Do they succeed? What qualities allow them to succeed or cause them to fail?

Eagleton's comment covers many works of literature, but critics also write extensively about individual works. You could use a critic's idea about a specific work as a starting point for an essay. You could write your essay in support of the idea or in disagreement with it. For an explanation of how to find critical interpretations of individual works, see the treatment of sources in chapter 10, pp. 178–82. For a complete student essay based on a critic's comment, see the essay on Edwin Arlington Robinson's "Richard Cory" in chapter 13.

When you think of literary criticism, you may think only of published works. But don't forget your instructor and the other students in your class. Your instructor is a critic who "publishes" comments in class, out loud to you. And students often make interesting responses to the instructor and to one another. All of these comments can provide excellent starting points for essays. An example of such an essay is the sample essay in chapter 13 on Emily Dickinson's "Because I Could Not Stop for Death."

Your own knowledge   Students at all levels of achievement often fail to realize that they know a great deal and are learning all the time. If you are a college student, you may be taking an English course, but you are most likely taking other courses in a wide range of disciplines. All of this knowledge interconnects, even though for practical reasons colleges chop it up into schools, departments, and courses. You can and may bring this knowledge to bear on works of literature. Subject areas such as psychology, sociology, philosophy, design, art history, history of science, religious studies, cultural history, political history, even landscape gardening throw powerful beams of light on authors and literature. Ibsen's Hedda Gabler (in the play *Hedda Gabler*) is a deeply troubled person. Can you find in your psychology textbooks theories that would help explain her problems? Ernest Hemingway said in an early version of "Big Two-Hearted River" that he wanted to write the way the French Impressionist Paul Cézanne painted. Can you explain Hemingway's themes and methods by comparing his writing to Cézanne's pictures and theories of art? In the poem "Heritage" Countee

Cullen conveys an ambivalent attitude toward Africa. How does the American understanding (or misunderstanding) of Africa at the time he wrote the poem (1925) both mirror his attitude and help explain his frustration? Anton Chekhov wrote plays at the turn of the twentieth century. What happened in Russia at that time, politically and socially, that clarifies the intellectual currents in his plays?

Another kind of knowledge students often overlook or discount is their own experience. Most students have developed expertise outside the academic world—through work, travel, family activities, personal experience of many kinds—and this expertise sometimes can illuminate works of literature. Have you done some sailing? If so, you might be able to explain the complex maneuvers the young captain makes at the end of Joseph Conrad's "The Secret Sharer" and suggest what this knowledge tells us about the captain. (Is he taking a foolish, irresponsible risk?) Speaking of Conrad, have you been to Zaire, the setting of *Heart of Darkness*? If so, are vestiges of the colonialism he despises in that novel still there? What can you tell us about the landscape and atmosphere of the country that would help us better understand this puzzling novel? Have you seen any bullfights? If so, you might help the rest of us understand the symbolic meaning of bullfighting in Hemingway's fiction. Have you been the victim of prejudice? If so, you should be able to give insights into the dynamics of bigotry dramatized in Bernard Malamud's *The Assistant* and Richard Wright's *Black Boy*.

6. Use Exercises to Help You Think Creatively

Once you have identified your audience, fixed in your mind the qualities of a good topic, studied the work, and perhaps even read some criticism of the work, you may still need some way of finding *your* topic. After doing all these things, many people discover topics easily and are ready to proceed to the next stage—writing drafts of the essay. But you may be stuck. The following exercises are some approaches to help get you unstuck.

Conversing   Imagine yourself talking to a friend about the work you want to write about. Or, perhaps better, find a real person to talk to. Talk out loud. Keep your partner clearly in mind. You really want to explain this work to her. Say anything you want about the work—what you like and dislike about it, what interests you or does not interest you. But probably the most helpful thing to do is to summarize the work. Start at the beginning and move through the work carefully and thoroughly until you reach the end. Check the work for facts if you have to, but work from memory as much as possible. Summarize in such a way that your friend will understand the work clearly, even though she may not have read it. Imagine her interrupting when things are not clear. As you summarize, keep in mind that works of literature are *about* something. They develop ideas. Explain these ideas to your friend. Try to show her how the facts of your summary relate to these ideas.

Summarizing should help you get the facts straight, see relationships among the facts, and see how the facts add up to ideas. These relationships and ideas can become the subject matter for essays about the work. By talking out loud you get your mind working and push yourself toward developing interpretations of your own.

Outlining   Make an outline of the work. The outline should not be formal (complete sentences, Roman and Arabic numerals, and so forth), rather a list or a series of statements that indicate important aspects of the work. You will probably want to write the outline down, mainly so you can remember everything you have put in it. But you can also outline works in your head. The outline could focus on the whole work or one element of the work.

There are many possibilities for the organization of the outline. The outline could follow the spatial order of the work; that is, it could represent the major aspects or events in the order presented in the work. Or it could follow a chronological organization; that is, the order in which the events occur in time. One thought-provoking organization is to outline the work according to the journalist's questions: who, what, when, where, why, how. The first four questions will help you get the facts straight. The last two will get you thinking about relationships among the facts. Who are the important characters in the work? What are they like? What are their values and beliefs? What has happened before the work begins? What do the characters do? When is the action set? Is the time of the action important? Where does the action occur? Does the author attach meaning to the place of the work? Why does the action happen? How does it affect the characters? How does it affect your attitude toward their beliefs and what they do? You might find that one of the journalist's questions will lead you to other questions and therefore further interest in that aspect of the work. And this line of thought and narrowing focus can give you the topic for an essay.

Free writing   Choose a work or some aspect of a work and begin writing about it. Write for at least five minutes but no more than fifteen. During this time, don't stop writing. If you can't think of anything new to say, repeat your last sentence or something like "I can't think of anything else to say" over and over until something new occurs to you. Don't worry about sentence structure or correct usage. Write incomplete sentences if you wish.

The theory behind freewriting is that writing generates thought, even if some of what you write is repetitious or even nonsense. As you write you may create ideas you never knew you had. These may enlighten you about what is most interesting about a work and what lines of thought you might take in an essay. You may even find that a piece of freewriting provides not only the topic but a rough organization for a full-blown essay.

Brainstorming   *Brainstorming* means thinking freely about particular works of literature—letting your mind flow where it will, but keeping it focused on the works and, after a point, upon some aspects of the works. To brainstorm you need pen and paper—lots of paper. As ideas come to you, jot them down. Think of this activity as play, a game in which you talk to yourself. As you write, don't worry about spelling, making complete sentences, putting ideas in order. Include even your craziest ideas. Channel the flow of your thinking with questions such as these: Among the works I may write about, which do I like best? (If necessary, jot down the possibilities. Choose one.) What interests me most about the work? (Jot down these.) What do I dislike about the work? (Jot down these.) Why do I like or dislike these particular things? (Jot down your reasons.) Are there aspects of the work I would like to write about? (Jot down these. Choose one. For example, if you want to write about characterization, begin brainstorming about the characters in the narrative. Some of the questions and exercises under "characterization" in chapter 4 might help you get started.) If your ideas about one aspect of the work seem uninspired, move on to another aspect and brainstorm about that.

At a certain stage of the brainstorming process, you must shift from a noncritical to a critical look at what you have done. This is a process of organization—of subordination, arrangement, and elimination. You sort out, make connections, arrange your jottings into groups, and eliminate the unusable. Organization is still part of the play of brainstorming, even though it is a more controlled activity than the initial stages of brainstorming. Feel free, then, to try certain arrangements and relationships, then discard them if they do not work. Try even the strangest, most unlikely connections and see if logical relationships you had never thought possible actually emerge. If you have a list of ten items, see what groups of relationships you can establish within the list. If you see connections between some but not others (perhaps five out of the ten), keep the ones that connect and discard (cross out) the others. Then brainstorm about the qualities linking the remaining items. Try to summarize these qualities in one phrase or apply one question to them. This phrase or question could be your topic, and the five items, arranged in an order that seems to make sense as part of your developing argument, could provide the structure for a rough draft of the essay.

Perhaps it would be useful to see an abbreviated version of the brainstorming process applied to an actual work, Nathaniel Hawthorne's story "Young Goodman Brown." A student's train of thought might go something like this:

My purpose is to explain this work to my readers, but I do not have time to explain everything, so what should I explain?

Characterization in this story interests me most, but which characters should I write about? The most complex character is Brown himself, so for starters I will concentrate on him. Also, now that I think about it, all the other characters may just be figments of his imagination, so I am pretty sure that it will be Brown.

But what *about* Brown? We see at the end of the story that the journey into the forest, whether dream or not, does him harm; he is a changed person for the worse. So why does he go in the first place? And why does he keep on going once he gets into the forest?

[At this point, the student realizes she needs to reread the story, with these questions in mind.]

Now I see that Brown is reluctant to continue his journey but that each time he decides to go back, something happens to make him go farther. What happens? He learns something new each time. Brown, by the way, is incredibly naïve not to have thought about some of these things before.

This story, then, is really about knowledge and what knowledge can do to you.

But is Brown wrong to react the way he does at the end of the story, turning into a cynic, believing that everyone is phony, even his wife Faith? After all, everything that happened down there might have been a dream. Surely he knows that. But even if it were not a dream, haven't other people learned the same things—that their parents and the respected members of their society have done bad things? And what's more, should Brown have believed the Devil? Is the Devil a trustworthy authority on the way people really are? (I remember somewhere that the Devil has been called the "Prince of Lies.")

No. I feel that Brown reacts improperly. He should not have trusted the Devil. As a good Puritan, furthermore, he should have realized that all people are sinful, but that does not mean they can't also be good people and receive salvation.

Brown is partly to blame for what happens to him. This, I feel, is Hawthorne's point. Brown is too naïve, dangerously naïve.

I am going to write, then, about Brown's dangerous naïveté. The question I will try to answer is, To what extent is Brown to blame for what happens to him at the end of the story? Or, put another way, how is he wrong? My thesis will be that his naïveté leads him to trust the wrong person (the Devil) and mistrust the right people (Faith, the other villagers, and, I assume, the Devil's counterpart, God himself).

My method will be to raise these questions at the beginning of the essay, then show in each stage of his journey how naïvely credulous he is, with a particular emphasis on the story's conclusion. I will reveal my thesis at the end of the essay.

This student's reasoning about the story is probably not finished, because the writing process is itself a way of thinking. Once she begins writing, she may think of things that did not occur to her during the brainstorming process. She may change her mind about the topic— become more skeptical about its validity, or veer toward another one. But at least she has gotten started; and once you get started thinking and writing about a reasonable topic, you have overcome what many consider the hardest part of writing an essay.

7. Complete All the Steps in the Writing Process

As the illustration above indicates, you don't really finish choosing a topic until you complete the whole writing process. The writing process consists of four main sets of activities:

Prewriting

1. You study the subject.
2. You digest the subject (usually when your mind is relaxed—when you are jogging, eating, listening to music, walking, playing games).
3. You decide who your audience is, what they want to know about the subject, and the limitations on your essay (length, time you have to compose it).
4. You identify the kind of topic that will meet your audience's expectations and the limitations on your essay.
5. You concentrate on the subject and what you want to do with it (using search strategies like analysis and critical commentary).
6. You restudy the subject in light of your thinking.
7. You identify a topic (during other thinking sessions).

Drafting

1. You create a plan for a first draft of the essay. This plan includes your general line of reasoning and organization of it.
2. You write the first draft.
3. As you write, you rethink your topic, your plan of organization, and your line of reasoning.

Revising

1. You rewrite (one or more rough drafts).
2. As you write, you rethink your topic, your plan of organization, and your line of reasoning.

Editing

1. You produce a final draft and put it in correct form.
2. You "publish" the essay (in a college course, you turn it in).

All good writers must go through these four sets of activities. And although this outline of the writing process suggests a progression—first one step, then another, then another—it also indicates that the process produces constant revision. *Revision* means not just changing a few minor things here and there, like spelling mistakes, but "seeing again," and re-doing the essay in light of that fresh view of the subject. Revision is almost inevitable in the writing process because writing generates thought. As you write, new ideas bubble up into your consciousness. And revision goes on almost all the time until you say, "All right, that's enough," and type up a final draft. Take comfort in the ongoing nature of revision. Prewriting is the most difficult and frustrating stage of the writing process. If you get stuck in choosing a topic, forge ahead anyway and write yourself toward a topic.

So far in this book, we have dealt with the prewriting stage of the writing process. The next six chapters continue to suggest ways in which you can locate topics for your essays. Then in chapters 9 through 12 we take up the other stages of the writing process, getting from topic to first draft and putting the essay into final form.

3

⚜

How to Analyze Literature

YOU MAY BE influenced by this myth about how writing is done: A writer (usually impoverished) reposes languidly in a garret when suddenly a blinding flash of intuition strikes. The writer leaps to the desk and writes furiously, trying desperately to capture all the nuances of the inspiration before it evaporates. If an interruption occurs—a visitor, perhaps—the intuition leaves, never to return again. If by miraculous chance no interruption comes, the piece of writing emerges brilliantly, whole and flawless, no revisions necessary. This myth persists more as a description of how "creative" writers work— writers of fiction, poetry, and drama. But some people believe that it applies to all writing, even college essays. *Don't believe it.* This myth is false.

All writers must go through a process of analyzing their subject in order to write well about it. Some may know their subject so well, may be so practiced at analyzing it, that the time it takes them to do so seems incredibly quick. Others, often very gifted writers, take days, weeks, even years to complete the process of analysis. But this initial analysis is necessary and inevitable, no matter who does it. Good writers do have moments of "inspiration," but these are really occasions when something clicks in the brain as a result of—not in place of— analytical thinking.

ANALYSIS

Analysis means breaking something down into its components and discovering the relationships among them that give unity and coherence to the whole. Whether you write for college courses or for situations in the "real world," you will speak cogently about your subject only if you can analyze it with reasonable thoroughness. If, for example, you work for a computer manufacturer and must communicate about computers, you probably will make little sense unless you can analyze computers. The same is true for writing about literature. To analyze works of literature, you need to know what literature is— what typical components to expect and how those components usually work together. You may want to write about all the parts of a work, or about just one or two parts. But to do either, you must know what the parts are.

Analysis is an especially valuable tool for understanding works of literature. Once you have considered important aspects of a work, you should know the work very well indeed. You should have the details of the work firmly in mind, and you should have thought creatively about how you can interpret the work. For this reason, analysis is an effective method for studying for tests, especially if they focus on just a few works. It is also, needless to say, an excellent preparation for writing essays about literature. Such preparation need not examine *every* key aspect of a work; just knowing what the key aspects are gives you insight into where to look for fruitful areas of discussion. You may want to go directly to one aspect or consider briefly each of the key aspects, as if you were flipping through a card file, and then focus on the most intriguing.

This chapter is the first of four chapters explaining how to analyze literature. It offers a "definition" of literature, an overview that should help you begin the process of analysis. The three chapters following this one discuss the elements of three literary genres: fiction, drama, and poetry. The method of these chapters is first to describe important aspects of literature and then to list questions about them. Anyone thinking carefully about the aspects of literature would ask such questions. Apply them to the works you are studying. Use them to generate your own questions. Use all of these questions as tools to pry open the work and extract its meaning. See if one or more of them might provide the basis for an essay topic.

THE NATURE OF LITERATURE

There are enough mysterious elements in literature to make a complete definition impossible. Most critics who have tried to define it, however, agree on a few common elements.

Literature Is Language

The medium of literature is language, both oral and written. But not everything written or spoken is literature. Creators of literature use language in a special way, a way different from that of scientists or people using everyday speech. Scientists use language for its *denotative* value, its ability to provide symbols (words) that mean one thing precisely. For scientists, the thing that the symbol represents—the referent—is more important than the symbol itself. Any symbol will do, as long as it represents the referent clearly and exactly. Since emotions render meanings imprecise, scientists try to use symbols that eliminate the emotional, the irrational, the subjective.

Writers of literature, in contrast, use language *connotatively*. They may at times—as in realistic novels—emphasize denotation, but usually they employ the connotative meanings of language. Connotation is the meaning that attaches to words in addition to their explicit referents. A good example of the difference between denotation and connotation is the word *mother*, whose denotation is simply "female parent" but whose connotations include nurturance, warmth, unqualified love, tenderness, devotion, protection, mercy, intercession, home, childhood, the happier past. The connotative meanings of words are subjective, multiple, and sometimes arbitrary. Even scientific language becomes connotative once it enters everyday speech. When we see Einstein's formula $E = mc^2$, we no longer think just of "Energy equals mass times the speed of light squared" but of mushroom clouds, ruined cities, and a sad-eyed, long-haired genius padding about his house in bedroom slippers.

Writers of literature use language, in short, for its expressive and emotional qualities. But they also use it for itself. They are fascinated by its sounds, its rhythms, even its appearance on the page. Sometimes they become so interested in these qualities that they subordinate meaning to them. People who use language in everyday speech and writing also display a sensitivity to its sounds and subjective qualities, but writers of literature exploit these qualities more fully, more consciously, and more systematically.

As you read, then, pay attention to the way the author uses language. Is there anything unusual or purposeful in the author's choice of words (*diction*)? Does the author, for example, employ connotations and double meanings? Does the author use words you do not know? If so, look them up, especially if the work is poetry. Does the sentence structure (*syntax*) of the work seem unusual or especially appropriate for the work's other qualities? What *is* the syntax—can you analyze it? Are there sound qualities of the author's language that seem important? Does the author use punctuation in odd ways? Does the author write in an archaic style—that is, archaic even for the author's day? Why? Does the author speak in dialect or have characters do so? What does this add to the work? For a look at how questions like these can help develop arguments, see the sample essays on poetry in chapter 13, both of which explain how authors use language.

Literature Is Aesthetic

Another quality of literature is that it gives a unique pleasure. This aesthetic quality cannot be defined and described. It just *is*. Like various other aesthetic pleasures—music, patterns of color, sunsets, dance— literature is an end in itself.

All the elements of literature contribute to the pleasure it gives. But probably the most important is *form*, the order the writer imposes on the material—on language, characters, events, details, all of which he or she draws from the usually disorderly realm of real life. Take, for example, events. In real life, events are not necessarily related by cause and effect. Or if some events are related, many are not. Events don't necessarily lead to a conclusion. The murderer may not be caught, the cruel parent may go on being cruel, the economic crisis may not be resolved, the poor but honest youth may not be rewarded. So many things happen to us that it is hard to remember or even be aware of them all. We do not always know which events are important, which trivial. But literature can give order to events in the form of a *plot*. Unimportant events will be excluded, cause-and-effect relationships established, conflicts introduced and resolved. Events will be arranged in logical order so that they form a sequence with a beginning, a middle, and an end. They may even have suspense, so that we fearfully or gleefully anticipate what happens next. Plot, of course, is only one of a multitude of ways in which artists give order to material. They may also arrange language into orderly patterns, reduce characters to recognizable types, offer ideas that guide the reader toward a certain interpretation of the material, describe settings in a selective, logical way. In a good work of literature, all of the elements combine to create an *overall* order, an *overall* coherence.

As you read, look for anything that gives pattern or structure to the work. If the work is poetry, is it governed by traditional forms such as the sonnet or ballad? What are the patterns that inevitably emerge from these forms? If it is a play, does it have act and scene divisions? How long are these? What happens in each? If it is a narrative, does it have chapter divisions or sectional divisions of other kinds (indicated by the use of double spacings, numbers, or even paragraph indentations)? Does the author divide the work according to a time scheme—hours, days, months, years? Does the repetition of phrases, words, images, and metaphors mark sections of a work or tie the work together thematically? More subjectively, why does the work give you pleasure? What qualities in it appeal to you?

Literature Is Fictional

We commonly use the term *fiction* to describe prose works that tell a story (short stories and novels). In fact, however, all works of literature are "fictional" in the sense that the reader sets them apart from the facts of real life.

A work can be fictional in two ways. First, the writer makes up some of the materials. Some of the characters, events, dialogue, and settings exist only in the writer's imagination. He or she may draw upon real-life observations and experiences to create them; but when these appear in the finished work, they have been so altered that no one-to-one correlation can be said to exist between them and anything that actually exists or existed. Furthermore, the writer may ignore laws that govern the real world. An obvious example is fantasy fiction, wherein human beings fly, perform magic, confront dragons, remain young, travel through time, discover utopian kingdoms, metamorphose, live happily ever after, or where animals or other "creatures" take on human traits like speech and intelligence. But even historical fiction, which relies on actual events for some of its material, is fictional. It includes characters, dialogue, events, and settings that do not exist in history.

Second, in addition to a lack of factuality, the fictionality of literature lies in the artistic control the writer exercises over the work. This artistic control has the effect of stylizing the materials of the work and thus setting the work apart from the context of the real. This effect occurs even when the material of the work *does* accurately mirror the facts of real life or when it states ideas that can be verified in actual experience. Compare, for example, accounts of the same event written by a newspaper reporter and by a poet. Both writers may describe the event accurately, but the reporter makes his or her account correspond as exactly as possible to the event so that the reader will experience the details of the event, not the report of it. The poet, in contrast, makes his or her *poem* the object of experience. Through the use of language, the selection of details, the interpretation—stated or implied—of the event, the inclusion of devices such as metaphor, irony, and imagery, the poet makes the work an artifact, an object of enjoyment and contemplation in itself. The reader instinctively if not consciously recognizes it as different from the event itself. In this way, the work becomes "fictional." Because of this element of fictionality you can experience and even enjoy works whose subject would in real life be so depressing or horrifying as to be unendurable.

You can detect the fictional quality of a work most obviously by watching for those elements that depart from the facts of the real world. What historical facts does the author distort or add to? What facts about the physical world and physical laws does the author alter? Why does the author do this? Do these changes or additions destroy the plausibility or enjoyableness of the work?

Less obvious but equally important are those elements that make the work an object of scrutiny in and of itself, such as its use of language and its ordering of material. One of the most important effects of the fictionality of literature is the distance it creates between you and the material presented. This distance is both physical and psychological. You know, as you read, that you are not actually involved in the work's events. They are physically, safely removed from you. Thus you can give freer rein to your emotional reactions than you can for real events. It would be difficult to control your emotions were you to meet a real vampire, werewolf, or homicidal maniac. But you can indulge in, enjoy, and yet control your feelings of fright by confronting yourself with fictional ones. Some authors, however, try to reduce as much as they can the psychological distance between their fictional events and you. They want to draw you into the events so fully that, at least for the moment, you imagine you are involved in real events. In contrast, other authors, such as Nikolai Gogol, Henry Fielding, Washington Irving, and W. M. Thackeray, constantly remind you that their events are fictional. What, then, is the psychological distance between you and the material of the work? Does the author make you feel objective about it? Or are you deeply and emotionally caught up in it? How does the author minimize or empahsize this distance? Why does the author do it?

Literature Is True

Even though works of literature are "fictional," they have the capacity for being "true." This paradox creates one of the most important and pleasurable tensions in literature: the fictionality of literature against its truthfulness in conveying the reality of human experience. Literature can be faithful to the facts of reality, as in descriptive prose and poetry. But it can be true in two other, more important ways. First, it interprets the real world even when it distorts, ignores, or alters facts. Simple examples of the interpretive quality of literature are fables and fairy tales, whose characters and events may be fantastic but whose lessons are true to our own experience. Aesop's fox in the "sour grapes" story is like no fox in real life; he can reason and use language. But he behaves like a real person in similar circumstances, and the lesson we learn from his behavior is a shrewd commentary on human nature.

Unlike fables, however, most literature does not present its interpretations of life in the form of a moral tacked on at the end. Rather, the total form of a work represents its interpretation. A work of literature creates an imaginary "world," and this world embodies a theory about how the real world works. That is, it embodies a "world view." Authors may or may not be consciously aware of this theory, but their views of the real world inevitably influence their construction of an imaginary one. In turn, we can infer the authors' world views from the details of their created worlds. Thus, the world of George Orwell's *1984* is filled with crumbling buildings, frightened people, children who spitefully turn their parents over to the police, procedures whereby truth is systematically altered, masses of people trapped by their ignorance and selfishness, officials who justify any deed to achieve power. It is a world without love, compassion, justice, joy, tradition, altruism, idealism, or hope. The facts of this world are patently imaginary—Orwell himself placed them in the future—but they communicate Orwell's extremely pessimistic view of human nature and human institutions. Orwell shows that, given what he has observed of today's society, the terrible society he describes in *1984* could become a reality.

What specific devices do authors use to embody their world views in their works? Two important ones are the representation of *typical characters* and of *probable actions*. Because works of literature often clothe their worlds in manifold detail, they create the illusion of being real and thus unique. But the characters and events of literature cannot be unique if they are to be meaningful. We often encounter freakish, inexplicable events and people in real life, and they disturb us because we cannot place them within an orderly context. But we expect literature to give order to the chaos of real life, and it does so partly by exposing patterns of meaning in life. To do this, literature must conform to generally recognizable patterns of behavior and probability. J. R. R. Tolkien, for example, offers an array of fantasy creatures and kingdoms in *The Hobbit* and its sequel, *The Lord of the Rings*. Yet his characters, whatever they may look like, represent types of human behavior, and the events in which they participate represent human activities we recognize as characteristic of individuals, clans, organizations, and nations. The protagonists, Bilbo and Frodo Baggins, typify those gentle, kindly people who would much prefer to live in domestic obscurity but who are called on to play heroic roles in cataclysmic dramas. And the way they behave is probable, because it fits the types of people they are. They don't suddenly become supermen with supernatural powers. Like average people, they are vulnerable to superior strength and to their own fears and temptations. But they succeed because they exhibit the strengths of average people: perseverance, shrewdness, unselfishness, courage, and honesty.

Of course, world views expressed in works of literature are subjective. The authors are expressing *their* views of what the real world is like. Orwell's view is very different from Tolkien's. Orwell shows an average man rebelling against social corruption and failing miserably to do anything about it. He is weak, ineffective, and controlled by forces outside himself. In Orwell's world, good loses because people are too stupid or too greedy or too weak to overcome evil. Like Orwell, Tolkien also shows the average man as weak, but in his world view, the average person is innately good and potentially strong; such individuals can band together with others like themselves and overthrow evil. Orwell is pessimistic about human nature and the future of humanity; Tolkien is optimistic.

In addition to offering a world view, literature can be true by presenting the *experience* of reality. The experience may be new or old, unique or shared by many people. Whatever it is, the author uses his or her imagination to put us in the midst of it, to make us feel it. The result is that we understand it better.

An example is Jessamyn West's novel *The Massacre at Fall Creek*. In the afterword she says she had long been intrigued by a historical event that occurred in Indiana in 1824. A white judge and jury convicted four white men of killing Indians, and the men were hanged. As far as West could discover, this event marked the first time in United States history that white men convicted other white men for killing Indians. But she was unable to find much historical information on this episode. She wondered what it was like to be condemned to death for something that had up to then been approved, or at least tolerated? How must the people, Indians and whites alike, have felt about the event? West's novel is an answer to these questions. We do not have a record of what these people experienced, but through an act of imagination, West shows us what they *probably* experienced, because she can assess what most people would go through under those circumstances. Furthermore, she causes us to *feel* what they experienced. We live through the killings themselves, with all their gruesome details. We share with the whites the fear of Indian reprisal. We see the callousness of hardened Indian killers. We experience the dawning realization of some whites that Indians are human beings and have rights. We suffer the alienation felt by those who take unpopular moral stands. We partake of the circuslike atmosphere of the crowd come to see the hangings. We puzzle over the ambiguity of the ethical problem confronting the judge. We stand on the scaffold with the condemned.

An idea that underlies Jessamyn West's world view is that it is wrong to kill Indians. Or, to put it more generally, she shows that all human life is precious and therefore should not be wantonly destroyed. Like the ideas in most works of literature, this idea is not new or unusual. Compare it, for example, with Orwell's in *1984* (totalitarianism is dehumanizing) and Tolkien's in *The Lord of the Rings* (eternal vigilance is the price of freedom). But the abstract ideas that underlie works of literature almost *have* to be commonplace in order to be recognizable and thus universal. The profundity of literature lies in its imaginative reconstruction of the experience of commonplace ideas. We don't have to read *Anna Karenina* to learn that circumstances and moral blindness can drive a person to despair. We read it because Tolstoy, through Anna, makes us *feel what it is like* to have everything we care about taken from us little by little because of flaws in our character or because of blind chance.

Here are some questions that should help you analyze the "truths" within a work:

1. What are the work's basic ideas? Sometimes the author states them or has a character state them. Usually, however, authors present themes indirectly; you have to infer them from details in the works. Underline or mark events, dialogue, aspects of setting, or whatever that seem to develop a theme. For an extended treatment of theme in a work, see the next chapter (p. 52).

2. What is typical about the characters in the work? What do they do and say that identify them as typical? What ideas do the characters represent? That is, do their character types, attitudes, or philosophies represent a way of looking at the world that is important in the work? One character, for example, may be worldly wise and tolerant, another naïve and thoughtless, another greedy and miserly, still another fatalistic and pessimistic. To which of these views does the author seem sympathetic? Which predominates at the end of the work?

3. Sometimes authors deliberately depart from the typical and probable. Why do they do so? How does this departure reflect the author's ideas? For example, if a character is extraordinarily beautiful and graceful, the author may be using these traits to glamorize ideas the character expresses or believes.

4. What are the implications of titles and epigraphs? (An epigraph is a pertinent quotation put at the beginning of a work or chapter.) *The Grapes of Wrath* (taken from a line in "The Battle Hymn of the Republic"), *All the King's Men* (from the nursery rhyme "Humpty-Dumpty"), *Pride and Prejudice, Great Expectations, Measure for Measure* are examples of titles that represent the authors' judgment of what their works are about. What do these titles mean when applied to the contents of the work?

5. What themes does the author develop in other works? Sometimes you must read more than one work by an author to reconstruct the author's world view. Reading literary criticism is helpful here, because often the critics have already done the work for you; they have read an author's works and have drawn conclusions about themes.

6. What has the author said about the work—in speeches, interviews, lectures, and essays? These may be worth seeking out, especially if the work is puzzling. Flannery O'Connor's comments about "A Good Man Is Hard to Find" are very revealing about the story's possible meaning.

7. What has your instructor said about the meaning of the work? These comments, of course, also provide insights into the work's meaning. Mark those sections the instructor calls to your attention in class and reread them.

Literature Is Expressive

Literature is an expression of the individuals who write it. Their personalities, emotions, and beliefs are bound up in their works. Some authors may try to reduce their presence as much as possible, so that the work seems to be merely that of a faceless observer who transcribes or mirrors reality. Shakespeare's plays and Daniel Defoe's novels have this quality. Other authors make themselves and their feelings the obvious subject matter of their work. William Wordsworth, who wrote that poetry "is the spontaneous overflow of powerful feelings," is one example. Lord Byron and Thomas Wolfe are others. But whatever authors decide about the relationship between themselves and their subject matter, they inevitably stamp it with those qualities that belong uniquely to them. And when we read their works, we feel the force of their character and personality.

One result of the expressive aspect of literature is that we may be drawn to a work because we are drawn to the author. We are charmed or impressed by the author's presence in the work. And we may read other works by that writer because we want to experience more of him or her. We may read Jane Austen to experience Jane Austen, Ernest Hemingway to experience Ernest Hemingway. Another result—sometimes intended by the author—is that through the work we experience events and emotional reactions that may be outside our own experience. The work thus broadens the range of our experience.

The expressive element in works of literature is often elusive. It may be solely a matter of language, whereby the author maintains a consistent style from work to work. Jane Austen, for example, is witty and ironic. Or it may be a philosophical outlook that carries over from work to work. Or it may be an autobiographical treatment of events in the author's life. If the expressive aspect of literature interests you, your best bet is to read more than one work by an author and to read more about the author. What similarities of style, ideas, and events do you see present in the author's works? How would you characterize the author's "voice"—the author's unique way of writing? Where and how in the work does the writer make his or her presence felt and his or her ideas known?

Literature Is Affective

Often related to the expressive aspect of literature is its *affective* aspect—that is, its ability to create an emotional response in the reader. The aesthetic experience we discussed earlier is itself emotional, but other elements of literature create emotional reactions as well. As with the expressive aspect, the degree to which literature is affective varies from author to author. Some writers try to make their works as unemotional and intellectual as possible. Alexander Pope's poetry, for example, appeals to our reasoning ability and to our interest in witty wordplay. Henry James's novels present moral problems that take on the quality of complicated puzzles. In contrast, other works are awash in sentiment; they want us to feel deeply and sometimes to do something about the situations that evoke feelings in us, as in the case of reform fiction such as Charles Dickens's *Oliver Twist* and Harriet Beecher Stowe's *Uncle Tom's Cabin*. Some literary forms—tragedy, comedy, melodrama, the lament, the elegy—strive to elicit fairly specific emotional reactions from us.

The expressive and affective aspects of literature often work together. The author makes the reader feel what he or she has felt. In *Native Son*, Richard Wright puts us in the shoes of a young black man living in an urban ghetto. He intends for us to be shocked by the violent crimes Bigger Thomas commits. But then he wants us to feel what it is like to be a victim of racism and, by feeling it, to see this victimization as a cause of Bigger's crimes. Wright is black, and his point is that the frustration and hatred Bigger Thomas feels is typical of the way many black people in the United States feel, even though most have not committed violent crimes as Bigger has. Wright makes us aware of his feelings by causing us, through his novel, to feel what he has felt.

You can uncover the affective elements in works of literature in several ways. The most obvious is to ask, What emotions did the work raise in me? Another way is to ask, What emotional impact has the work had on others? Sometimes this impact is a matter of historical record, something you can read about, as in the case of the effect *Uncle Tom's Cabin* had on readers before the Civil War. You can also simply ask people questions: How did you like this book? How did it make you feel? Once you identify the emotional reactions the work typically draws from readers, you might ask, What reactions was the author *trying* to create? Does the work achieve this effect?

FOR FURTHER STUDY

Defining literature is an intriguing but prickly enterprise. Any definition raises objections and counterdefinitions. This chapter conforms largely to the view of literature in the opening section of René Wellek and Austin Warren's *Theory of Literature* (New York: Harcourt, 1942). Two works that take different and stimulating approaches are Terry Eagleton's *Literary Theory: An Introduction* (Minneapolis: U of Minnesota P, 1983) and John M. Ellis's *The Theory of Literary Criticism: A Logical Analysis* (Berkeley: U of California P, 1974).

4

How to Analyze Fiction

THIS CHAPTER begins an explanation of how to analyze the genres of literature. The word *genre* comes from French and means "type" or "kind." To identify literary genres, then, is to classify literature into its kinds. Literary critics sometimes disagree about how to classify literature. Some say the genres of literature are tragedy, comedy, lyric poetry, satire, the ode, the elegy, and so forth. But for our purpose, it will be useful to classify literature into three broad "kinds": fiction, poetry, and drama. This chapter begins with the most popular genre, fiction.

THE NATURE OF FICTION

As a descriptive term, *fiction* is misleading, for although fiction does often include made-up or imaginary elements, it has the potential for being "true": true to the nature of reality, true to human experience. The intellectual activity that most resembles fiction is history. Both attempt to create a world that resembles the multiplicity and complexity of the real world. Both attempt to speculate about the nature of the real world. But fiction is different from history in key ways, and these differences help reveal the nature and uniqueness of fiction.

The most obvious difference is that writers of fiction can make up facts but that historians must take facts as they find them. In works of history, historians cannot manufacture facts to fill in the gaps of their knowledge. Consequently, the fictional world is potentially more complete and coherent than the historical world. Not only can writers of fiction produce facts at will, they can produce them to fit a coherent plan. If they have an optimistic view of reality, for example, writers can include only positive and affirming facts. Furthermore, they can know more about their worlds than historians (or anyone else) can know about the real world. They can enter their characters' minds, look into the heavens, create chains of cause and effect, foresee the future. A second difference is that writers of fiction must establish some principle of order or coherence that underlies their work. They must establish at least an aesthetic order, and they may also impose a philosophical order upon their materials. Although historians often do both, they need do neither. Like newspaper reporters, historians need only record events as they occur, no matter how unrelated or senseless they may seem. A third difference is that writers of fiction must build conflict into their worlds, whereas historians need not. The events of history are not inevitably characterized by conflict, but the events of fiction always are.

All three of these differences point to qualities that make fiction innately enjoyable—its imaginative, orderly, and dramatic qualities. But two more differences reveal an equally important aspect of fiction—the kinds of reality it deals with and thus the kinds of truth it attempts to expose. The fourth difference, then, is that writers of fiction celebrate the separateness, distinctness, and importance of all individuals and all individual experiences. They assume that human experiences, whatever they are and wherever they occur, are intrinsically important and interesting. In contrast, historians record and celebrate human experiences that affect or represent large numbers of people—wars, rises and falls of civilizations, technological innovations, economic developments, political changes, social tastes and mores. If historians discuss individuals at all, it is because they affect or illustrate these wider experiences. Henry Fleming, the protagonist of Stephen Crane's novel *The Red Badge of Courage,* has no historical importance. As far as history is concerned, he is an anonymous participant in the Civil War battle of Chancellorsville, one soldier among thousands. Even his deeds, thoughts, and feelings do not necessarily represent those of the typical soldier at Chancellorsville. Yet in the fictional world they are important because they are *his* deeds, thoughts, and feelings. We are interested in him not for his connection with an important historical event but simply because he is a human being.

Finally, a fifth difference is that writers of fiction see reality as welded to psychological perception, as refracted through the minds of individuals. In contrast, historians present reality as external to individuals and thus as unaffected by human perception. Both historians and writers of fiction, for example, deal with time. But time for the historian is divisible into exact, measurable units—centuries, decades, years, months, weeks, days, hours, minutes, seconds. Time, for historians, is a river in which individuals float like so many pieces of driftwood. In contrast, writers of fiction present time as an experienced, emotional phenomenon, as a river flowing *inside* the mind. Its duration is not scientifically measurable but rather is determined by states of mind, the familiar when-I-am-happy-time-goes-fast, when-I-am-sad-time-goes-slow phenomenon. Other aspects of reality take on a similar psychological dimension within works of fiction. A house may not be haunted, but the character perceives it as such out of fear and anxiety. A mountain may not be steep, but the character perceives it as such out of fatigue and aching muscles.

THE ELEMENTS OF FICTION

This explanation of the nature of fiction should help you know generally what to expect from it. But fiction, poetry, and drama all have more specific characteristics, and knowing what these are will help you analyze a work by isolating and examining its elements. The rest of this chapter defines some of the elements of fiction. It provides questions after each definition. And it gives "Thinking on Paper" exercises. Use the definitions, questions, and exercises as tools for studying the details of the work, for collecting facts from the work, and for developing your own ideas about the work.

Plot

Put simply, *plot* is what happens in a narrative. But this definition is too simple. A mere listing of events, even in the order in which they occur, is not plot. Rather, writers of fiction arrange fictional events into patterns. They select these events carefully, they establish causal relationships among events, and they enliven these events with conflict. A more complete and accurate definition, then, is that plot is a pattern of carefully selected, causally related events that contains conflict. Although writers of fiction arrange events into many patterns, the most common is that represented by the *Freytag pyramid*, shown here, which was developed by the German critic Gustav Freytag in 1863. Although Freytag meant this diagram to describe a typical five-act tragedy, it may be adapted to apply to most works of fiction. At the beginning of this pattern is an *unstable situation*, a conflict that sets the plot in motion. The author's *exposition* here explains the nature of the conflict. He or she introduces the characters, describes the setting, and provides historical background. The author next introduces a series of *events*, all related by cause. One event may cause another event, which in turn causes another event, which causes the next event (husband gets angry with wife, who gets angry with kids, who get angry with dog, who sulks in the basement). Or several events may be linked to the same cause (a series of deaths at the beach, all caused by a monster killer shark). Whatever the causal relationship among events, each event intensifies the conflict so that the plot "rises" toward a *climax*.

The climax is the most intense event in the narrative. The rest of the story—the *falling action*—is usually brief. It contains events that are much less intense than the climax and that lead toward the resolution of the conflict and toward a *stable situation* at the end. Another term for falling action is *dénouement*, a French word meaning "unravelling."

An example of the Freytag pyramid is the stereotypical fairy tale in which the youngest son must seek his fortune (unstable situation: he has no source of income, no home). He goes into a far country whose king is offering a prize, the hand of his daughter for anyone who can accomplish three tasks. The hero successfully completes all three (rising action and climax: each task is increasingly difficult, but the third is a humdinger). The king praises the hero but does not want his daughter to marry a commoner. The hero reveals that he is not, as he seems, a mere peasant but the son of a nobleman (falling action/dénouement: the conflicts now are minor and easily resolved). The hero marries the princess and lives happily ever after (stable situation: the hero has eliminated the initial conflict since he now has a wife, a source of income, and a home).

There are two general categories of conflict: external and internal. *Internal conflicts* take place within the minds of characters. An example is the good person who wrestles inwardly with temptation. *External conflicts* take place between individuals or between individuals and the world external to individuals (the forces of nature, human-created objects, and environments). The climactic shootout in an American western is an example of a physical external conflict, but not all external conflicts are physical or violent. A disagreement between two people is also an external conflict.

The forces in a conflict are usually embodied by characters, the most relevant being the protagonist and the antagonist. The term *protagonist* usually means "main character," but it might be helpful sometimes to think of the protagonist as someone who is fighting for something. The *antagonist* is the opponent of the protagonist; the antagonist is usually a person, but can also be a nonhuman force or even an aspect of the protagonist—his or her tendency toward evil and self-destruction, for example. Although a protagonist sometimes fights for evil—Macbeth, for example— we usually empathize with the protagonist and find the antagonist unsympathetic.

Questions about plot   Probably the single most revealing question you can ask about a work of literature is, What conflicts does it dramatize? For fiction, this is a crucial question. You can break it down into subquestions, each of which might produce an interesting essay topic: What is the main conflict? What are the minor conflicts? How are all the conflicts related? What causes the conflicts? Which conflicts are external, which internal? Who is the protagonist? What qualities or values does the author associate with each side of the conflict? How is the main conflict organized? Where does the main climax occur? Why does it occur? Is there more than one "main" climax? How is the main conflict resolved? Which conflicts go unresolved? Why?

An example of how you can use these questions to interpret fiction is Ernest Hemingway's story "Hills Like White Elephants." The story consists almost entirely of a dialogue between a young woman and man who are waiting for a train at a tiny station in the Spanish countryside. We learn that they have traveled widely, that they are intimate, that they are lovers. But they are in conflict. About what? The conflict they bring out into the open and discuss aloud concerns an abortion. The woman is pregnant, and the man urges her to have an abortion. He keeps telling her that the abortion will be "simple," "perfectly natural," and will make them "all right" and "happy." But she resists. She asks if after the abortion "things will be like they were and you'll love me." She says that they "could get along" without the abortion.

Gradually we realize that although the immediate conflict is over the abortion, there is a deeper, unspoken conflict. This more important conflict—the main conflict—is over the nature of their relationship.

The man wants the abortion because it will allow him to continue the rootless and uncommitted relationship he has enjoyed with the woman up to now. The woman, however, wants a more stable relationship, one that having the child would affirm, one that she has apparently believed the man wanted too. Hemingway resolves the conflict by having the woman realize, in the face of the man's continued insistence on the abortion, that the relationship she wants with the man is impossible. Examining the story's main conflict in this way helps to reveal several important things about the story. At first glance, it seems to have little "action," but examining the conflict reveals what its action is. Studying the conflict also helps to illuminate the characters: the man is selfish and obstinate, the woman is idealistic and somewhat innocent. And analyzing the conflict points to the meaning or theme of the story. Hemingway seems to support the woman's view of the way a loving relationship should be. He makes her the protagonist, the more sympathetic character of the two. Because examining conflict in works of literature is crucial to understanding them, such a study is a rich source of essay topics, perhaps the richest. This discussion of "Hills Like White Elephants" is but one of many examples of what an essay might do with conflict.

Thinking on Paper About Plot

1. On one side of a page, list the external conflicts of the work. On the other side, list the internal conflicts. Draw a line between the external and internal conflicts that seem related.

2. List the key conflicts. For each conflict, list the ways in which the conflict has been resolved, if it has.

3. Describe the turning point or climax. Explain what conflicts are resolved. List the conflicts that are left unresolved.

4. List the major structural units of the work. Summarize what happens in each unit.

5. List the qualities of the protagonist and antagonist.

6. List the qualities that make the situation at the beginning unstable. List the qualities that make the conclusion stable.

7. List the causes of the unstable situations at the beginning and throughout the work.

Characterization

Characters are the people in narratives, and *characterization* is the author's presentation and development of characters. Sometimes, as in fantasy fiction, the characters are not people. They may be animals, or robots, or creatures from outer space, but the author gives them human abilities and human psychological traits. Thus they really are people in all but outward form.

There are two broad categories of character development: simple and complex. The critic and fiction writer E. M. Forster coined alternate terms for these same categories: *flat* (simple) and *round* (complex) characters. Flat characters have only one or two personality traits and are easily recognizable as stereotypes—the shrewish wife, the lazy husband, the egomaniac, the stupid athlete, the shyster, the miser, the redneck, the bum, the dishonest used-car salesman, the prim aristocrat, the absent-minded professor. Round characters have multiple personality traits and therefore resemble real people. They are much harder to understand and describe than flat characters. No single description or interpretation can fully contain them. An example of a flat character is Washington Irving's Ichabod Crane, the vain and superstitious schoolmaster of "The Legend of Sleepy Hollow." An example of a round character is Shakespeare's Hamlet. To an extent all literary characters are stereotypes. Even Hamlet is a type, the "melancholy man." But round characters have many more traits than just those associated with their general type. Because it takes time to develop round characters convincingly, they are more often found in longer works than in shorter ones.

Authors reveal what characters are like in two general ways: directly or indirectly. In the *direct* method, the author simply tells the reader what the character is like. Here, for example, is Jane Austen telling us, very early in her novel *Pride and Prejudice*, what Mrs. Bennet is like:

> She was a woman of mean understanding, little information, and uncertain temper. When she was discontented she fancied herself nervous. The business of her life was to get her daughters married; its solace was visiting and news.

When the method of revealing characters is *indirect*, however, the author shows us, rather than tells us, what the characters are like through what they say about one another, through external details (dress, bearing, looks), and through their thoughts, speech, and deeds.

Characters who remain the same throughout a work are called *static* characters. Those who change during the course of the work are called *dynamic* characters. Usually, round characters change and flat characters remain the same. But not always. Shakespeare's Sir John Falstaff (in *Henry IV, Parts I and II*), a round character, is nonetheless static. Dynamic characters, especially main characters, typically grow in understanding. The climax of this growth is an *epiphany*, a term that James Joyce used to describe a sudden revelation of truth experienced by a character. The term comes from the Bible and describes the Wise Men's first perception of Christ's divinity. Joyce applied it to fictional characters. His own characters, like Gabriel Conroy in "The Dead," perfectly illustrate the concept. Often, as in "The Dead," the epiphany occurs at the climax of the plot.

Questions about characters   You can ask many revealing questions about characters and the way they are portrayed: Are they flat, round, dynamic, or static? Do they change? How and why do they change? What steps do they go through to change? What events or moments of self-revelation produce these changes? What do they learn? Does what they learn help or hinder them? What problems do they have? How do they attempt to solve them? What types do they represent? If they are complex, what makes them complex? Do they have traits that contradict one another and therefore cause internal conflicts? Do they have conflicting attitudes about something? Do they understand themselves? Do they experience epiphanies? When, why, and what do their epiphanies reveal—to them and to us? How do they relate to one another? What pleasures and conflicts do their relationships with one another cause? Does the author want us to compare one character with another? Do the characters have speech mannerisms, gestures, or modes of dress that reveal their inner selves? Is the character sad, happy, or in-between? Is the character mentally disturbed?

But the overriding questions that any character analysis attempts to answer are simply, What is the character like? What are the character's traits?

An example is the woman in Hemingway's "Hills Like White Elephants," discussed above. Hemingway drops hints that indicate something about her personality. She compares the Spanish hills to white elephants, a comparison that at first seems capricious but later suggests an imaginative, even artistic quality that the man cannot comprehend. After she senses the man's true motivation for wanting the abortion, she looks out over the fields of ripe grain, the trees, the river, and the mountains beyond, and tells the man that "we could have all this" but that "every day we make it more impossible." She seems to connect the appreciation of nature, the sympathy they could feel for it, with the moral quality of their relationship. But because their relationship must remain superficial, she says that the landscape "isn't ours any more." Once again, the man lacks the imagination to make the connection, and he fails to grasp her moral point. Hemingway seems to admire the woman's ability to make these comparisons. It underscores her more obvious and admirable desire for a profound and lasting relationship. Another thing we learn about the woman is that she is a dynamic character. At the beginning of the story she does not fully recognize the falseness of her relationship with the man. She seems genuinely to hope for something better. But by the end of the story she knows the truth and, from all appearances, has changed as a result. At the beginning she is innocent and dependent on the man for her happiness; by the end she has lost her innocence and has become independent.

Thinking on Paper About Characterization

1. List the traits of the main characters in the story. List the characters in ascending order of complexity (least complex to most complex).

2. Describe the ways the author reveals the traits of a character.

3. Write a description of a complex character in which you try to account for every trait of the character.

4. Describe the emotional reaction a character has to an important event or events.

5. Describe each event that influences a character's change. For each event, explain what happens to the character and how the character changes (from what to what).

6. Write a paragraph explaining why a character changes.

7. Describe the scene in which a character has an epiphany. Explain what happens and what the character comes to see.

8. Mark the places in which the author or other characters make revealing statements about a character.

Theme

Theme is perhaps the most obvious statement of the "truth" of a work. This discussion of theme, then, is a continuation of the discussion in chapter 3 (on pages 37–41) of how literature is true. *Theme* is the central idea in the work—whether fiction, poetry, or drama. It is the comment the work makes on the human condition. It deals with four general areas of human experience: the nature of humanity, the nature of society, the nature of humankind's relationship to the world, and the nature of our ethical responsibilities. Theme answers questions such as these: Are human beings innately "sinful" or "good"? Does fate (environment, heredity, circumstance) control us, or do we control it? What does a particular social system or set of social practices (capitalism, socialism, feudalism, middle-class values and practices, genteel English country life, urban life, rural life, bureaucracy) do for—and to—its members? What is right conduct and wrong conduct, and how do we know?

For many readers, theme is an attractive element because it gives works meaning; it makes them relevant. But searching for theme has its pitfalls. To avoid them you should know several characteristics of theme. First, the theme of a work is *not* the same as the subject or topic of a work. Learn to distinguish between them. The *subject* is what the work is about. You can state the subject in a word or phrase. The subject of Shakespeare's Sonnet 116 (pages 113–14) is love. In contrast, theme is what the work *says* about the subject. The statement of a work's theme requires a complete sentence, and sometimes several sentences. The theme of Sonnet 116 is "Love remains constant whether assaulted by tempestuous events or by time."

Second, a work's theme must apply to people outside the work. For example, it is incorrect to say that the theme of "Rip Van Winkle" is "Rapid change in his environment threatens Rip's identity." This statement is true, but it is not the theme. Remember, theme is the comment the work makes *on the human condition*. Therefore, you must state theme in such a way as to include people in general, not just the characters in the story. A correctly stated theme for "Rip Van Winkle," then, would be "Rapid change in environment causes *many people* to feel their identity threatened." Stating theme in a work of literature means that you move from concrete situations within the work to generalizations about people outside the work. In this way, literature becomes a form of philosophy—universal wisdom about the nature of reality.

A third characteristic of theme is that many works have more than one subject and thus more than one theme. This is especially true of complex works. A subject of Tolstoy's *Anna Karenina* is clearly sacred versus profane love. But another, equally important subject is social entrapment. One theme of *Anna Karenina*, then, is that people should not abandon "sacred" commitments, like marriage and parenthood, for extramarital "loves," no matter how passionate and deeply felt they may be. This theme emerges from Anna's desertion of her husband and child for Count Vronsky. But an alternate theme is that people, through little fault of their own, can become trapped in painful, long-lasting, and destructive relationships that they want desperately to escape. This theme emerges from Anna's marriage. When she was very young, Anna married an older man whom she now realizes is too petty, prim, and self-absorbed to satisfy her generous and passionate nature. So discordant is her relationship with her husband that it seems no less "immoral" than her affair with Vronsky. Tolstoy, in other words, draws complex, even contradictory lessons from Anna's adultery. She is not simply the sinful person; she is also the driven person. And this combination of traits characterizes the condition of many people.

Fourth, some works may not have a subject or a theme. There may be so many contradictory or incompletely developed elements in a work that it is impossible to say for sure what the work means. Examples of such works are Edgar Allan Poe's "The Raven" and "The Fall of the House of Usher."

Fifth, the subjects and themes of complex works can rarely be covered completely. Even when the author says what the work means, you cannot exclude other possibilities. To get at a work's theme, you must seek patterns in the concrete world that the author creates. You must extrapolate from the evidence. But you can rarely see all the evidence at once or see all the possible patterns that are inherent in them. The best you can do is support your interpretations as logically and with as much evidence as you can. You may disagree with the author's conclusions about a given subject—with his or her theme. But your job is first to identify and understand the work's theme and then, if you are writing about it, to represent it fairly. To do this, however, is not necessarily to agree with it. You are always free to disagree with an author's world view.

Sixth, theme may be a presentation of a problem rather than a moral or message that neatly solves the problem. Robert Penn Warren's novel *All the King's Men*, for example, raises the problem of morality in politics. A question the novel seems to ask is, How can political leaders in a democratic society do good when citizens are apathetic and easily misled? The character who embodies this question is a well-meaning and gifted politician who uses corrupt and violent means to attain good ends. By telling his story, Warren dramatizes the question. But he never really answers it. You cannot pull a neat moral out of the story of this character's rise and fall. Rather, to state the "theme" of this novel—or one theme—you need to summarize as accurately as you can the problem Warren presents in the way he presents it. You could explain how the problem is worked out in this one character's life, but you could not necessarily generalize from that to all people's lives.

Questions about theme   The key questions for eliciting a work's theme are, What is the subject (that is, what is the work about)? Then, What is the theme (that is, what does the work say about the subject)? And, finally, In what direct and indirect ways does the work communicate its theme? In "Hills Like White Elephants," Hemingway does not state his subject and theme directly, but given his development of conflict and characterization, it seems fair to say that his subject is love (or loving relationships) and that one possible theme might be something like this: "Loving relationships are impossible without unselfish commitment from both partners."

We said that theme deals with four areas of human experience. One strategy for discovering a work's theme is to apply questions about these areas to the work. Here are some suggestions: First, what image of humankind emerges from the work? From the way the author presents characters, can you tell if the author thinks people are "no damned good" (Mark Twain's phrase), or does the author show people as having redeeming traits? If people are good, what good things do they do? If they are flawed, how and to what extent are they so? Second, does the author portray a particular society or social scheme as life-enhancing or life-destroying? Are characters we care about in conflict with their society? Do they want to escape from it? Are they trapped by it? Do they ultimately find a secure place in it without sacrificing their dignity or values? What causes and perpetuates this society? Revolutionary upheavals? Good people trying to do right? Blind tradition? If the society is flawed, how is it flawed? Does the author show preference for one society by contrasting it with another?

Third, what control over their lives do the characters have? Do they make choices in complete freedom? Are they driven by forces beyond their control? What controls them? Are they aware of these controlling forces? Does Providence or some grand scheme govern history, or is history simply random and arbitrary? Fourth, what are the moral conflicts in the work? Are they clear-cut or ambiguous? That is, is it clear to us exactly what is right and exactly what is wrong? When moral conflicts are ambiguous in a work, right often opposes *right*, not wrong. What are the rights in opposition to one another? Does right win in the end? To what extent are characters to blame for their actions? (Presumably, persons who have no free choice, who are driven by forces beyond their control, cannot be blamed for their actions.) Do ethical decisions emerge from situations or do they come from preconceived notions of right and wrong (from the Bible, for example, or from cultural tradition)? Is one set of moral values in opposition to another?

Another strategy for discovering a work's theme is to answer this question: Who serves as "moral center" of the work? The moral center is the one person whom the author vests with right action and right thought (that is, what the *author* thinks is right action and right thought), the one character who is clearly "good" and who often serves to judge other characters. Not every work has a moral center; but in the works that do, its center can lead you to some of the work's themes. In Dickens's *Great Expectations*, for example, the moral center is Biddy, the girl who comes to Pip's sister's household as a servant. She is a touchstone of goodness for Pip, and when he strays from the good, his talks with Biddy and his remembrance of her help bring him back to it. *Great Expectations* is largely about morality (subject), and by studying Biddy we can uncover some of Dickens's ideas about morality (theme).

When identifying a work's moral center, answer questions such as these: What does the author do to identify this person as the moral center? (Part of your argument may be simply to show that a character is indeed the moral center.) What values does the moral center embody? Is the moral center flawed in any way that might diminish his or her authority? What effect does the moral center have on the other characters and on us? If a work does not have a moral center, why not? What do we gain or lose from not having one?

Thinking on Paper About Theme

1. List the subject or subjects of the work. For each subject, state a theme. Put a check next to the ones that seem most important.

2. Explain how the title, subtitle, epigraph, and names of characters may be related to theme.

3. Describe the author's attitude toward human behavior.

4. Describe the author's attitude toward society. Explain the representation of social ills and how they might be corrected or addressed.

5. List the moral issues raised by the work.

6. Name the character who is the moral center of the work. List his or her traits.

7. Mark statements by the author or characters that seem to state themes.

Setting

Setting includes several closely related aspects of a work of fiction. First, setting is the physical, sensuous world of the work. Second, it is the time in which the action of the work takes place. And third, it is the social environment of the characters: the manners, customs, and moral values that govern the characters' society. A fourth aspect—"atmosphere"—is largely but not entirely an effect of setting.

Questions about place   You should first get the details of
the physical setting clear in your mind. Where does the action take
place? In what planet, country, locale? What sensuous qualities does the
author give to the setting? What does it look like, sound like, feel like?
Do you receive a dominant impression about the setting? What impression, and why?

Once you have answered these questions, you can move on to a
more interesting one: What relationship does place have to characterization and theme? In some novels, geographical location seems to have
no effect on characters. Indoors or out, in one locale or another they
behave the same. In other novels, such as those of Thomas Hardy or
Joseph Conrad, place affects the characters profoundly. Here is Hamlin
Garland depicting the relationship of environment to the process of
making decisions:

> A cornfield in July is a hot place. The soil is hot and dry;
> the wind comes across the lazily murmuring leaves laden with a
> warm sickening smell drawn from the rapidly growing, broad-
> flung banners of the corn. The sun, nearly vertical, drops a flood
> of dazzling light and heat upon the field over which the cool
> shadows run, only to make the heat seem the more intense.
>
> Julia Peterson, faint with fatigue, was toiling back and
> forth between the corn rows, holding the handles of the double-
> shovel corn plow while her little brother Otto rode the steaming
> horse. Her heart was full of bitterness, and her face flushed with
> heat, and her muscles aching with fatigue. The heat grew terri-
> ble. The corn came to her shoulders, and not a breath seemed
> to reach her, while the sun, nearing the noon mark, lay pitilessly
> upon her shoulders, protected only by a calico dress. The dust
> rose under her feet, and as she was wet with perspiration it
> soiled her till, with a woman's instinctive cleanliness, she shud-
> dered. Her head throbbed dangerously. What matter to her that
> the king bird pitched jovially from the maples to catch a wan-
> dering bluebottle fly, that the robin was feeding its young, that
> the bobolink was singing? All these things, if she saw them, only
> threw her bondage to labor into greater relief.

In this story, "Among the Corn Rows," Garland shows geographical
environment pressuring Julia Peterson into a decision that will affect
the rest of her life. Garland has already told us that her parents treat her

harshly and force her to work too hard. By emphasizing one sensuous quality, the heat, Garland makes us feel the hardship of her life. She has dreamed of a handsome suitor who will take her away from the farm and give her a life of ease, but the heat makes her feel that anything would be better than this misery. So when a young farmer happens along just after the incident described here and offers her a life of respect and only normal difficulty, she marries him. Garland shows that Julia's environment leads her to settle for less than she really wants. She is not free to choose exactly as she would choose.

Questions about time   Three kinds of time occur in fiction, thus three types of questions about time are important. First, at what period in history does the action take place? Many stories occur during historical events that affect the characters and themes in important ways. Margaret Mitchell's *Gone with the Wind* and Tolstoy's *War and Peace* are examples. To answer this question you may have to do background reading about the historical period. Tolstoy and Mitchell give you a great deal of historical information in their fiction, but many authors do not. In either case, you may need to supplement facts in the work with what you can find out elsewhere.

Second, how long does it take for the action to occur? That is, how many hours, days, weeks, years are involved? Authors often use the passage of time as a thematic and structuring device; the mere fact that some specific amount of time has passed may be important for understanding characters. Years go by in Alice Walker's *The Color Purple*, for example, allowing her characters to grow and change. But because of her method of telling the stories—through letters—we are not immediately aware of how much time passes until near the end of the book. Because we read the letters one after the other, we get the illusion of time passing quickly. In fact, the letters are written at long intervals, which means that we must consciously slow down the time of the novel to understand its effect on the characters. What clues, then, does the author give to indicate how much time is passing? Is the passage of time in the work relevant to characterization and theme? Is it important to the plausibility of the plot? If an author seems to obscure how much time is passing, why? Does the author use time as a structuring device?

Third, how is the passage of time perceived? Time may seem to move very slowly or very quickly, depending on a character's state of mind. Thus our recognition of how a character perceives time helps us understand the character's internal conflicts and attitudes.

In *Jane Eyre*, for example, Charlotte Brontë intertwines length of time and perception of time. Jane, the narrator, describes her stays at various "houses." She spends about the same amount of time at each house, but the length of her description of each stay is proportional to the value she places on it. She devotes 100 pages (in the Penguin edition) to her stays with the Reeds and at Lowood, and 100 pages to her stay with the Rivers family. But she devotes 235 pages to her stay at Thornfield, where she falls in love with Mr. Rochester. The effect of these unequal proportions is to slow down the time spent at Thornfield and thus to emphasize Jane's emotional reaction to the experiences she has there.

Brontë uses this slowing-down method with specific events as well. In fact, the novel is a collection of highly charged, intensely felt moments in Jane's life that seem to last far longer than they actually do. The novel opens, for example, with Jane's imprisonment in the hated "red room" of the Reed mansion. As her anger subsides, she becomes aware that the room is "chill," "silent," and "solemn." She recalls that Mr. Reed died there. In a mirror she sees her "glittering eyes of fear moving where all else was still." Daylight "forsakes" the room. She feels "oppressed, suffocated" at thoughts of Mr. Reed's death and the possibility of her own. When she sees a light on the wall, she thinks it is a ghost. She screams. Mrs. Reed rushes to check on her. She thrusts Jane back into the room and locks the door. Jane faints from hysteria. The length of this description corresponds to Jane's perception of time, which in turn corresponds to her fear of the room. Each detail is like the tick of a loud clock.

What, then, is the relationship between the length of narrated events and the amount of time in which they occur? Is the author purposely slowing down or speeding up our perception of time? Why? What mental states or internal conflicts does a character's perception of time reveal?

Questions about social environment   Often the social environment represented in a work is of little importance. Sometimes, in fact, there is virtually no social environment. But when it does seem important, a good essay topic should emerge from these questions: What is the social environment portrayed in the work—the manners, mores, customs, rituals, codes of conduct of a society? What does the author seem to think about them? (Approving? Ambivalent? Disapproving?) How do they affect the characters? Sinclair Lewis spends much of his novel *Babbitt* describing the social environment of his fictional midwestern city, Zenith. And then he shows that the pressure to conform to this environment is almost irresistible. His characters sometimes want to rebel against this pressure, but they are too weak to do so without extreme guilt or without threat to their economic and social security. Their social environment determines their behavior and entraps them.

Questions about atmosphere   *Atmosphere* refers to the emotional reaction that we and—usually—the characters have to the setting of a work. Sometimes the atmosphere is difficult to define, but it often inheres in the sensuous quality of the setting. Our emotional reaction to the Hamlin Garland passage above is pain, discomfort, weariness, and oppression, mainly because of his emphasis on the thermal sense, the sense of hot and cold. Your most fruitful questions about atmosphere will probably be, What methods does the author use to create the work's atmosphere? What does the author achieve by creating this atmosphere? Why does the author create this particular atmosphere? Sometimes, the author's purpose may simply be to play upon your emotions. Poe, for example, wants to scare us. Garland's purpose, however, is more meaningful. He seems to want to convince us of a philosophical point: physical environment affects human behavior. Joseph Conrad in *Heart of Darkness* creates an atmosphere of mystery, foreboding, and imminent danger to reflect his hatred of colonialism and his belief that "civilized" people are capable of the worst barbarities.

Thinking on Paper About Setting

1. Mark the most extensive or important descriptions of physical place. Underline the most telling words and phrases.

2. Characterize physical locales, such as houses, rooms, outdoor areas.

3. Explain the relationship to the physical place that one or more of the main characters has. Explain the influence that place exerts on the characters.

4. Arrange the main events in chronological order. Indicate when each event occurs.

5. Mark passages where a character's emotional state affects the way the passage of time is presented to us.

6. List the historical circumstances and characters that occur in the work. Explain their importance.

7. List the patterns of behavior that characterize the social environment of the work. For example, people drink heavily, go to church, have tea, gamble, throw parties, go dancing, cruise around in cars, get in fights, marry, have children, cheat in business, wander restlessly, and so forth.

8. Mark scenes in which the author or characters express approval or disapproval of these patterns of behavior.

9. Explain the influence one or more of these patterns has on a character or characters.

10. Mark sections that contribute to atmosphere. Underline key words and phrases.

11. List the traits of the atmosphere.

Point of View

Point of view is the author's relationship to his or her fictional world, especially to the minds of the characters. Put another way, point of view is the position from which the story is told. There are four common points of view, four positions the author can adopt in telling the story.

Omniscient point of view   In the omniscient position, the author, not one of the characters, tells the story, and the author assumes complete knowledge of the characters' actions and thoughts. The author can thus move at will from one place to another, one time to another, one character to another, and can even speak his or her own views directly to the reader as the work goes along. The author will tell us anything he or she chooses about the created world of the work. Many of the great eighteenth- and nineteenth-century novels utilize an omniscient point of view; examples are Hawthorne's *The Scarlet Letter*, Hardy's *Tess of the D'Urbervilles*, and Fielding's *Joseph Andrews*.

Limited omniscient point of view   When the limited omniscient position is used, the author still narrates the story but restricts (limits) his or her revelation—and therefore our knowledge—of the thoughts of all but one character. This character may be either a main or peripheral character. One name for this character is "central consciousness." A device of plot and characterization that often accompanies this point of view is the character's gradual discovery of himself or herself until the story climaxes in an epiphany (see pages 50–51). Examples of the limited omniscient point of view are Hawthorne's "Young Goodman Brown," Crane's "The Open Boat," and, for the most part, Jane Austen's *Pride and Prejudice*. Sometimes the author restricts the point of view so severely that we see everything solely through the mind of a single character, like sunlight filtered through the leaves and branches of a tall tree. The later fiction of Henry James experiments with this severe restriction of the limited omniscient point of view. His story "The Beast in the Jungle" and his novel *The Ambassadors* are examples. Other writers, such as James Joyce, Virginia Woolf, and William Faulkner, carry James's experiments further with a "stream of consciousness" technique, which puts the reader literally in the mind of a character. In the first section of Faulkner's *The Sound and the Fury* we experience the chaotic thoughts of a mentally retarded man, and we view the novel's world solely through his mind. A short story that uses a stream-of-consciousness technique is Katherine Anne Porter's "The Jilting of Granny Weatherall."

First-person point of view   In the first-person position, the author is even more restricted: one of the characters tells the story, eliminating the author as narrator. Whereas in the limited omniscient point of view the author can reveal anything about one character, even things the character may be dimly aware of, here the narration is restricted to what one character *says* he or she observes. The character-narrator may be a major character who is at the center of events or a minor character who does not participate but simply observes the action. Examples of first-person narratives are Dickens's *Great Expectations*, Twain's *Huckleberry Finn*, F. Scott Fitzgerald's *The Great Gatsby*, Poe's "The Cask of Amontillado," and Melville's "Bartleby the Scrivener." An unusual use of the first-person point of view is the epistolary narrative, which reveals action through letters. (An *epistle* is a letter and *epistolary* means written in letters.) Samuel Richardson's *Pamela*, Henry James's "A Bundle of Letters," and Alice Walker's *The Color Purple* are all epistolary narratives.

Objective (dramatic) point of view   In the objective position, the author is more restricted than in any other. Though the author is the narrator, he or she refuses to enter the minds of any of the characters. The writer sees them (and lets us see them) as we would in real life. This point of view is sometimes called "dramatic" because we see the characters as we would the characters in a play. We learn about them from what they say and do, how they look, and what other characters say about them. But we don't learn what they think unless they tell us. This point of view is the least common of all. Examples are Hemingway's "Hills Like White Elephants" and "The Killers," Stephen Crane's "The Blue Hotel," and Shirley Jackson's "The Lottery."

Tone *Tone* is also an aspect of point of view since it has a great deal to do with the narrator. Tone is the narrator's predominant attitude toward the subject, whether that subject be a particular setting, an event, a character, or an idea. The narrator conveys his or her attitude through the way narrative devices are handled, including choice of words. Sometimes the narrator will state point-blank how he or she feels about a subject; more often, the narrator's attitude is conveyed indirectly. Jack Burden, the narrator of Robert Penn Warren's *All the King's Men*, maintains a flippant and cynical tone through most of the narration. Jake Barnes, the narrator of Hemingway's *The Sun Also Rises*, maintains a stoical, hardboiled tone. Dr. Watson, the narrator of the Sherlock Holmes stories, manifests a bemused, surprised tone.

Questions about point of view Point of view is important to an understanding of a story in two main ways. First, the author may choose a particular point of view in order to emphasize one character's perception of things. Point of view also influences *our* perception of things. The omniscient narrator can tell us what a character thinks, but the limited omniscient and first-person points of view make us *experience* what the character thinks. To make the emphasis even more emphatic, an author may include several points of view in the same work. Dickens in *Bleak House* shuttles back and forth between a first-person narrative and an omniscient narrative. We see that the first-person narrator has a more limited view of things than the omniscient narrator. Point of view here becomes a means of developing character and of making a point about the limits of human perception.

Second, point of view is important when you suspect the trustworthiness of the narrator. A preliminary question is, Who tells the story? But a searching follow-up question is, Can you trust the narrator to tell you the truth about the events, characters, and setting of the story? You can almost always trust omniscient narrators. But you should be suspicious about first-person narrators and the "centers-of-consciousness" characters in limited omniscient stories. Sometimes these characters distort what they observe. Ask, then, if circumstances such as their age, education, social status, prejudices, or emotional states should make you question the accuracy or validity of what they say and think. Ask, also, if the author differentiates between his or her view of things and the characters' views.

Mark Twain makes such a distinction in *Huckleberry Finn*. When Huck sees the Grangerford house, he says, "It was a mighty nice family, and a mighty nice house, too. I hadn't seen no house out in the country before that was so nice and had so much style." He proceeds to describe the interior with awe and reverence. But although Huck is impressed with the furnishings, Twain clearly is not. We recognize Twain's attitude from the details Huck provides: the unread books, the reproductions of sentimental paintings, the damaged imitation fruit, the crockery animals, the broken clock, the painted hearth, the tablecloth "made out of beautiful oilcloth," the piano "that had tin pans in it." Huck also shows his admiration for Emmeline Grangerford's poetry by reproducing some of it to share with us. But we see, as Twain wants us to see, that the poetry is awful.

Finally, Huck is awestruck by the family's aristrocratic bearing: "Col. Grangerford was a gentleman, you see. He was a gentleman all over; and so was his family. He was well born. . . . He didn't have to tell anybody to mind their manners—everybody was always good mannered where he was." Yet he fails to see, as Twain and we see, the ironic contrast between the family's good manners and its conduct of an illogical, murderous feud with another family. Twain's handling of point of view in this novel helps to develop both character and theme. By presenting Huck's credulous view of things, it develops Huck as an essentially innocent person. By ironically contrasting Twain's view to Huck's, it underscores the author's harsher and more pessimistic perception of "reality."

Once you have determined a work's point of view, good essay topics should emerge from two general questions: Why has the author chosen this point of view? What effects does it have on other elements of the story—theme, characterization, setting, language? Some follow-up questions are these: What effect does the author's point of view have on us and the way we view the world of the work? For example, if the point of view is first person, we have a much more limited view than if it is omniscient. The omniscient point of view makes us feel as though we understand everything about the world of the work, as though everything revealed by the omniscient narrator is true. What perspective of the world, then, does the author want us to have? Also, what do we learn about the nature of human perception from the author's handling of first person and especially limited omniscience? Henry James's limited omniscience often shows people as blind to the needs and desires of other people and of themselves as well. If the point of view is first person, is the narrator telling the story to someone? If so, to whom? How do they react? What do we learn about the narrator from that fact? Try this question on Poe's "The Cask of Amontillado," for example, and see what you come up with. If the point of view is objective (dramatic), does it seem as though the narrator is emotionally uninvolved and rationally objective about the characters and events? What do we gain by not being able to enter the characters' minds?

Thinking on Paper About Point of View

1. Identify the point of view of the story. Describe how the story would change if it were told from each of the other points of view.
2. List the main characters in the story. Write a paragraph on one or more characters, explaining how the story would be different if that character were narrating it.
3. Mark places where the narrator or central consciousness differs from our view of reality or fails to see important truths that we or other characters see.
4. Mark places that are particularly expressive of the narrator's tone. List the characteristics of tone.

Irony

Authors use irony pervasively to convey their ideas. But irony is a diverse and often complex intellectual phenomenon difficult to define in a sentence or two. Generally, *irony* makes visible a contrast between appearance and reality. More fully and specifically, it exposes and underscores a contrast between (1) what is and what **seems** to be, (2) between what is and what **ought** to be, (3) between what is and what one **wishes** to be, and (4) between what is and what one **expects** to be. Incongruity is the method of irony; opposites come suddenly together so that the disparity is obvious to discriminating readers. There are many kinds of irony, but four are common in literature.

Verbal irony   Verbal irony is perhaps the most common form of irony. Most people use or hear verbal irony daily. In verbal irony, people say the opposite of what they mean. For example, if the day has been terrible, you might say, "Boy, this has been a great day!" The hearer knows that this statement is ironic because of the speaker's tone of voice and facial or bodily expressions or because the hearer is familiar with the situation and immediately sees the discrepancy between statement and actuality. Understatement and overstatement are two forms of verbal irony. In *understatement*, one minimizes the nature of something. "It was a pretty good game," one might say after seeing a no-hitter. Mark Twain's famous telegram is another example of understatement: "The reports of my death are greatly exaggerated." In *overstatement* one exaggerates the nature of something. After standing in a long line, you might say, "There were about a million people in that line!"

Why do people use verbal irony? The answer is that verbal irony is more emphatic than a point-blank statement of the truth. It achieves its effect by reminding the hearer or reader of what the opposite reality is and thus providing a scale by which to judge the present reality. Verbal irony often represents a mental agility—wit—that people find striking and, as with the Mark Twain retort, entertaining. Verbal irony in its most bitter and destructive form becomes *sarcasm*, in which the speaker condemns someone by pretending to praise him:

> Oh, you're a real angel. You're the noble and upright man who wouldn't think of dirtying his pure little hands with company business. But all along, behind our backs, you were just as greedy and ruthless as the rest of us.

Situational irony   In situational irony, the situation is different from what common sense indicates it is, will be, or ought to be. It is ironic, for example, that General George Patton should have lived through the thickest of tank battles during World War II and then, after the war, have been killed accidentally by one of his own men. It is ironic that someone we expect to be upright—a minister or judge—should be the most repulsive of scoundrels. Authors often use situational irony to expose hypocrisy and injustice. A profound example is Hawthorne's *The Scarlet Letter*, in which the townspeople regard the minister Arthur Dimmesdale as sanctified and angelic when in fact he shamefully hides his adultery with Hester Prynne, allowing her to take all the blame.

Attitudinal irony   Situational irony results from what *most* people expect, whereas attitudinal irony results from what one person expects. In attitudinal irony, an individual thinks that reality is one way when, in fact, it is a very different way. A frequent example in literature is the naive character—Fielding's Parson Adams, Cervantes's Don Quixote, Dickens's Mr. Micawber, Voltaire's Candide—who thinks that everyone is upright and that everything will turn out for the best, when in fact the people he or she meet are consistently corrupt and the things that happen to him or her are destructive and painful.

Dramatic irony   Dramatic irony occurs in plays when characters state something that they believe to be true but that the audience knows to be false. An example is the play *Oedipus Rex*. Like all Greek tragedies, *Oedipus Rex* dramatizes a myth that its audiences knew. Thus when Oedipus at the beginning boasts that he will personally find and punish the reprobate who killed King Laius, the audience recognizes this boast as ironic. Oedipus does not know, but the audience knows, that he himself is the unwitting murderer of Laius. Although dramatic irony gets its name from drama, it can occur in all forms of literature. The key to the existence of dramatic irony is the reader's foreknowledge of coming events. Many works become newly interesting when you reread them, because you now know what will happen but the characters do not; this dramatic irony intensifies characterization and makes you aware of tensions that you could not have known about during your initial reading.

Questions about irony   The first question to ask is, What are the most obvious ironies in the work? The second is, How are the ironies important? What, for example, are their implications? Shirley Jackson's "The Lottery" is layered with irony. An essay might deal with one of its ironies, such as the ironic contrast between the placid country-town setting and the horrible deeds done there. The setting is everyone's nostalgic image of the ideal American small town, with its central square, post office, country store, cranky old men, gossipy housewives, laconic farmers, mischievous children, settled routine, and friendly atmosphere. Is Jackson implying, then, that "normal" American communities conduct lotteries to decide which of their members is to be destroyed by the others? The answer is yes, she is suggesting just this. Americans are guilty of conducting "lotteries," perhaps not exactly in this manner, but with equal arbitrariness and cruelty. Instead of making this point directly, however, she implies it through the use of irony. And she achieves a much greater emphasis than if she were to state her accusation directly. She shocks us by associating something that we all agree is horrible with a way of life that up to now we had thought was "normal" and benign. The irony packs an emotional wallop that at least gets our attention and, she hopes, will get us thinking.

Other, more specific, questions about irony are these:

Verbal irony: If characters constantly use verbal irony, why? What do we learn about their attitudes toward the world? Does their verbal irony usually take the form of sarcasm? Are they, then, bitter, disappointed people or simply realistic? Does their disappointment stem from selfishness or altruistic idealism?

Situational irony: What are the most obvious situational ironies? What are the less obvious ones? Which are more important? Do the less obvious ironies contradict or reinforce the more obvious ones? Do the situational ironies result from fate or human actions? Are the characters aware of the situational ironies? At what point do they become aware of them? By pointing out situational ironies, what is the author trying to say to us? Should we blame the characters for creating situational ironies or not understanding them? Does the author, for example, want *us* to do something about them—to reform society and ourselves?

Attitudinal irony: What attitudes do the characters have that contradict reality? Are we supposed to admire the characters who misconstrue the world, or blame them for being naïve and deluded? What troubles do they encounter because of their attitudes?

Dramatic irony: What do you know about coming events or past events in the work that the characters do not know? When and what do they say that triggers this disparity? What does the author want us to think of them when they say these things? Are we supposed to sympathize with them, or blame them for not being farsighted? What effect does dramatic irony have on the plot? Does it, for example, make the plot suspenseful? Are any of the ironies in the work funny? Do they disturb you? Are they too painful and serious for laughter? What is the author's attitude toward them? Do *you* share the author's attitude?

Thinking on Paper About Irony

1. Mark examples of verbal irony, either by the narrator or other characters. Explain how a character's verbal irony helps characterize him or her.

2. Mark episodes in which a character's beliefs and expectations are contradicted by reality. Explain the importance to characterization of these episodes.

3. List instances of situational irony; identify people, for example, whom we expect to behave in one way but who behave quite differently. Explain the importance to theme of these instances.

Symbolism

In the broadest sense, a symbol is something that represents something else. Words, for example, are symbols. But in literature, a *symbol* is an object that has meaning beyond itself. The object is concrete and the meanings are abstract. Fire, for example, may symbolize general destruction (as in James Baldwin's title *The Fire Next Time*), or passion (the "flames of desire"), or hell (the "fiery furnace"). Symbols, however, are not metaphors; they are not analogies that clarify abstractions, such as the following metaphor from Shakespeare's Sonnet 116: love

> is an ever-fixèd mark,
> That looks on tempests and is never shaken.

Here, the abstract concept (the referent) is "love" and the clarifying concrete object is the stable mark (buoy, lighthouse, rock) that tempests cannot budge. A symbol, in contrast, is a concrete object with no clear referent and thus no fixed meaning. Instead, it merely suggests the meaning and, in an odd way, partly *is* the meaning. For this reason, the meaning of symbols is difficult to pin down. And the more inexhaustible their potential meaning, the richer they are.

There are two kinds of symbol: public and private. *Public* (conventional) *symbols* are those that most people would recognize as meaning something fairly definite. Examples of public symbols are the cross, the star of David, the American Eagle, flags of countries, the colors red (for "stop") and green (for "go"), the skull and crossbones.

Private symbols are unique to an individual or to a single work. Only from clues in the work itself can we learn the symbolic value of the object. There are many examples of private symbols in literature. In F. Scott Fitzgerald's *The Great Gatsby*, there is an area between the posh Long Island suburbs and New York City through which the major characters drive at various times and which Fitzgerald calls a "valley of ashes." It is a desolate, grey, sterile place, and over it all broods a partly obliterated billboard advertisement that features the enormous eyes of Doctor T. J. Eckleburg, an optometrist. Fitzgerald invests this area with symbolic meaning. He associates it with moral decay, urban blight, the oppression of the poor by the wealthy, meaninglessness, hell, and violent death. At one point he connects the eyes with failure of vision, at another with God, who sees all things. But we never know exactly what the valley of ashes represents; instead, it resonates with many possible meanings, and this resonance accounts for its powerful impact on readers.

Questions about symbolism   Not every work uses symbols, and not every character, incident, or object in a work has symbolic value. You should ask the fundamental question, What symbols does the work seem to have? But you should beware of finding "symbols" where none were intended. A second question, then, is necessary to the believability of any essay you might write on symbols: How do you know they are symbols? Or, What does the author do that gives symbolic meaning to the elements you mention? Once you answer this question to your own—and your reader's—satisfaction, you can move on to a third and more interesting question: What does the symbol mean? You could, for example, write about the symbolic meaning of rain in Hemingway's *A Farewell to Arms*. The following dialogue between Frederic Henry and Catherine Barkley strongly suggests that Hemingway intended a symbolic meaning for rain; it also suggests what the symbol represents:

> "It's raining hard." [Frederic says]
> "And you'll always love me, won't you?" [Catherine replies]
> "Yes."
> "And the rain won't make any difference?"
> "No."
> "That's good. Because I'm afraid of the rain."
> "Why? . . . Tell me."
> "All right. I'm afraid of the rain because sometimes I see me dead in it."
> "No."
> "And sometimes I see you dead in it. . . . It's all nonsense. It's only nonsense. I'm not afraid of the rain. I'm not afraid of the rain. Oh, oh, God, I wish I wasn't." She was crying. I comforted her and she stopped crying. But outside it kept on raining.

Throughout the novel, Hemingway's recurrent association of rain with destruction of all kinds broadens its significance from a mere metaphor for death to other and more general qualities, such as war, fate, alienation, foreboding, doom, "reality." Because of these associations, the last sentence of the novel is more than just a description of the weather: "After a while I went out and left the hospital and walked back to the hotel in the rain." The sentence seems to suggest that Frederic is stoically and bravely facing the harsh realities—including Catherine's death, the war, the arbitrariness and cruelty of fate—represented by the rain.

Thinking on Paper About Symbolism

1. List the symbols in the work.
2. Mark the descriptions or episodes that give the symbols meaning.
3. List each symbol's meanings.

OTHER ELEMENTS

In this chapter we have treated the elements most obviously identified with fiction. But other elements are also sometimes important in fiction: dialogue, description, metaphor, poetic use of language, diction. We will discuss these other elements in the next two chapters.

FOR FURTHER STUDY

Booth, Wayne C. *The Rhetoric of Fiction.* Chicago: U of Chicago P, 1961.

Forster, E. M. *Aspects of the Novel.* New York: Harcourt, 1954.

Poe, Edgar Allan. Reviews of Hawthorne's *Twice-Told Tales.* Published first in *Graham's Magazine,* April and May 1842; widely reprinted since.

Scholes, Robert, and Robert Kellogg. *The Nature of Narrative.* New York: Oxford UP, 1966.

Stevich, Philip, ed. *The Theory of the Novel.* New York: The Free Press, 1967.

Wellek, René, and Austin Warren. *Theory of Literature.* New York: Harcourt, 1956.

Poe in his reviews of Hawthorne's *Twice-Told Tales*, while on one hand declaring Hawthorne a "man of the truest genius" and on the other accusing him of "plagiarism," also lays out the theoretical basis for the modern short story. He says, among other things, that the story should create a single impression with the greatest economy of means. His essay "The Philosophy of Composition" (1846) applies much the same principles to poetry. E. M. Forster was an important twentieth-century English novelist, and his *Aspects of the Novel* is a beautifully written, compelling defense of what he thinks constitutes good fiction. In this book Forster coins and explains the terms "flat" and "round" characters, but he does much more. Wayne C. Booth in *The Rhetoric of Fiction* makes many cogent comments about the nature of fiction at the same time that he argues a thesis. His thesis is that fiction is rhetorical—that it offers comments on the nature of reality and uses various devices to persuade us that these comments are valid. *The Theory of the Novel* is a collection of essays and excerpts; it tries to represent some of the best thinking on all the elements of fiction. Scholes and Kellogg's *The Nature of Narrative* is a closely reasoned and highly suggestive analysis of narrative in fiction as well as in other genres. Wellek and Warren's *Theory of Literature* is a difficult but brilliant book about the nature of literature; it discusses all the genres but is especially good on fiction. It has greatly influenced the discussion of literature in this book.

5

How to Analyze Drama

DRAMA CONTAINS many of the elements of fiction. Like fiction, drama contains plot, characters, theme, and setting. Like fiction, drama uses irony and symbolism. And indeed, you can read a play as you would a short novel, using your imagination to fill in all the "missing" material you typically find in fiction—character description, background information, vivid action scenes. Similarly, drama often contains many of the elements of poetry, and you can read the poetic passages in plays just as you read any poetry. Because of the great similarity of drama to fiction and poetry, the definitions, questions, and exercises stated in the preceding chapter on fiction and in the following chapter on poetry are all equally valid for drama. Use them to study specific plays systematically and to generate ideas that you might turn into essay topics.

THE NATURE OF DRAMA

Drama is different from fiction and most poetry in one essential way: It is meant to be performed. Some theorists of drama argue that a play is incomplete *until* it is performed. According to the critic Bernard Beckerman in *Dynamics of Drama,* "a play is a mere skeleton; performance fleshes out the bones." When you read a play, you miss qualities the playwright intended as a part of the play. For one thing, you miss the audience, whose physical presence and reactions to the performance influence both the performance and your perception of the play. For another, you miss the set designers' vision of the atmosphere and physical world of the play. You miss the interpretive art of the actors and the illusion they can create of real life unfolding before your eyes. You miss the physical and emotional *experience* of drama that a production can give you.

This is not to say that reading a play carefully is not worth doing. Sometimes you miss aspects of plays during performance that most people can catch only when reading the play. This is especially true of plays written in poetry. Shakespeare, for example, has Romeo and Juliet, when they first meet, not only exchange comments that play upon a complex metaphor (a pilgrim coming to a shrine), but he molds their exchange into a sonnet. It is unlikely that a playgoer, upon hearing this exchange, would think, "Aha! That was a sonnet!" Rather, you notice poetic devices such as rhyme scheme and involved patterns of imagery only in reading carefully. And even if your purpose is to produce the play, you must read carefully, because productions are based upon interpretations of the plays. "Literary" devices such as this sonnet may not be immediately recognizable by the audience, but they provide clues to how the playwright wanted the play performed. In fact, everything in the play is a clue to its ideal performance and thus deserves studious attention.

To read a play with an eye to how the play might be produced, therefore, is to understand the play as the playwright conceived it. Since we discuss the elements of fiction and poetry in chapters 4 and 6, we will concentrate in this chapter on how you can use the potential performance of drama as a means of understanding its elements.

THE ELEMENTS OF DRAMA

Plot

Because the playwright has only a short time (two hours or so) to develop plot and because the playwright's audience experiences the play in one sitting, with little immediate opportunity to review it, the playwright must keep the plot simple and clear enough for an audience to grasp during the length of the performance. This means that the playwright cannot indulge in numerous subplots or in intricate plot complications; otherwise the playgoer would become confused. Playwrights, therefore, limit the number of characters in the play. (The fewer the characters, the simpler the plot can be.) Playwrights also emphasize conflict to keep the audience involved in the action and establish easily discernible patterns of cause and effect.

Although the playwright can present physical action without having to use words, the action (and the conflict implicit in the action) must be understandable to the audience. The most important and almost inevitable means for doing this is dialogue—people talking to people. Playwrights, then, strive to make every word of dialogue help move the plot forward. The near inevitability of dialogue also means that playwrights focus largely on conflicts between people rather than conflicts between people and nonhuman forces. In contrast, fiction need not represent characters' words or thoughts and so is freer to depict conflicts between people and nonhuman forces. Jack London's short story "To Build a Fire" does give the thoughts of the protagonist; but otherwise there is no "dialogue," just the author's record of the protagonist's conflict with the harsh Yukon landscape. It would be very difficult for a play to duplicate this kind of conflict. Plays sometimes do portray conflicts between people and nonhuman forces, but these conflicts are revealed through dialogue and usually through conflicts between the characters.

Because the time and space for a presentation is limited, certain kinds of action—battles and sports activities, for example—cannot be represented fully or literally on the stage. These activities must be concentrated or symbolized. A duel onstage, for example, might represent an entire battle; a plantation house that in act one is sparkling new but in act four is ramshackled might represent the activities that have brought a once-grand family to the brink of ruin. Sometimes the playwright has activities occur offstage. A character might describe events that have just taken place, but the audience does not see these events. It learns about them only through the dialogue.

The actions that take place during the presentation of the play— onstage or offstage actions—are usually only a part of a larger series of events. Bernard Beckerman helpfully distinguishes the two sets of actions by the terms *plot* (what occurs during the play) and *story* (what occurs before, during, and after the play). The plot of *Oedipus Rex*, for example, is Oedipus's attempt to rid Thebes of a blight and his resulting discovery of who he is and the nature of his crimes. The story of the play is Oedipus's entire history, starting with his parents' attempt to kill him when he was an infant and ending with his death at Colonus. Some plays feature a plot that is only a small part (but usually a very important and climactic part) of a story. Other plays feature a plot that is almost equivalent to the story. Shakespeare's *Macbeth*, for example, has almost no important past and future events; nearly all the action occurs within the play itself. Thus the plot and story of *Macbeth* are nearly equivalent. The events in *Hamlet*, however, occur after a murder and a marriage and, long before that, a war between Denmark and Norway, all of which profoundly affect the action within the play itself; the conclusion of the play, furthermore, suggests something of what the future of Denmark will be like under its new ruler, the Norwegian king Fortinbras.

The plotting in drama depends in part on establishing *audience expectations* of what will happen in the immediate future, as the play is unfolding. Both fiction and poetry, in contrast, focus more on what has already happened. The playwright, of course, predetermines the events in a play; but as we watch, we experience the illusion that the action is occurring in the present and that neither we nor the characters know what will happen next. This effect of expectation is heightened in drama, because as we watch the play we have little time to reflect on what has happened, whereas when we read a novel we at least have the choice of pausing and thinking about what we have read. Playwrights often rely heavily on what they predict our expectations will be, given certain kinds of action and certain kinds of characters. They may choose to fulfill our expectations or to surprise us by thwarting them.

The *structural divisions* of plays affect plot. Playwrights usually provide structural divisions to give playgoers physical relief—a few moments to stand up, walk about, stretch, or reflect (however briefly) on what they have seen. Structural divisions also serve to allow set changes. In addition to such performance considerations, structural divisions also mark off segments of the plot. *Formal structural divisions* are those specified in the play or the program—acts and scenes. *Informal structural divisions* can be smaller units within an act or scene, units not identified as such by the playwright but that nonetheless have a self-contained quality. In formal structural units, the playwright might call for the curtain to come down, the lights to go off, or the characters to leave the stage to signal the end of a unit. Shakespeare often ends his units with a couplet. In informal units, none of these things may happen; instead, the units may just flow together. Characteristic of all of them, however, is a rising action, a climax, and possibly a brief falling action. The climax of these units is usually a moment of revelation, either to the main characters, to other characters, or to the audience. An example is Hamlet's recognition at the climax of the play-within-a-play scene that King Claudius has murdered Hamlet's father, the former king. All of the units of a play contribute to the rising action of the entire play and lead finally to its main climax.

Questions about plot   We said that plot in drama needs to be relatively simple and clear. In the play you are studying, is it? If not, why would the playwright want to create confusion about the important conflicts and cause-and-effect relationships? Sometimes the playwright *tries* to make such confusion. Congreve in *The Way of the World*, for example, creates a pattern of relationships so confusing that an audience is hard put to figure out who has done what to whom, especially at the breakneck speed the play is usually performed. He probably does this on purpose to indicate the complicated texture of Restoration upper-class society and the difficulty of finding one's way through it safely and honorably. Basic questions, of course, are, What are the main conflicts? What has caused the conflicts existing at the beginning of the play? What causes the conflicts that emerge during the course of the play? Who is in conflict with whom? Why? Are any of the characters in conflict with forces larger than just individuals—society, for example, or fate? How are the conflicts resolved?

What actions occur offstage? Why does the author elect to place some actions offstage and other actions onstage? In *Macbeth*, for example, Shakespeare has the murder of King Duncan (at the beginning of the play) occur offstage, but later he has the murder of Banquo and, in another scene, the murder of Macduff's family (or part of it) occur onstage. Why, then, does he choose to put one murder offstage and other murders onstage? Questions that should lead to answers to this are, How do the characters react to the offstage events? What does the playwright want us to learn from the characters' reactions? Shakespeare probably places Duncan's murder offstage because he wants the audience to focus attention on Macbeth and Lady Macbeth's reaction to the murder. Related questions are, What does the playwright use to represent or symbolize action that occurs offstage? What do we learn about the nature of the actions from these representations? When Macbeth returns from killing Duncan, he carries the murder weapons, all covered with blood. His hands are covered with blood. When Lady Macbeth returns from smearing blood all over the sleeping guards, *her* hands are covered with blood. The more we see of this blood and the more they talk about it, the more grisly, and physical, and sticky the murder seems. Without actually describing the murder, Shakespeare uses a physical image, blood, and the characters' reaction to it to signal what the murder was like.

What is the "plot" of the play? What is the "story"? If the plot is only part of the story, why does the playwright choose this part? What has happened before the play begins? What will happen afterward? As Beckerman points out, if the plot is only part of a larger or ongoing story, then the characters are more likely to seem at the mercy of forces beyond their control; whereas, if the plot and story are roughly equivalent, the characters will seem more free to choose and mold their own fate. The plot of *Romeo and Juliet*, for example, is only one episode—the final episode, we hope—of a generations-long, murderous, and absurd family feud. Romeo and Juliet are, therefore, "star-crossed" and "death-marked"; try as they will, they cannot escape the undertow of their families' history. Even Prince Escalus, the only person in the play with both power and good sense, can do nothing to avert the concluding tragedy. Macbeth and Lady Macbeth, in contrast, choose to do evil at the beginning of the play and thus give rise to the forces that destroy them.

What expectations does the plot call up in the audience? Does the playwright fulfill those expectations? If not, how and why not? Most traditional comedy, for example, offers young lovers as staple characters. We expect the lovers, after suitable complications, to find happiness together, usually signaled at the end by betrothal or marriage. But sometimes the playwright introduces potential lovers, gives us something like a light comic tone, creates comic complications, but thwarts our expectations that they will marry. Examples are Etherege's *The Man of Mode*, Molière's *The Misanthrope*, and Shaw's *Mrs. Warren's Profession*. Another example is Chekhov's *The Cherry Orchard*, which he called a comedy, even though it is not always played as such. In this play, the mian character, Lopakhin, and the adopted daughter of the family he is trying to rescue from economic disaster, seem meant for each other. There is much talk throughout the play of their marrying. Such a marriage would seem to be good for both of them. They agree to marry. And since they are sympathetic characters, the audience wants them to marry. Yet they never do. Why does Chekhov create the expectation and even hope of their marriage and then abort it? The answer to this question provides insight into Chekhov's purposes in *The Cherry Orchard*; and since he uses the same device in other plays—*Three Sisters*, for example—the answer throws light on his entire dramatic method.

What are the formal structural divisions of the plays? How many of them are there—three acts, four, five? How do the formal divisions reflect the playwright's purposes and materials? Oscar Wilde's *The Importance of Being Earnest*, for example, is divided into three acts. The first act takes place in London, the second and the third in the country. This division reflects the double-identity motif in the plot, because the main character pretends to have two identities, a city identity and a country identity. The first two acts reflect these opposing identities. The third act, however, synthesizes the two. Events and revelations allow the main character to bring his city and country identities into one happy whole. The structure of the play, then, neatly reflects the "thesis, antithesis, synthesis" pattern of oppositions and resolution of oppositions.

What are the informal units of the play? For *all* the units, what are the climaxes of each? What is revealed in the climax—to the main character featured in the unit, to other characters, to the audience? How is a particular unit important to the whole play? What is the main climax of the play? Why is it the "main" climax? What do you learn from it? Is there more than one climax that might qualify as the main climax? Why does the playwright include more than one?

Thinking on Paper About Plot

1. List the conflicts revealed in each major section of the play (usually acts, but sometimes scenes).

2. Explain how one or more of these conflicts is first made evident. Pay close attention to dialogue.

3. Summarize how a conflict is developed through the whole play and how it is resolved.

4. Summarize the events, either in the past or present, that cause conflict. If there is one event that caused or causes all the conflicts, summarize it in detail and explain why and how it is so important.

5. List the external conflicts. Explain how they are represented on stage. Through dialogue? Through physical action? Through symbolic stage props?

6. List the events that precede the action of the play. Explain the effect, if any, of these prior events on the action.

7. Summarize the events in each major structural unit of the play. Explain the relationship of the play's units to the plot's structure. Show how the action in each unit rises to a climax.

8. Mark some informal structural divisions in the play. Note the rising action and climax of these units.

9. Describe one important scene in detail. Explain how the characters' actions and dialogue reveal conflict. Explain the importance of the scene to the whole play.

10. Describe the climax of the play. Explain what conflicts are resolved.

11. List the main plot and the subplots. Explain the relationship of the subplots to the main plot.

12. List the events that occur offstage. Explain why the playwright has one or more of these occur offstage rather than onstage.

13. Summarize the situation at the beginning of the play and state what you expect to happen. Explain how the play does or does not fulfill those expectations.

Characterization

As with plot, the playwright must keep character portrayal simple enough for an audience to understand during the course of a single performance. Therefore, the playwright must rely heavily on flat characters, especially stereotyped ("stock") characters, whose personalities and moral traits are easily caught and remembered by the audience. The playwright may even use unsubtle stratagems of dress, dialect, physical movements, and names to communicate these traits. In Restoration and eighteenth-century comedy, for example, the names signal the traits of comic flat characters: Mrs. Loveit, Sir Fopling Flutter, Snake, Pert, Mr. Oldcastle, Lady Wishforit, Lady Sneerwell, Smirk, Handy. The playwright must also rely on static characters more heavily than dynamic characters, because restricted performance time limits the opportunity to make character changes plausible.

Edward Pixley has pointed out that when the play is dominated by flat characters, the excitement of the plot emerges from external conflicts; the focus is on action. When the play includes round characters, the excitement of the plot emerges from internal conflicts, or an interplay between external and internal conflicts; the focus is on characterization. In Wilde's *The Importance of Being Earnest*, for example, all the characters are flat and artificial; the charm of the play lies not in character development but in the witty language, in the mild satire rippling through the dialogue, and in the plot complications resulting from the confusion of identities. In contrast, Ibsen's *Hedda Gabler* presents a complex, round character, Hedda herself; and the interest of the play lies in what she will do next and why she will do it. Hedda does not change during the play, but her character traits intensify and become clearer to the audience. Round characters, therefore, hold the audience's attention by changing or, if they don't change, by becoming more intense. In either case, continual revelations about the characters grip the audience's interest.

Although the playwright may depend to an extent on exterior details to reveal character traits, the playwright's most important device for character development is dialogue—what the characters say and what they say about one another. But performance time is limited; the words of the dialogue cannot describe the character fully. Playwrights, therefore, rely heavily upon implication in the dialogue and upon "gaps"—information left out—to indicate what characters are like and what physical things they might be doing. Some critics mark this distinction with the terms *text* for the written dialogue and *subtext* for the implications and gaps. All literary genres make use of implication and gaps, but drama and poetry almost *must* rely on them because both genres are such compressed forms of communication.

A simple example of text and subtext is the scene near the beginning of *Hamlet* in which Hamlet, after a long absence, meets his university friends Horatio and Marcellus. The night before this meeting, Horatio and Marcellus have seen the ghost of Hamlet's father. But Hamlet doesn't know about the ghost; instead, he complains about his mother's marrying so soon after his father's death:

> HAMLET. Would I had met my dearest foe in heaven
> Or ever I had seen that day [the wedding day], Horatio!
> My father—methinks I see my father.
> HORATIO. Where, my lord?
> HAMLET.   In my mind's eye, Horatio.
> HORATIO. I saw him once. 'A was [he was] a goodly king.

If you were the actor playing Horatio, how would you say the line "Where, my lord?" The "gap" here is the nature of Horatio's response to Hamlet's statement, "My father—methinks I see my father." To fill the gap, you have to determine from the context how Horatio takes that statement (Shakespeare doesn't tell you how, as a novelist might), and you have to communicate his reaction to the audience by the way you say the line and by your physical demeanor. You might phrase the line as an incredulous question: "What? You see your father? But how could you, he's dead?" Or you might say it as a reflection of what you take to be Hamlet's witty mood: "I know you're joking, Hamlet. But tell me anyway. Where do you see your father?" Probably, however, you should say it in astonishment, as if you take it literally. After all, *you* have seen the ghost of Hamlet's father just a few hours before. You probably think Hamlet has now spotted the ghost, and so you say, "Good Lord, do you see it too? Where?" And you look fearfully around, trying to see the ghost too. When Hamlet indicates that he is only remembering his father, you calm down. At this point you might pause and make appropriate gestures to indicate your shift from fear and astonishment to calmness. The fact that you *have* made such a shift is indicated by your response to Hamlet: "Yes. Once, when the king was alive, I saw him too. He was an impressive looking king." This last statement shows that Horatio has moved from thinking about a supernatural phenomenon (the ghost) to thinking about a natural one (Hamlet's father when he was alive).

This brief example illustrates the greatest value of understanding a play's subtext. By "reading" the implications and the gaps in the play, you uncover the inner states of the characters—what is going on in their minds and what their hidden nature is. You also establish a correspondence between the character's inner state and what the character says and does (the character's outer state). Interpretation of subtext is essential for actors, who must figure out how to say the dialogue and what to do onstage. But it is important for readers, too, even though a reader may not work out intonation and physical movements in as much detail as actors do. The reason is that a character's inner world is the key to the character's makeup and actions. Horatio, in the example above, is a flat character, and the problem of exposing his inner state is relatively uncomplicated. But doing so gives the performance—whether seen by an audience or imagined by a reader—vividness. Horatio springs to life. He is not just an automaton reading lines; he is a real person. As for round characters, the difficulty of uncovering their inner states is much greater. Yet that is part of their fascination. Great characters like Oedipus, Macbeth, Hamlet, and Hedda Gabler grip our imaginations just because their inner states are complex and mysterious. The only way we can expose these inner states is by interpreting the subtext of the play.

Closely related to subtext in drama is *mask wearing*. Nearly every play employs the mask as a device for developing plot and characterization. Juliet wears a "mask"—pretends to be different from the way she really is—in order to fool her parents and run away with Romeo. Hamlet puts on a mask of madness to root out the murderer of his father. Hedda pretends to be the contented housewife in order to secure the wealth and social status she thinks she deserves. Macbeth and Lady Macbeth pretend to be the loyal servants and gracious hosts of King Duncan while plotting his murder. The audience may be fully aware of the mask and thus the disparity between appearance and reality, as, for example, in Juliet's case. Or the audience may be as unaware of the mask at first as are the other characters in the play, as in Hedda's case. And sometimes the mask-wearers are themselves unaware or partially unaware of their masks; that is, they deceive themselves. Oedipus, for example, doesn't know that he is masking his true identity of king-murderer. In all cases, both plot and characterization turn on revelation—the tearing away of the mask. At these moments of revelation, the audience and at least some of the characters see the reality behind the mask. Often the final unmasking comes at the climax of the plot. In *Othello*, for example, the climax occurs when Iago's mask is ripped away before Othello's shocked eyes.

Questions about characterization and plot   If the characters are flat, what are their dominant traits and what is their function in the plot? How do they help establish the conflicts in the plot? If the characters are dynamic, how do they change—from what to what? If they are static, do their traits intensify or become clearer as the play moves on? What are the important places of revelation? What do we learn about the characters? What do they learn about themselves? If the characters are round, what can you learn from the subtext of the play about their inner states? What clues in what they say and *do not say* lead you to conclusions about their thoughts and about hidden aspects of their makeup? Apply this question to specific scenes. A pattern of characterization should emerge by the end of the play. A good subject for an essay would be your interpretation of the subtext of one important scene, or of several scenes that establish a pattern.

What "masks" are the characters wearing? Who is hiding what from whom? How important is mask wearing to the plot? (Does the whole plot hinge on it, or only one part of the plot?) When are the masks removed? What causes their removal and what are the results? In general, how would you play a particular character if you were the actor? What would your bearing—your physical appearance—be? Hedda Gabler, for example, is aristocratic, proud, and forceful; she seems strong but has an inner fragility. Her rival, Thea, is hesitant, unsophisticated, and afraid; she seems weak but has an inner strength. If you were acting these characters, how would you present yourself physically to convey these qualities? How would you show that Hedda seems strong but is in fact weak? You may not actually act Hedda, of course, but determining a physical presence for her forces you to analyze her and thus understand her better.

Thinking on Paper About Characterization

1. List the character traits of each major character.

2. List the devices, such as dress, names, and gestures, that help establish the traits of a character.

3. Describe in detail the traits of a complex character, especially contradictory and seemingly inexplicable traits.

4. Explain a character's motivations for doing the things he or she does. Focus especially on what the character wants, both from the situations of the play and from life. Explain the situations from which the character's motivations emerge.

5. Describe the strategies a character devises for getting what he or she wants. Explain how effective those strategies are.

6. Describe the miscalculations a character makes and the effect they have.

7. Summarize how a character intensifies, changes, or comes into sharper focus for the audience. Trace the intensification, change, or focus through each major unit of the play. Explain what causes it.

8. Summarize a scene in which a major character faces a crisis. Explain what we learn about the character from the character's words and actions.

9. Summarize a scene in which a major character has a startling or affecting revelation. Explain what the revelation is, what causes it, and its effect on the character's future.

10. Explain how you would portray one of the characters in an important scene. Show how your performance would reveal the character's inner state.

11. Explain the relationship a major character has with all the other major characters. Describe the alliances and conflicts the character has with the other characters. Describe the attitudes the character has toward the other characters and their attitudes toward him or her.

12. If there is one character who exerts control, intentionally or unintentionally, over other characters, describe the character in detail and explain the source and nature of that control. Describe the other characters' reactions to that control.

13. Explain the effects on a character of not having power and therefore of feeling powerless.

14. Explain the limits and constraints placed on a major character (by other people, by society, by physical circumstances) and how the character responds to these limits and constraints.

15. List the masks established at the beginning of the play. Explain why a character wears a mask.

16. Trace one or more of these masks through the play. Explain how effectively the mask accomplishes the character's purpose.

17. Summarize the scene in which the mask is dropped. List the effects of the mask's being dropped.

Setting

Because of the limited time and space of dramatic productions, a play cannot create a "world" in the same detail and breadth a novel can. The worlds of novels like Tolstoy's *War and Peace* and Hugo's *Les Miserables*, with their multitude of characters, scenes, physical places, and battles, are impossible to show in drama. Rather, such worlds can be represented only fragmentarily. The playwright must use a shorthand method of presenting setting so that the playgoer grasps enough information about the setting to understand whatever relationship setting might have to characterization and theme. Sometimes the relationship is minimal, sometimes very close. *Setting* in drama is the same as in fiction: the social mores, values, and customs of the world in which the characters live; the physical world; the time of the action, including historical circumstances.

The playwright has three main ways of communicating setting to an audience. First, we learn about setting from the characters' dialogue, dress, and behavior. In Sheridan's *School for Scandal*, we know immediately that the world of this play is leisured upper-class English society. We know this from the elaborately polite and mannered way in which the characters carry themselves and from the names they so freely drop—Sir Harry Bouquet, Lord Spindle, Captain Quinze, Lady Frizzle, the Dowager Lady Dundizzy. In *Hedda Gabler* the conversations between Hedda and Judge Brack let us know that they are aristocrats and that Hedda's husband and his family are middle class. Second, we learn about setting from the sets produced by the set designer. Sheridan doesn't tell us what the interiors for *School for Scandal* should look like. He says simply that throughout the play the setting is "London" and that in act one it is "Lady Sneerwell's house." A set designer, however, would do research on the interior design of fashionable homes in late-eighteenth-century England and produce that image on stage. The set, in short, should "say" that these people are aristocrats.

Third, we learn about setting from the knowledge we *bring* to the performance. The playwright alludes to the nature of the setting and assumes we will fill in the details. As Americans, for example, we have relatively little trouble understanding the setting of Arthur Miller's *The Crucible*, even though it is set in seventeenth-century New England. Miller expects us to know something about the Salem witch trials and about the McCarthy "witch hunts" of the 1950s, and most Americans who see that play do know about them.

A problem surfaces, however, when the audience does not have the supplemental information to complete the setting of the play— audiences from other cultures or other time periods. Chekhov's plays are a case in point. *The Cherry Orchard*, for example, plays against a background of Russian history that Chekhov assumes we know: the reform acts of Czar Alexander II (1855–81), including the freeing of the serfs in 1861 and the establishing of the *zemstvo* system of local self-government; Alexander's assassination by anarchists in 1881; the rigid autocracy of the next czar, Alexander III (1881–94); and the ineffectual and repressive reign of his successor, Nicholas II (1894–1917), which revived revolutionary movements in the late 1890s. *The Cherry Orchard* turns on the passing of a decrepit aristocratic order and the arising of a vigorous middle class and financial order. For us even to recognize this concern, it helps to know a little history. Otherwise, we will be confused about why the aristocrats are so nostalgic, whimsical, and impractical in the face of imminent financial disaster. Chekhov wants us to see that their attitude is both a result of and a cause of this historical change.

A choice a playwright and set designer have in designing the sets is whether or not to give them symbolic value. Sets need not be symbolic. The sets in *School for Scandal* will probably always be a literal suggestion of aristocratic drawing rooms and mean nothing more than that. To create the illusion of real rooms, the set designer can lavishly use physical detail—furniture, wallpaper, decorative doodads, architectural features, paintings, clothes. But aspects of sets can take on symbolic or representational meaning. The simplest representational set is probably a bare stage, which can represent anything the playwright wants—a battlefield, a heath, a forest, a gothic cathedral. The playwright can be blatantly symbolic, assigning obvious meanings to physical objects. Thornton Wilder does this in *Our Town* when he uses stepladders to represent houses. The playwright can also combine a realistic with a symbolic method. In *Hedda Gabler*, for example, Ibsen calls for solidly "real" things to be put in the two rooms we see of the Tesman house—an armchair, footstools, sofa, tables, french windows, flowers in vases. But certain objects—Hedda's pistols, the portrait of General Gabler (Hedda's father), and the piano—become closely associated with her and her psychological disorders. Equally suggestive are the two rooms, one a large, elegant drawing room located in the front part of the stage, and the other a smaller sitting room located in back. In act one Hedda's piano is in the drawing room, but in act two it is out of sight in the back room. In fact, as the play proceeds, the back room becomes more and more "Hedda's room" and the drawing room "Tesman's room." Even the portrait of General Gabler is in the back room. At the end of the play, Hedda retreats to the back room, pulls the curtains, frantically plays the piano, and shoots herself. It is as if the back room represents an increasingly restricted physical and emotional space for Hedda, until at last it becomes her prison and coffin.

Questions about setting What do you learn about the setting from characters' behavior and dialogue? What kind of sets does the play seem to call for? Does the playwright specify sets or say anything about the setting? What sets would enhance the playwright's intentions? What costumes would you have the actors wear? What costumes would best fit particular characters? Does the play seem to require background knowledge on your part to understand its setting? If so, what is it? Does the author want the sets to be presentational (realistic) or representational (symbolic)? What are the symbolic possibilities in particular objects or in larger portions of the set? What relationships does setting have to characterization? Are the characters, for example, influenced or impelled or trapped by the setting? What emotional feel—atmosphere—does the setting have? What devices does the playwright call for or that you could improvise that would help create that atmosphere? What relationships does setting have to theme? Can you tell what the playwright's own view toward the setting is from clues in the play? Does the playwright, for example, approve or disapprove of the setting?

Thinking on Paper About Setting

1. For each major unit of the play, describe the place where the action occurs. If the playwright gives a description of the place, summarize the description in your words. If the playwright does not give a

description, use information from the dialogue to construct a description. Explain the relationship of place to action, characterization, and theme.

2. Identify the time of day of each unit of the play. Explain how the time of day is represented on stage and its effect on the characters and the action.

3. Identify the time of year of each unit of the play. Explain the relationship of time of year to action, characterization, and theme.

4. Identify the historical period of the play. Give any background information that would be useful for understanding the play. Explain the relationship of the historical period to action, characterization, and theme.

5. Describe the atmosphere of each major unit of the play.

6. Describe the events of which the action of the play is a part. For example, the action may be a skirmish in a major war; the skirmish takes place onstage, the war offstage. Explain the circumstances of the war and how the skirmish fits in.

7. Describe the costumes the characters wear. Explain the relationship between costumes, characterization, and theme.

8. Describe your design for the physical world—sets, costumes, sounds, lighting, the works—of one major unit of the play. Explain the reasons for your choices.

9. List the details of setting that have symbolic value. Explain what each symbolizes. Explain the relationship of symbolism to characterization and theme.

10. Explain each major character's attitude toward the setting.

Theme

Playwrights build themes into their plays through the development and interrelationship of all the elements of drama, most of which are the same as for fiction. Three methods of developing theme, however, are particularly noteworthy: repetitions, symbols, and contrasts. All three lend themselves well to drama. Audiences can pick up on them easily during performances.

Repetitions can take many forms—a character's performing the same gesture over and over again, repeating the same phrase, stating the same idea, or appearing at regular intervals. But for repetitions to relate to theme they must develop ideas. Shakespeare does just that in *Hamlet* by repeating and intertwining three concepts: Denmark as "rotten," human beings as sinful, and the king's role as crucial to the health of the state. He characterizes Denmark by repeatedly comparing it to a garden overrun with weeds and to a diseased body, analogies borne out by Hamlet's partial madness and Ophelia's complete madness and suicide. He has key characters dwell on the sinful nature of humankind. The queen says that her own soul is "sick," "as sin's true nature is." The king says that his "offense is rank, it smells to heaven" because it has "the primal eldest curse" upon it of Cain's murder of Abel. And Hamlet says that even the best people seem to have "some vicious mole of nature in them" that leads them from purity to corruption. (All three of these statements connect sin to sickness.) The corrupt state of Denmark, Shakespeare implies, is the result of the king's sin. For, as one character says, the king is like the hub of a wheel whose spokes connect to "ten thousand lesser things." Whatever the king does affects everyone in the state.

As we have said, *symbolism* can enrich setting. But in fact symbolism bears on both characterization and theme as well. It is often hard to separate the effect of symbolism on all three elements. In *Hedda Gabler*, for example, Ibsen uses a contrast between Hedda's and Thea's hair to symbolize their different character traits. Hedda's hair is thin and dull; Thea's is thick and luxuriant. Hedda dates her long-standing rivalry with Thea from their school days, when even then Hedda threatened to "burn off" Thea's hair. Hedda seems at times to want to inspire people to create, but her efforts end up as destructive; whereas Thea has an innate and unconscious gift for inspiring creativity. This wellspring of inspiration and fertility is symbolized by Thea's hair, which helps explain Hedda's animosity toward it. It's hard to say just what Ibsen's themes in *Hedda Gabler* are; he may simply be trying to present, not explain, Hedda's mysterious perversities. But one implication of the hair symbolism may be that creativity is a mysterious quality existing even in someone as innocent and nonintellectual as Thea and that it may not have anything to do with the intellectual sharpness and forcefulness characterizing people like Hedda. Whatever Ibsen's themes are, they are inextricably bound up with his characterization of Hedda and Thea.

A simpler—because easier to interpret—example of thematic symbolism occurs in Lorraine Hansberry's *A Raisin in the Sun*. Mrs. Younger, the main character, is the mother of a large extended family, but her environment—a stultifying, roach-infested, inner-city tenement—has kept her from giving the best of life to her children. The house she wants to buy in the suburbs becomes equivalent to new "earth" in which her children and grandchild can "grow," because, as she says, they are her "harvest." To emphasize the analogy between the house and a garden, Hansberry has Mrs. Younger constantly dream of working in the garden at the new house, and as a moving present, her children give her garden tools. But the most visible symbol of Mrs. Younger's frustrations and aspirations is a malnourished houseplant she has been trying for years to nurture. The audience sees the plant sitting in the window. Mrs. Younger fusses over it. Her children chide her for messing with it at all. But she persists. The last thing we see her do is say goodbye to the oppressive apartment and carry the plant out the door. At the new house, it will revive in the sunshine and clean air of a better world. The message is clear: People are like plants; they become healthy—mentally, morally, and physically—only in hospitable environments.

Like symbolism, *contrast* is a device for developing not just theme but characterization and plot as well, and contrast usually bears on all three. We have already seen many examples of contrast in the plays we have discussed so far: romantic love (Romeo and Juliet) versus social requirements (the Montagues and the Capulets), Thea versus Hedda, Macbeth versus Duncan, old Russia versus new Russia, Hamlet's father versus the new king. Often playwrights repeat scenes and circumstances but vary them in such ways that the similarities and differences create aesthetic and thematic effects. *Macbeth* illustrates the aesthetic device of "framing" the work by putting nearly identical events at the beginning and end. At the beginning, Scotland has just defeated Norway. The traitorous Thane of Cawdor is executed, and Macbeth triumphantly displays the head of another rebel by putting it on a stake. As a reward for valor, the king designates Macbeth the new Thane of Cawdor. At the end of the play, another battle is fought and Macbeth is killed as a "usurper," his head cut off and held aloft as a sign of revenge and victory. Ironically, Macbeth has changed places with the first Thane of Cawdor in both name and nature, and the circumstances of their deaths are almost identical.

A more far-reaching example of contrast is the Surface brothers in Sheridan's *School for Scandal*. Joseph Surface pretends to be good, but he is in fact selfish and destructive. Charles Surface leads a carefree and careless life; he seems to be a wastrel, but he is in fact generous and honest. Their uncle and benefactor, Sir Oliver Surface, a brusque but warmhearted man, has just returned to England after a long absence and wants to ferret out the true nature of his two potential heirs. To do this he visits each brother separately, disguised as someone else. Both scenes are so similar that an audience cannot fail to notice the similarity;

Sheridan uses the similarity to contrast the brothers. The first scene, with Charles, does indeed expose his good qualities. The audience now knows how the scene will go and gleefully awaits the second scene, in which the despicable Joseph will almost certainly be exposed. This contrast not only develops plot and character; it also points a moral— that the appearance of goodness is worthless without the practice of goodness.

Questions about theme   What repetitions occur in the play? Which of these would be obvious to an audience? Which are so subtle that only careful reading will uncover them? In particular, what analogies and ideas are repeated throughout the play? What patterns of meaning can you make out of these repetitions? How do the patterns interrelate? Are any of the repetitions contradictory?

What symbols does the author deliberately establish? How do you know they are symbols? That is, what comments or actions establish them as symbols? What do the symbols seem to mean? Are the meanings fairly easy to discover? Or are the meanings subtle and elusive? Why would the playwright make them elusive, if they are?

What contrasts does the playwright establish? How thorough and extensive are the contrasts? Are they a major quality of the play—as they are in *School for Scandal*—or just momentary and briefly suggestive? Which are the obvious contrasts and which are the not-so-obvious contrasts? In *Romeo and Juliet*, for example, we easily spot the contrast between the lovers and the parents, but other contrasts are suggestive: Romeo is different from Juliet and is perhaps partly to blame for their deaths; Prince Escalus is different from the parents; the nurse's attitude toward love contrasts starkly with Juliet's; the friar's attitude toward love is different from Romeo's. Any one or a combination of these contrasts would make a good subject for an essay. How is contrast related to the conflicts in the plot? Hedda and Thea are not only different from each other; they are in conflict. What values, then, do the contrasting sides of a conflict manifest? How do these values tie in to the playwright's possible themes?

Thinking on Paper About Theme

1. List the subjects of the play (the issues or problems the play seems to be about). State themes for each of these subjects (what the play seems to be saying about these issues and problems).

2. Mark speeches and sections of dialogue that help develop a particular theme. Look especially for "the big speech," which will typically be longer than most and will forcefully state a theme. Hamlet's "To be or not to be" speech is an example. There may be more than one "big speech." Summarize them in your own words and explain how the actions of the play develop their ideas.

3. Explain in detail how an important scene helps develop themes.

4. Trace the development of one theme through the play. Mark all the passages that help develop this theme. Summarize the plot as it relates to this theme.

5. List the images (sensuous images, metaphors) that recur in the play. Explain what ideas they seem to develop.

6. List other repetitions (characters' actions and words, characters' obsessions, scenes, details of setting). Explain their relationship to characterization and theme.

7. List the symbols in the play. For each symbol, list its meanings.

8. Describe the important contrasts in the play (of characters, scenes, values, actions, physical objects). Explain how these contrasts help expose character traits and develop theme.

9. Describe contrasts between what seems to be true and what is true. Explain how this kind of contrast helps develop theme.

Irony

The presence of an audience at performances of plays affects profoundly the way plays are written and the way productions are conceived. The actors, of course, pretend to be real people, involved in real human relationships. But unlike real life, these fictional activities are attended to by an audience of total strangers. It is as if the front wall of your neighbor's house were taken away and the whole neighborhood were standing outside, watching everything your neighbors were doing, hearing everything they were saying. One decision a playwright or producer has is whether to exclude or include the audience from participation in the play. If the choice is to exclude the audience, the production assumes that no one is watching. There is a marked physical and psychological distance between the performance and the audience (the performance lighted, the auditorium dark; the performance up on stage, the audience down and away from the stage), and the actors pretend the audience is not there. If the choice is to include the audience, then measures are taken to bring the audience "into" the play. The physical distance between performance and audience may be reduced (by building the stage out into the auditorium or by having the actors circulate among the audience). The actors may look at the audience, gesture to it, or talk to it as if the audience were another person. Shakespeare's drama includes these possibilities with its numerous asides and soliloquies.

One prominent and powerful device that relies entirely on the presence of an audience, and on what the audience is thinking, is dramatic irony. *Dramatic irony* in effect does acknowledge the presence of the audience, because it gives the audience the privilege of knowing things the characters do not know but almost certainly will soon know. Dramatic irony occurs when characters say or do something that has meaning the audience recognizes but the characters do not. The concept of dramatic irony can be extended to all situations in which characters are blind to facts the audience knows. Sometimes only the audience is aware of the ironic contrast between the character's words or actions and the truth; sometimes the audience shares this knowledge with other characters onstage.

In the two parallel scenes in *School for Scandal,* for example, the audience knows that Sir Oliver Surface is wearing a mask to test his nephews, and of course Sir Oliver knows but the nephews do not. So the audience recognizes as ironic everything the nephews do and say that works for or against their self-interest, particularly in the case of Joseph, who would treat Sir Oliver with meticulous courtesy if only he knew who he was. In another scene from this play, Lady Teazle hides behind a screen while her husband, unaware of her presence, talks about her. When he says that he wants to leave her a lot of money upon his death but that he does not want her to know about it yet, we recognize his statement as ironic, because we know and he doesn't that Lady Teazle has heard everything.

One of the most powerful examples of dramatic irony occurs in the last scenes of Shakespeare's *Othello.* Before Desdemona goes to bed, she sings a song about a man who accuses his love of being promiscuous. She asks Emilia, her woman in waiting, if any woman could so treat her husband. Emilia says that some might for the right "price," but Desdemona says that she could not do so "for the whole world." The audience recognizes her comments as ironic, because Othello, unbeknownst to Desdemona, is nearly insane with the belief that she is a "whore" and plans to kill her for it. Later, when Othello is strangling Desdemona, he boasts that even if he is "cruel" he is at least "merciful," because he will kill her quickly without allowing her to "linger in . . . pain." But his "mercy" contrasts horribly with our knowledge of her innocence and the quality of mercy she justly deserves. And when he defends his murder to Emilia, he says,

> Cassio did top her. Ask thy husband [Iago] else.
> O, I were damned beneath all depth in hell
> But that I did proceed upon just grounds
> To this extremity. Thy husband knew it all.

We know, and poor Othello is about to find out, that Iago has betrayed him and that he has in truth had no "just grounds" for the "extremity" of his deed.

Questions about irony To what extent does the playwright seem to want the audience involved in the action? How would you perform such audience-involving devices as soliloquies and asides? To whom, for example, would you have the actors make asides? What advantages are there in performing the play as if the audience is not there? Do certain kinds of drama lend themselves better to audience involvement than others? Comedy, for example, seems automatically to invite audience participation. Why and how?

Like fiction and poetry, drama uses all kinds of irony. Verbal irony is very prevalent, for example, simply because drama relies so heavily on dialogue. Sometimes the director and actors themselves must decide whether particular lines are ironic. When Thea, for example, tells Hedda about inspiring Loevborg to write his book, Hedda interjects comments like these: "Poor, pretty little Thea"; "But my dear Thea! How brave of you!"; "Clever little Thea!" It is almost certain that Hedda means these statements ironically. The actress would probably say them, then, with enough sarcasm to let the audience know how Hedda really feels about Thea's successes, but with not enough bite to let the slow-witted Thea pick up on the irony.

What are the ironies, then, in the play you are studying? How do they relate to characterization and theme? Most importantly, what dramatic ironies does the playwright build into the play? How do they serve as "exclamation points" to emphasize character traits and ideas? Do the dramatic ironies—such as Othello's repeated description of Iago as "honest"—create a pattern of revelation or meaning? Why do the dramatic ironies appear where they do in the play? That is, does dramatic irony serve as a device for structuring the play?

Thinking on Paper About Irony

1. Explain the extent to which the play seems to invite audience participation.
2. Mark the instances in the play of dramatic irony. Explain what the dramatic irony reveals about characterization and theme.
3. Mark the instances of verbal irony. Explain what the verbal irony reveals about the characters who use it.
4. List the instances of situational irony. Explain the importance of situational irony to characterization and theme. (For a definition of situational irony, see chapter 4.)
5. List the instances of attitudinal irony. Explain the importance of attitudinal irony to characterization and theme. (For a definition of attitudinal irony, see chapter 4.)

Subgenres

The best-known subgenres of drama are tragedy and comedy, but there are many others: melodrama, theater of the absurd, allegory, comedy of manners, the spectacle, the masque, modern drama, farce, tragicomedy. Some, like musicals, opera, and ballet, shade into other art forms. Although our purpose in this book is not to define subgenres, you may find fruitful essay subjects in such definitions.

Definitions of *tragedy*, for example, usually begin with the first and most famous definition, Aristotle's *Poetics*. Aristotle based his definition on an inductive examination of Greek tragedy, and he seems in particular to have had Sophocles's plays in mind. His definition focuses primarily on the effect of the play on the audience and on the nature of the tragic hero. The hero, he says, inspires "pity" and "fear" in the audience: pity because the hero doesn't deserve his fate, fear because the hero's fate could be anyone's. The audience, in other words, identifies deeply with the tragic hero. The hero is noble but flawed. He has one principal flaw—in Sophocles, usually the flaw of pride. This flaw Aristotle called a *hamartia*, literally a "miscalculation." Because of the hero's flaw, he suffers emotionally and experiences a reversal of fortune, moving abruptly from a high place (high social position, wealth, responsibility, purity) to a low place. Before this reversal occurs, the hero understands for the first time his flawed state and his error-filled ways. This moment is the "recognition" and usually occurs at the climax of the play. The hero recognizes that he is responsible for his deeds and that they contradict a moral order inherent in the entire cosmos. The effect of the play on the audience is to induce a *catharsis*, a feeling of emotional release and exuberance.

Aristotle planned to write as comprehensively on *comedy* as on tragedy, but either that part of the *Poetics* was lost or he never got around to it. It is hard to see, however, that he could have made comedy any less enigmatic than it still appears to us. For comedy is difficult to pin down, both artistically and psychologically. Numerous essays have been written trying to explain why people laugh, and all are speculative. Laughter is only one of the puzzling aspects or products of comedy. Most people would agree on some of the aspects of comedy. Comedy is the depiction of the ludicrous, and the ludicrous is a gross departure from the serious. Therefore, in order to see something as comic, you must first understand what is "serious." Drama communicates to a community of playgoers, so the comic in drama is closely related to what the community *thinks* is serious. If the community thinks that proper attire for men is a business suit, tie, and polished shoes, then a gross distortion of that dress—by a clown in a circus, for example— would be comic. The basic methods of signaling the ludicrous are incongruity and exaggeration. It is incongruous for a haughty, spiffily dressed man, walking nose in the air, to slip and fall face first into a mud hole or to be hit in the face with a cream pie. Furthermore, comedy must cause no pain to the audience. This means that the audience cannot identify as deeply with comic figures as it does with tragic figures. And it means that the method of presentation—language, acting, setting—must communicate an air of fantasy. Through its methods and style, the production constantly says, "This isn't true. It's only a joke." The fantasy element in comedies helps explain why they almost always end happily, whereas tragedies end unhappily. Finally, the characters in comedy are more "realistic" than in tragedy. They are more like us, whereas in tragedy they are, even in their flawed state (sometimes *because* of their flawed state), far nobler than we are.

Questions about subgenres   Definitions of genres and subgenres are useful only if they help you understand specific works. Aristotle was trying to understand Greek tragedy, so it does non-Greek tragedies an injustice to apply rigidly his definition to them. The same goes, really, for anyone's definition of a subgenre, because literature is too various and complex a phenomenon to fit neatly into categories. You should use definitions like Aristotle's as insights into the probable nature of a work, and base your questions on those insights. You can take every part of these definitions of tragedy and comedy and turn each into a probing question aimed at a specific work: What is the character's major flaw? Does he or she have more than one flaw? When does the recognition scene occur? What does the character recognize? What incongruities cause the comedy? What do the incongruities reveal about the playwright's attitude toward the characters and setting? Are there hints of satire in these incongruities? How does the playwright establish the detachment necessary for us to laugh?

You might also apply definitions like these to works that do not quite fit the categories and see what you come up with. Some people regard *Hedda Gabler* as something like a "tragedy" but not exactly an Aristotelian tragedy. Will any parts of Aristotle's definition apply to *Hedda Gabler*? Which fit well, which do not? Does Hedda have a "tragic flaw"? Is she responsible for her actions? Is she to blame for the harm she does? Does she have a moment or moments of recognition? Is she nobler than we are? Does she experience a "reversal"? How does the audience feel after seeing or reading the play? Does the audience experience pity and fear for Hedda or just despise her?

Some of the most interesting questions about subgenres emerge from plays that mix subgenres. Why, for example, are there comic elements in Shakespeare's tragedies? What is *The Cherry Orchard*—a comedy, a tragedy, or both? Are we supposed to laugh or cry at the fate of Chekhov's ineffectual aristocrats? If Aristotle's definition or someone else's has no explanation for a particular feature of a play, can you invent an explanation of your own?

Thinking on Paper About Subgenres

1. If you know the category the play belongs to (tragedy, comedy, farce, etc.), find a good definition of the category. List the characteristics of the category.

2. Take one item from the list and explain how well it applies to the play. If Hamlet is a tragic character, for example, what might be his tragic flaw? What constitutes his reversal? When does he experience a recognition? How does the audience respond to him?

FOR FURTHER STUDY

Aristotle. *The Poetics*. Various editions.

Beckerman, Bernard. *Dynamics of Drama: Theory and Method of Analysis*. New York: Drama Book Specialists, 1979.

Bentley, Eric. *The Playwright as Thinker: A Study of Drama in Modern Times*. New York: Harcourt, 1967.

Corrigan, Robert W., ed. *Tragedy: Vision and Form*. San Francisco: Chandler, 1965.

———. *Comedy: Meaning and Form*. New York: Harper, 1981.

Esslin, Martin. *An Anatomy of Drama*. New York: Hill and Wang, 1976.

———. *The Theatre of the Absurd*. Garden City: Doubleday, 1969.

Kernodle, George, Portia Kernodle, and Edward Pixley. *Invitation to the Theatre*. 3rd ed. San Diego: Harcourt, 1985.

Styan, J. L. *The Elements of Drama*. Cambridge: Cambridge UP, 1969.

Kernodle, Kernodle, and Pixley's *Invitation to the Theatre* and Esslin's *An Anatomy of Drama* are both general introductions to the elements of drama. Beckerman's *Dynamics of Drama* and Styan's *The Elements of Drama* concentrate on the performance aspects of drama. Beckerman attempts to establish a critical vocabulary and a system for analyzing drama as a performed art. Aristotle's *Poetics* is perhaps the most famous book ever written on literature. It contains his analysis of tragedy, with a few glances at comedy. Corrigan's books on comedy and tragedy anthologize essays and excerpts about these two complex subgenres. They deal with elements such as form, character types, language, and world view. Bentley's *The Playwright as Thinker* deals with the emergence of "modern" drama at the end of the nineteenth century and discusses the importance of playwrights such as Shaw, Ibsen, Strindberg, Brecht, and Sartre. Esslin's *The Theatre of the Absurd* defines and exemplifies post-World War II theatre by covering playwrights such as Samuel Beckett, Eugène Ionesco, Jean Genet, Harold Pinter, Edward Albee, and Arthur Kopit.

6

How to Analyze Poetry

POETRY SHARES many elements with its sister genres, drama and fiction. And indeed, many works of drama and fiction are written in the form of poetry. Plays by Shakespeare, Goethe, Molière, Marlowe, Maxwell Anderson, and T. S. Eliot; narrative works by Homer, Chaucer, Dante, Longfellow, Whittier, Jeffers, Milton, Spenser, Tennyson, and Browning are examples. But poetry is usually different from prose drama and fiction in several key ways. In general, it is more concentrated—that is, poetry says more in fewer words. Poets achieve this concentration by selecting details more carefully, by relying more heavily on implication (through figurative language, connotation, and sensuous imagery), and by more carefully organizing the form of their poetry (through rhythmic speech patterns and "musical" qualities, such as rhyme). Because of the relative shortness of poetry and because of its greater concentration, it demands a more complete unity than prose fiction; nearly every word, sound, and image contributes to a single effect.

Poetry is a complex subject. The following is a *brief* survey of its elements, with questions and exercises that should lead you to discover good essay topics.

THE ELEMENTS OF POETRY

Characterization, Point of View, Plot, Setting, and Theme

Some poems—"narrative" poems—are very similar to prose fiction and drama in their handling of characterization, point of view, plot, and setting. Thus many of the same questions that one asks about a short story, novel, or play are relevant to these poems. Most poems, however, do not offer a "story" in the conventional sense. They are usually brief and apparently devoid of "action." Even so, a plot of sorts may be implied, a place and time may be important, a specific point of view may be operating, and characters may be dramatizing the key issues of the poem. In any poem there is always one "character" of the utmost importance, even if he or she is the only character. This character is the speaker, the "I" of the poem. Often the speaker is a fictional personage, not at all equivalent to the poet, and may not be speaking to the reader but to another character, as is the case in Marvell's "To His Coy Mistress" and Browning's "My Last Duchess." The poem might even be a dialogue between two or more people, as in ballads such as "Edward" and "Lord Randal" and in Frost's "The Death of the Hired Man." Thus the poem can be a little drama or story, in which one or more fictional characters participates. But more typically, one character, the "I," speaks of something that concerns him or her deeply and personally. Such poems are called "lyric" poems because of their subjective, musical, highly emotional, and imaginative qualities. They are songlike utterances by one person, the "I."

Questions about characterization, point of view, plot, setting, and theme In analyzing poetry, your first step should be to come to grips with the "I" of the poem, the speaker. You should answer questions such as these: Who is speaking? (Remember that the speaker is often not the poet.) What characterizes the speaker? To whom is he or she speaking? What is the speaker's tone? What is the speaker's emotional state? Why is he or she speaking? What situation is being described? What are the conflicts or tensions in this situation? How is setting—social situation, physical place, and time—important to the speaker? What ideas is the speaker communicating? Try to answer these questions for each section of the poem. A good exercise is to summarize the meaning of each part of the poem in your own words.

Matthew Arnold's "Dover Beach" provides an example of how you can use most of these questions to get at the central meaning of a poem.

DOVER BEACH

MATTHEW ARNOLD

The sea is calm to-night.
The tide is full, the moon lies fair
Upon the straits; on the French coast the light
Gleams and is gone; the cliffs of England stand,
Glimmering and vast, out in the tranquil bay.
Come to the window, sweet is the night-air!
Only, from the long line of spray
Where the sea meets the moon-blanched land,
Listen! you hear the grating roar
Of pebbles which the waves draw back, and fling,
At their return, up the high strand,
Begin, and cease, and then again begin,
With tremulous cadence slow, and bring
The eternal note of sadness in.

Sophocles long ago
Heard it on the Aegean, and it brought
Into his mind the turbid ebb and flow
Of human misery; we
Find also in the sound a thought,
Hearing it by this distant northern sea.

The Sea of Faith
Was once, too, at the full, and round earth's shore
Lay like the folds of a bright girdle furled.
But now I only hear
Its melancholy, long, withdrawing roar,
Retreating, to the breath
Of the night-wind, down the vast edges drear
And naked shingles° of the world.

°beaches covered with pebbles

> Ah, love, let us be true
> To one another! for the world, which seems
> To lie before us like a land of dreams,
> So various, so beautiful, so new,
> Hath really neither joy, nor love, nor light,
> Nor certitude, nor peace, nor help for pain;
> And we are here as on a darkling plain
> Swept with confused alarms of struggle and flight,
> Where ignorant armies clash by night.

Since Dover is an English port city, one of several points of departure for the European continent, the speaker has apparently stopped for the night on his way to Europe. As he looks out of his hotel window, he speaks to another person in the room, his "love" (last stanza). Arnold traces the speaker's train of thought in four stanzas. In the first stanza, the speaker describes what he sees, and his tone is contented, even joyous. He sees the lights on the French coast, and he sees the high white cliffs of Dover "glimmering" in the moonlight. He invites his companion to share the glorious view. But as he describes the sound of the surf to her, his tone alters slightly; the sound reminds him of "the eternal note of sadness." This melancholy tone deepens in the second stanza. There the speaker connects the sea sound with a passage in Sophocles, probably the third chorus of *Antigone*, which compares the misery of living under a family curse to the incessant roar of a stormy sea beating against the land.

In the third stanza, the remembrance of Sophocles's comparison leads the speaker to make a more disturbing comparison of his own. He likens the sea to faith—apparently religious faith, both his own and that of his age. He says that at one time the "Sea of Faith" was full but now has withdrawn, leaving a "vast," "drear," and coarse world. By the fourth stanza, the speaker has fallen into despair. He says that what merely looks beautiful—the panorama seen from his window—is only a false image of the world, which in reality is absurd and chaotic. He has only one hope, his companion, whom he now urges to be true to him as he is true to her. The speaker, in short, is an erudite, thoughtful, but deeply troubled person. The poem takes him from momentary contentedness to near hopelessness. The stimulus for his train of thought is the place of the poem—Dover Beach—and the companion to whom he addresses his remarks. All these elements—thoughts, place, and companion—are interrelated.

Thinking on Paper About Characterization, Point of View, Plot, Setting, and Theme

Many of the exercises one does on poetry consist of marking the poem itself. You might, then, photocopy the poem and write on the photocopy rather than the book. Some photocopy machines will enlarge images. Since poems are often published in small print, taking advantage of this feature would allow you to see the poem better and have more space to write. You might want to make more than one copy of the poem. Use different copies for marking different aspects of the poem.

1. Find the subject, verb, and object of every sentence in the poem. Sometimes this will be easy; reading poetry will be like reading clear prose. But sometimes it will not. Because poetry often conforms to structural requirements and because it is a condensed form of communication, sentence structures are sometimes distorted and words are left out. In such cases, you will have to put the sentence in normal order and insert missing words.

2. Paraphrase the poem. This is one way to make sure you understand every sentence.

3. Identify the speaker of the poem. Underline the words and phrases that help characterize the speaker and bring out the speaker's concerns. Describe in detail the traits of the speaker and of any other characters in the poem.

4. Describe the situation of the poem: where the speaker is, what time of day it is, what season of the year, what historical occasion, to whom the speaker is speaking, why. List the external and internal conflicts of the poem.

5. State the issues that concern the speaker (what the poem is about). Explain the speaker's ideas (the themes of the poem). Note any changes in the speaker's mood or ideas as the poem moves from unit to unit. Explain what the speaker is trying to accomplish.

6. Describe the speaker's tone (angry, lyrical, hopeful, bitter, nostalgic, sarcastic, compassionate, admiring, sorrowful, amused, etc.). Note any changes of tone.

7. If the speaker is not the poet, describe the poet's attitude toward the speaker and to the issues raised by the poem. Indicate any differences between the poet's attitude and the speaker's.

8. Describe important contrasts made in the poem. Explain their relationships to characterization and theme.

9. Relate the poem's title to its themes.

10. Explain any allusions in the poem. An *allusion* is a reference to historical events and people, to mythological and biblical figures, and to works of literature. Allusions always invite comparison between the work at hand and the items referred to. An example of an allusion is Arnold's reference to Sophocles in "Dover Beach." Arnold invites us to bring the weight of Sophocles's tragedies to bear on the subject matter of his poem. An allusion is a compact way of adding meaning to the work. Explain, then, the implications of the allusions.

Diction

Basically, *diction* refers to the poet's choice of words. Poets are sensitive to the subtle shades of meanings of words, to the possible double meanings of words, and to the denotative and connotative meanings of words. As we saw in chapter 3, *denotation* is the object or idea—the referent—that a word represents. The denotation of a word is its core meaning, its dictionary meaning. *Connotation* is the subjective, emotional association that a word has for one person or a group of people. Poets often choose words that contribute to the poem's meaning on both a denotational and a connotational level. You should be alert to such choices.

Questions about diction   You should examine the words in a poem for all their possible shades and levels of meaning. Then you should ask how these meanings combine to create an overall effect. Note the effect that connotation creates in William Wordsworth's "A Slumber Did My Spirit Seal":

A SLUMBER DID MY SPIRIT SEAL

WILLIAM WORDSWORTH

A slumber did my spirit seal;
　　I had no human fears—
She seemed a thing that could not feel
　　The touch of earthly years.

No motion has she now, no force;
　　She neither hears nor sees;
Rolled round in earth's diurnal course,
　　With rocks, and stones, and trees.

THE ELEMENTS OF POETRY **105**

In order to create the stark contrast between the active, airy girl of the first stanza with the inert, dead girl of the second, Wordsworth relies partly on the connotative effect of the last line. We know the denotative meaning of "rocks and stones and trees," but in this context the emotional or connotative meaning is unpleasant and grating. Rocks and stones are inanimate, cold, cutting, impersonal. And although we usually think of trees as beautiful and majestic, here the association of trees with rocks and stones makes us think of tree roots, of dirt, and thus of the girl's burial. The rocks and stones and trees are not only nonhuman, they confine and smother the girl. Another example of connotation is the word *diurnal*, which means "daily." But the Latinate *diurnal* has a slightly more formal connotation than the prosaic *daily*. The effect of the word is to make the processes of nature—death, the revolving of the earth, the existence of rocks and stones and trees—seem remote, remorseless, and inevitable.

Be alert for wordplay—double meanings and puns. The speaker in Andrew Marvell's "To His Coy Mistress," for example, tries to persuade a reluctant female to make love with him. His argument is that time is running out and unless we take opportunities when they appear, we will lose them. He concludes his speech with a pun:

> Thus, though we cannot make our sun
> Stand still, yet we will make him run.

That is, we cannot stop time (make the sun stop), but we can bring about new life (a child: "son"), which is one way of defeating decay and death. Some poets, such as e. e. cummings, make imaginative wordplay a dominant trait of their poetry. In "anyone lived in a pretty how town," cummings uses pronouns on two levels of meaning. The words *anyone* and *noone* mean, on the one hand, what we expect them to mean ("anybody" and "nobody"); but on the other hand they refer to two people, male and female, who fall in love, marry, and die.

Thinking on Paper About Diction

1. Circle all the words you do not know. Look them up in the dictionary.

2. Underline words that seem especially meaningful or well chosen. For each word, explain denotations and connotations.

3. Underline any wordplay, such as double meanings and puns. Explain what the wordplay adds to the sense of the poem.

4. Underline any uses of unusual words—slang, profanity, archaisms, foreign language words, made-up words. Explain what qualities and meanings these words add to the poem. Discuss how the poem would be different without them.

5. Identify the level of diction in the poem (formal, informal, colloquial, slangy, dialect). Explain what the poem gains from the use of this level. Explain what it would lose by changing to a different level.

6. Explain how the choice of words contributes to the speaker's tone.

Imagery: Descriptive Language

When applied to poetry, the term *imagery* has two meanings. First, imagery represents the descriptive passages of a poem. Although the word *imagery* calls to mind the visual sense, poetic imagery appeals to all the senses. Sensuous imagery is pleasurable for its own sake, but it also provides concreteness and immediacy. Imagery causes the reader to become personally, experientially involved in the subject matter of the poem. Furthermore, the poet often uses descriptive imagery to underscore other elements in a poem. The selection of detail and the vividness imparted to images help create tone, meaning, and characterization.

An example of descriptive imagery is the first stanza of John Keats's narrative poem "The Eve of St. Agnes":

> St. Agnes' Eve—Ah, bitter chill it was!
> The owl, for all his feathers, was a-cold;
> The hare limped trembling through the frozen grass,
> And silent was the flock in woolly fold;
> Numb were the Beadsman's fingers, while he told
> His rosary, and while his frosted breath,
> Like pious incense from a censer old,
> Seemed taking flight for heaven, without a death,
> Past the sweet Virgin's picture, while his prayer he saith.

This stanza appeals to the thermal sense (the chill of the evening, the frozen grass), the sense of touch (the beadsman's numb fingers), the visual sense (the beadsman saying his rosary before the picture of the Virgin), the sense of motion (the hare trembling and limping through the grass, the beadsman's frosted breath taking flight toward heaven), and the sense of sound (the silent flock, the sound of the beadsman's monotonous prayer). But the dominant sensuous appeal is to the thermal sense. Keats uses every sensuous image in the stanza to make us feel how cold the night is.

Imagery: Figurative Language

Critics today use *imagery* in a second sense. They use it to mean figurative language, especially metaphor. *Figurative language* is the conscious departure from normal or conventional ways of saying things. This could mean merely a rearrangement of the normal word order of a sentence, such as the following: "Sir Gawain the dragon slew" or "This do in remembrance of me." Such unusual rearrangements are called "rhetorical" figures of speech. But much more common and important to poetry is a second category of figurative language: tropes. *Tropes* (literally, "turns") extend the meaning of words beyond their literal meaning, and the most common form of trope is metaphor. *Metaphor* has both a general and a specific meaning. Generally, it means any analogy (an *analogy* is a partial similarity between two things upon which a comparison may be based). Specifically, metaphor means a particular kind of analogy and is contrasted with the simile. A *simile* is a comparison of two things that are essentially different, and it is signaled by the use of *like* or *as*; for example, "Her tears were like falling rain." The following stanza from Shakespeare's "Fair Is My Love" contains several similes (indicated by the added italics):

> Fair is my love, but not so fair as fickle;
> *Mild as a dove*, but neither true nor trusty;
> Brighter than glass, and yet, *as glass is, brittle;*
> Softer than wax, and yet, *as iron, rusty;*
> A lily pale, with damask dye to grace her;
> None fairer, nor none falser to deface her.

A metaphor also compares things that are essentially unlike, but it eliminates the comparative words and thus equates the compared items. For example, "My heart was a tornado of passion." The poem "Love Is a Sickness" by Samuel Daniel contains several metaphors (indicated here by the italics):

LOVE IS A SICKNESS

SAMUEL DANIEL

Love is a sickness full of woes,
  All remedies refusing.
A plant that with most cutting grows,
  Most barren with best using.
                Why so?
More we enjoy it, more it dies,
If not enjoyed it sighing cries,
                Hey ho.

Love is a torment of the mind,
  A tempest everlasting,
And Jove hath made it of a kind
  Not well, nor full, nor fasting.
                Why so?
More we enjoy it, more it dies,
If not enjoyed it sighing cries,
                Hey ho.

Analogies can be directly stated or implied. The similes and metaphors in the above poems by Shakespeare and Daniel are directly stated analogies; but when Daniel in the last lines of each stanza says that love "sighs," he implies a kind of analogy called *personification;* he pretends that love has the attributes of a person. When the poet develops just one analogy throughout the whole poem, the analogy is called an *extended metaphor.* Thomas Campion's "There Is a Garden in Her Face" contains an extended metaphor comparing the features of a woman's face to the features of a garden:

THERE IS A GARDEN IN HER FACE

THOMAS CAMPION

There is a garden in her face,
Where roses and white lilies grow,
A heavenly paradise is that place,
Wherein all pleasant fruits do flow.
There cherries grow, which none may buy
Till "Cherry ripe!"° themselves do cry.

°A familiar cry of London street vendors

Those cherries fairly do enclose
Of orient pearl a double row;
Which when her lovely laughter shows,
They look like rosebuds filled with snow.
Yet them nor peer nor prince can buy,
Till "Cherry ripe!" themselves do cry.

Her eyes like angels watch them still;
Her brows like bended bows do stand,
Threatening with piercing frowns to kill
All that attempt with eye or hand
Those sacred cherries to come nigh,
Till "Cherry ripe!" themselves do cry.

Questions about imagery   Imagery is an important—
some would argue the most important—characteristic of poetry. You
should always identify the imagery of a poem. Ask, then, what senses
the poet appeals to and what analogies he or she implies or states
directly. But you should also ask, *Why* does the poet use these particular
images and analogies? In "Dover Beach," for example, Arnold meaningfully uses both descriptive and metaphorical imagery. He emphasizes two senses, the visual and the aural. He begins with the visual—
the moon, the lights of France across the water, the cliffs, the tranquil
bay—and throughout the poem he associates hope and beauty with
what the speaker sees. But the poet soon introduces the aural sense—
the grating roar of the sea—which serves as an antithesis to the visual
sense. These two senses create a tension that mirrors the conflict in the
speaker's mind. The first two stanzas show the speaker merely drifting
into a perception of this conflict, connecting sight with hope and sound
with sadness. But by the third stanza, he has become intellectually alert
to the full implications of the conflict. He signals this alertness with a
carefully worked out analogy, his comparison of the sea with faith. By
the fourth stanza, he sums up his despairing conclusion with a stunning
and famous simile:

And we are here as on a darkling plain
Swept with confused alarms of struggle and flight,
Where ignorant armies clash by night.

This final analogy achieves several purposes. First, it brings the
implication of the descriptive imagery to a logical conclusion. No

longer can the speaker draw hope from visual beauty; in this image, he cannot see at all—it is night, the plain is dark. He can only hear, but the sound now is more chaotic and directly threatening than the mere ebb and flow of the sea. Second, the analogy provides an abrupt change of setting. Whereas before the speaker visualized an unpeopled plain, now he imagines human beings as agents of destruction. He implies that a world without faith must seem and be unavoidably arbitrary and violent. Finally, the analogy allows the speaker to identify his own place in this new world order. Only loyalty is pure and good, so he and his companion must cling to each other and maneuver throughout the world's battlefields as best they can.

Thinking on Paper About Descriptive Language

1. Mark the descriptive images. For each image, name the sense appealed to. Characterize the dominant impression these images make.

2. Explain the relationship of descriptive images to the speaker's state of mind.

3. Describe how the descriptive images create a sense of the time of day and season of the year.

4. Note any progression in the descriptive images; for example, from day to night, hot to cold, soft to loud, color to color, slow to fast.

5. Explain how the descriptive images help create atmosphere and mood. Slow movements, for example, are conducive to melancholy; speed to exuberance and excitement.

Thinking on Paper About Figurative Language

1. Mark the similes in the poem. Underline or circle the words that signal the comparisons (words such as *like, as, similar to, resembles*). Explain the implications of the analogies (that is, what they contribute to the meaning of the poem).

2. Mark the metaphors in the poem. Explain the implications of the analogies.

3. Mark any personification in the poem. Underline the words and phrases that make the personification clear.

4. Poets often use analogies to help make an abstract quality, such as "love" or "my love's beauty" or "my current predicament" or "the destructive effect of time" or "God's grandeur," concrete and knowable. They do so by comparing the abstract quality to something the reader knows well. Almost always this "something" is a physical object or

reality. Name the abstract quality the poet wants to clarify and the object the poet is comparing it to. List the qualities of the object. Explain how the comparison has clarified the abstraction.

5. List the senses appealed to in each analogy. Describe the dominant sensuous impression created by the analogies.

Rhythm

All human speech has rhythm, but poetry regularizes that rhythm into recognizable patterns. These patterns are called *meters*. Metrical patterns vary depending on the sequence in which one arranges the accented (á) and unaccented (ă) syllables of an utterance. The unit that determines that arrangement is the foot. A *foot* is one unit of rhythm in a verse. Probably the most natural foot in English is the iambic, which has an unaccented syllable followed by an accented syllable (ăá). Here are the most common metrical feet:

iamb (iambic) ăá	ăbóve
trochee (trochaic) áă	lóvelў
anapest (anapestic) ăăá	ŏvĕrwhélm
dactyl (dactylic) áăă	róyăltў
spondee (spondaic) áá	bréak, bréak

Poets further determine the arrangement of metrical patterns by the number of feet in each line. The following names apply to the lengths of poetic lines:

monometer (one foot)
dimeter (two feet)
trimeter (three feet)
tetrameter (four feet)
pentameter (five feet)
hexameter (six feet)
heptameter (seven feet)
octameter (eight feet)

A very common line in English poetry is iambic pentameter; it contains five iambic feet. Shakespeare wrote his plays in iambic pentameter, and the sonnet is traditionally composed in iambic pentameter (see pages 119–20 for some examples).

Another feature of line length is that each line may have a fixed number of syllables. When people speak of iambic pentameter, they usually think of a line containing five accented syllables and ten syllables in all. Even if the poet substitutes other feet for iambs, the number of syllables in the line comes out the same—ten for iambic pentameter, eight for iambic tetrameter, six for iambic trimeter, and so forth. When a line of poetry is measured by both accents and syllables, it is called *accentual-syllabic*. Most English poetry is accentual-syllabic, as in these iambic tetrameter lines from "To His Coy Mistress":

> Hăd wé bŭt wórld ēnoúgh, ańd tiŕne,
> Thĭs cóyneš̆s, ládў̆, weŕe nŏ críme.

Each line has four iambic feet—four accented syllables, eight syllables in all. But not all English poetry is accentual-syllabic. Sometimes it is just accentual. Traditional ballads, for example, often count the number of accents per line but not the number of syllables:

> "O whére hae ye beén, Lord Rańdal, my són?
> O wheŕe hae ye beén, my hańdsome young mán?"
> "I hae beén to the wild wood; móther, maƙe my bed soón,
> For I'm weáry wi huńting, and fáin wald lie doẃn."

The third line of this stanza contains five accented syllables but twelve (not five) syllables. The first two lines contain four accents but ten (not eight) syllables. And the last line contains four accents but twelve (not eight) syllables. The important factor in purely accentual lines is where the accent falls; the poet can freely use the accents to emphasize meaning. One of the accents in line three, for example, falls on *wild*, which expresses the treacherous place from which Lord Randal has returned.

Because individuals hear and speak a language in different ways, *scanning* a poem (using symbols to mark accented and unaccented syllables and thus identify its metrical pattern) is not an exact science. Some poets establish easily recognizable—often strongly rhythmical— metrical patterns, and scanning their poems is easy. Other poets use more subtle rhythms that make the poetic lines less artificial and more like colloquial language. The best poets often deliberately depart from the metrical pattern they establish at the beginning of the poem. When you scan a poem, therefore, do not force phrases unnaturally into the established metrical pattern. Always put the accents where you and most speakers would normally say them. The poet probably intends for them to go there.

When you scan a poem, be alert for caesuras. A *caesura* is a strong pause somewhere in the line. You mark a caesura with two vertical lines: ‖. Consider the caesuras in this jump-rope rhyme:

> Cinderella, dressed in yellow,
> Went upstairs ‖ to kiss a fellow.
> Made a mistake; ‖ kissed a snake.
> How many doctors did it take.
> One, two, three, four . . .

A likely place for a caesura is in the middle of the line, and if the meter of the poem is tetrameter, then a caesura in the middle neatly divides the line in half. Such is the case in lines 2 and 3 of this poem. A caesura may also occur near the beginning of a line or near the end. Or there may be no caesuras in a line, as is probably the case in lines 4, 5, and possibly 1 of this poem. Caesuras often serve to emphasize meaning. Caesuras in the middle of lines, for example, can emphasize strong contrasts or close relationships between ideas. In line 3, both the caesura and the rhyme of "mistake" with "snake" link the abstraction (the mistake) with the action (kissing the snake).

A profound example of the relationship between meaning and caesura—indeed, between meaning and all the qualities of poetic sound—is Shakespeare's Sonnet 129:

SONNET 129

WILLIAM SHAKESPEARE

> Th' expense of spirit ‖ in a waste of shame
> Is lust in action; ‖ and, till action, lust
> Is perjured, murderous, bloody, full of blame,
> Savage, extreme, rude, cruel, not to trust;
> Enjoyed no sooner ‖ but despisèd straight: 5
> Past reason hunted; ‖ and no sooner had,
> Past reason hated, ‖ as a swallowed bait,
> On purpose laid ‖ to make the taker mad:
> Mad in pursuit, ‖ and in possession so;
> Had, having, and in quest to have, extreme;   10
> A bliss in proof; ‖ and proved, a very woe;

> Before, a joy proposed; ‖ behind, a dream.
> All this the world well knows; ‖ yet none knows well
> To shun the heaven ‖ that leads men to this hell.

Here Shakespeare establishes a pattern of contrasts and similarities, and he uses caesura and other sound devices to establish them. One of these devices is the accentual pattern. Like most sonnets, this one has ten syllables per line and is supposed to be iambic pentameter. But for many of these lines, Shakespeare has only four accents per line, not five. This allows him to make some of his comparisons equal in weight. Line 5, for example, has a strong caesura and four accented syllables:

> Enjóyed no soóner ‖ but despiśèd straíght.

The effect is to contrast strongly the two emotional states, pleasure and guilt; and since Shakespeare puts guilt last, he gives it more weight. Lines 11 and 12, however, contain caesuras and five accents each, making the two-part divisions within the lines unequal. Note how this relates to the meaning of the lines:

> A bliśs in próof; ‖ and próved, a véry wóe;
> Befóre, a jóy propósed; ‖ behínd, a dréam.

The "weaker" sides of the lines contain the pleasure part of the equation and emphasize the brevity and insubstantial quality of pleasure; the "strong" sides emphasize either naïve expectation or guilt.

Questions about rhythm   Metrics has many uses in poetry. It provides a method of ordering material. It creates a hypnotic effect that rivets attention on the poem. Like the rhythmic qualities of music, it is enjoyable in itself. Children, for example, take naturally to the strongly rhythmic qualities of nursery rhymes and jump-rope rhymes; jump-rope rhymes, in fact, are that rare form of literature that children teach each other. But probably the greatest importance of metrics is that it establishes a pattern from which the poet can depart. Good poets rarely stick to the metrical pattern they establish at the beginning of the poem or that is inherent in a fixed form, like the sonnet. Sonnet 129, above, is a striking example. Sometimes they depart from the established pattern to make the language sound more colloquial. Such is partly the case in "Dover Beach" and Browning's "My Last Duchess," both of which are spoken by fictional characters. Sometimes poets depart from the pattern to emphasize specific parts of the poem's content. This is why you should be sensitive to the natural rhythms of the language when you scan a poem. Take, for example, these lines from Sonnet 129: Lust is like

a swallowed bait,	7
On purpose laid to make the taker mad:	8
Mád iñ pūrsúit, añd iñ pösséssiōn só;	9
Hád, hávinğ, añd iñ quést tō háve, extréme;	10
A bliss in proof; and proved, a very woe;	11
Before, a joy proposed; behind, a dream.	12

All of these lines fit the iambic scheme except lines 9 and 10. Why? Because Shakespeare wants to emphasize certain words in these two lines, particularly the first words in each. The accents in line 10 are especially emphatic, for the accents emphasize the past ("had"), the present ("having"), the future ("quest" and "have"), and the psychological and moral nature of all three ("extreme").

Questions to ask about rhythm in poetry, then, are these: What metrical pattern does the poem use? What is appealing about the pattern? How closely does the poet stick to the established pattern? If closely, why and what effect is the poet striving for? For example, does the poem have a singsong quality? If so, why does the poet do this? "To His Coy Mistress" is a poem that adheres with little variation to its iambic tetrameter pattern. How is Marvell's choice to do this fitting for his dramatic situation (man addressing woman) and his subject? What variations from the established pattern does the poet make? Why? What words and ideas do these variations emphasize? Does the poet establish a pattern of emphasis? How does the poet use pauses within each line? What are the strong pauses (caesuras) and the weaker pauses? When the poet uses pauses to break a line into smaller units, what relationships do the units have? Are there cause-and-effect relationships or comparison-and-contrast relationships between them?

Thinking on Paper About Rhythm

1. Count the number of syllables for each line. Write the number at the end of the line.
2. Read the poem aloud, then mark the accented and unaccented syllables of each line.
3. Draw a vertical line between each foot in the line.

4. Identify the metrical pattern (iambic, trocheeic, etc.) and the length of the lines (pentameter, hexameter, etc.).

5. Use two vertical lines to mark the caesuras in the poem. Explain how the caesuras relate to the sense of each line.

6. Underline the places where the poet departs from the established metrical pattern of the poem. Explain how these departures relate to the sense of each line. Show which words are emphasized by the departures.

7. Explain the appropriateness of the metrical pattern to the poem's meaning.

8. Describe how easy it is to read the poem aloud. Does the metrical pattern slow you down? Or does it allow you to read smoothly? Explain how the difficulty or ease of reading the metrical pattern relates to the poem's meaning and purpose.

Sound

Poets delight in the sound of language and consciously present sounds to be enjoyed for themselves. They also use them to emphasize meaning, action, and emotion, and especially to call the reader's attention to the relationship of certain words. Rhyme, for example, has the effect of linking words together. Among the most common sound devices are the following:

onomatopoeia—the use of words that sound like what they mean ("buzz, "boom," "hiss," "fizz").

alliteration—the repetition of consonant sounds at the beginning of words or at the beginning of accented syllables ("the woeful woman went wading Wednesday").

assonance—the repetition of vowel sounds followed by different consonant sounds (O, the groans that opened to his ears").

consonance (or *half-rhyme*)—the repetition of final consonant sounds that are preceded by different vowel sounds (the beast climbed fast to the crest").

rhyme—the repetition of accented vowels and the sounds that follow. There are subcategories of rhyme:

masculine rhyme (the rhymed sounds have only one syllable: "man-ran," "detect-correct").

feminine rhyme (the rhymed sounds have two or more syllables: "subtle-rebuttal," "deceptively-perceptively"). ·

internal rhyme (the rhymed sounds are within the line).

end rhyme (the rhymed sounds appear at the ends of lines).

approximate rhyme (the words are close to rhyming: "book-buck," "watch-match," "man-in").

Edgar Allan Poe's "To Helen" illustrates many of these sound devices:

TO HELEN

EDGAR ALLAN POE

Helen, thy beauty is to me
Like those Nicean barks of yore, — masculine rhyme/end rhyme
That gently, o'er a perfumed sea,
alliteration The weary, way-worn wanderer bore
To his own native shore.   5

consonance On desperate seas long wont to roam   6
Thy hyacinth hair, thy classic face
Thy Naiad airs have brought me home — approximate rhyme   8
To the glory that was Greece
And the grandeur that was Rome.

assonance Lo! in yon brilliant window-nich   11
How statue-like I see thee stand! — internal rhyme
The agate lamp within thy hand,
Ah! Psyche, from the regions which
Are Holy Land!

Questions about sound   It's easy to lose yourself in an analysis of the mechanical intricacies of a poem's sound structure and forget why you are making the analysis in the first place. You want to ask, What sound devices does the poet use? But you also should ask, Why does the poet use them? How do they help establish the poem's tone, atmosphere, theme, setting, characterization, and emotional qualities? In Poe's "To Helen," for example, the alliteration in the fourth line ("*w*eary, *w*ay-*w*orn *w*anderer") underscores the fatigued state of the wanderer. The consonance of "seas" and "airs" in lines 6 and 8 emphasizes the contrast between them; one is "desperate" but the other assuages despair. And the assonance in line 11 ("*in* yon br*i*lliant w*i*ndow-n*i*ch"), with its emphasis on high, tight, "i" sounds, helps to characterize the luminousness of the place where Helen, statue-like, stands.

Be especially alert to the relationships between ideas established both by rhyme, and most notably by internal rhyme and end rhyme. Rhyme, of course, is a musical device that makes the sound of the poem attractive to the ear, but it can be used meaningfully as well. Turn back to Sonnet 129, and examine the complex sound associations Shakespeare creates there. The words sound rough and almost painful, with their harsh consonants, all of which illustrate the frustrated and frenetic emotional state Shakespeare ascribes to lust. Note the variation on "s" sounds in the first line.

Th' expense of spirit in a waste of shame

Line 3 begins a list of qualities, and Shakespeare divides and associates them through assonance and alliteration: Lust

Is perjured, murderous, bloody, full of blame.

The words *perjured* and *murderous* are linked by assonance (the "er" sounds), and they focus on evil deeds (falsehood, murder), which leads to the second half of the line. The words *bloody* and *blame* are linked by alliteration, and they focus on the results of evil deeds, especially murder: blood and guilt. The linkages signaled by the poem's end rhyme are also meaningful: shame/blame, lust/not to trust, no sooner had/make the taker mad, extreme/dream, yet none knows well/leads men to this hell.

In the poem you are analyzing, what linkages of meaning are there to *all* the sound qualities of the words—especially to the obvious ones, such as alliteration, internal rhyme, and end rhyme? What light do these linkages throw on the themes of the entire poem?

Thinking on Paper About Sound

1. Underline instances of alliteration, assonance, and consonance in the poem. Explain the relationship between these devices and the sense of the lines where they occur.

2. Circle rhymed words. Explain what similarities and contrasts the rhymed words call attention to.

3. Circle words that have meaningful or attractive sound qualities, such as onomatopoetic words. Explain how these words add to the poem's sense.

4. When the sounds of a poem are harsh and grating, the effect is called *cacophony*. When they are pleasing and harmonious, the effect is called *euphony*. Underline instances of cacophony or euphony. Explain how they relate to the poem's sense.

5. Describe any sound devices in the poem that catch you by surprise. Explain how and why the poet uses such surprises.

Structure

Poets give structure to their poems in two overlapping ways: by organizing ideas according to a logical plan and by creating a pattern of sounds. Arnold arranges "Dover Beach" in both ways, as do most poets. He divides the poem into four units, each of which has a pattern of end rhyme, and he arranges the whole poem rhetorically—that is, by ideas. Each unit elaborates a single point, and each point follows logically from the preceding one.

Perhaps the most common sound device by which poets create structure is end rhyme, and any pattern of end rhyme is called a *rhyme scheme*. Rhyme scheme helps to establish another structural device, the *stanza*, which is physically separated from other stanzas by extra spaces and usually represents one idea.

Stanzas typically have the same structure: the same number of lines, length of lines, metrical patterns, and rhyme schemes. Poets, of course, can create any rhyme scheme or stanza form they choose, but they often work instead within the confines of already established poetic structures. These are called *fixed forms*. Stanzas that conform to no traditional limits, such as those in "Dover Beach," are called *nonce forms*. The most famous fixed form in English is the *sonnet*. Like other fixed forms, the sonnet provides ready-made structural divisions by which a poet can organize ideas. But it also challenges poets to mold unwieldy material into an unyielding structure. The result is a tension between material and form that is pleasing both to poet and reader.

All sonnets have fourteen lines of iambic pentameter. There are two kinds of sonnets, both named for their most famous practitioners. A *Shakespearean sonnet* rhymes abab/cdcd/efef/gg and has a structural division of three quatrains (each containing four lines) and a couplet. A *Petrarchan sonnet* rhymes abbaabba in the octave (the first eight lines) and cdecde in the sestet (the last six lines). Poets often vary the pattern of end rhyme in these kinds of sonnets, and this is especially true of the sestet in the Petrarchan sonnet. Note, for example, the following sonnet by Wordsworth. Each kind of sonnet has a *turn*, a point in the poem at which the poet shifts from one meaning or mood to another. The turn in the Shakespearean sonnet occurs between lines 12 and 13 (just before the couplet). The turn in the Petrarchan sonnet occurs between the octave and the sestet. In both forms, the part of the poem before the turn delineates a problem or tension; the part after the turn offers some resolution to or comment on the problem, and it releases the tension.

SONNET 116

WILLIAM SHAKESPEARE

Let me not to the marriage of true minds	a	
Admit impediments. Love is not love	b	
Which alters when it alteration finds,	a	
Or bends with the remover to remove:	b	4
Oh, no! it is an ever-fixèd mark,	c	
That looks on tempests and is never shaken;	d	
It is the star to every wandering bark,	c	
Whose worth's unknown, although his height be taken,	d	8
Love's not Time's fool, though rosey lips and cheeks	e	
Within his bending sickle's compass come;	f	
Love alters not with his brief hours and weeks,	e	
But bears it out even to the edge of doom.	f	12
If this be error and upon me proved,	g	
I never writ, nor no man ever loved.	g	14

three quatrains; turn →; couplet

Shakespeare molds the ideas and images of this poem to fit its form perfectly. He states the theme—that love remains constant no matter what—in the first quatrain. In the second, he says that cataclysmic events cannot destroy love. In the third, he says that time cannot destroy love. Finally, in the couplet, he affirms the truth of his theme.

THE WORLD IS TOO MUCH WITH US

WILLIAM WORDSWORTH

octave {	The world is too much with us; late and soon,	a
	Getting and spending, we lay waste our powers;	b
	Little we see in nature that is ours;	b
	We have given our hearts away, a sordid boon!	a ___ 4
	This Sea that bares her bosom to the moon,	a
	The winds that will be howling at all hours,	b
	And are up-gathered now like sleeping flowers,	b
turn →	For this, for everything, we are out of tune;	a ___ 8
sestet {	It moves us not.—Great God! I'd rather be	c
	A Pagan suckled in a creed outworn;	d
	So might I, standing on this pleasant lea,	c
	Have glimpses that would make me less forlorn;	d
	Have sight of Proteus rising from the sea;	c
	Or hear old Triton blow his wreathèd horn.	d ___ 14

Wordsworth uses the structure of the Petrarchan sonnet to shape his ideas. In the octave he states his general theme—that materialistic values and activities dull our sensitivity to nature. But he divides the octave into two quatrains. In the first he states his theme; in the second he exemplifies it. He then uses the sestet to suggest an alternate attitude, one that might produce a greater appreciation of nature's mystery and majesty.

Questions about structure   You can find definitions of many fixed forms by looking them up in handbooks of literature (see the reading list at the end of this chapter)—ballad, ode, heroic couplet, Alexandrine stanza, rhyme royal stanza, Spenserian stanza, and so forth. But since poets do not always use fixed forms, and since there are many ways to give poetry structure, you should try to answer this question: What devices does the poet use to give the poem structure? Does the poet use rhyme scheme, stanzas, double spaces, indentations, repetition of words and images, line lengths, rhetorical organization? As with rhythm and sound, a follow-up question is of equal consequence: How does the poem's structure emphasize or relate to its meaning? An example of such a relationship is the final stanza of "Dover Beach," in which Arnold uses end rhyme to emphasize opposing worldviews:

Ah, love, let us be true	a
To one another! for the world, which seems	b
To lie before us like a land of dreams,	b
So various, so beautiful, so new,	a
Hath really neither joy, nor love, nor light,	c
Nor certitude, nor peace, nor help for pain;	d
And we are here as on a darkling plain	d
Swept with confused alarms of struggle and flight,	c
Where ignorant armies clash by night.	c

The rhyme scheme of the first four lines is almost the same as the next five lines; the only difference is the addition of the fifth line. This similarity divides the stanza in half, and the difference in rhymes corresponds to the difference of the ideas in the two halves.

Thinking on Paper About Structure

1. Mark the rhyme scheme of the poem or stanza. (Use the three examples on pp. 120, 121, and 122 as models for doing this.)
2. Draw horizontal lines between each division of the poem or unit of the poem. In a sonnet, for example, mark divisions between quatrains, couplets, octaves, and sestets. (Use the poems mentioned in the first question.)
3. Summarize the meaning of each division of the poem. In a Shakespearean sonnet, for example, summarize the meaning of each quatrain and the couplet. In a Petrarchan sonnet, summarize the meaning of the octave (and the quatrains within the octave) and the sestet. For both kinds of sonnet, indicate how the meaning changes after the turn.
4. Within the poem or stanza, summarize the relationships between ideas suggested by the end rhyme. A couplet, for example, wherever it may appear in the poem or stanza, almost always states one idea or indicates a close connection between the sense of the two lines.
5. If one or more lines are shorter or longer than most of the others, describe the effect of that different length on the sense and impact of the poem or stanza.
6. Account for variations from the established rhyme scheme. Explain how the variations relate to the sense of the poem or stanza.

7. Describe and explain the significance of subtle differences between sections or stanzas in a poem. Ballads, for example, often rely on *incremental repetition,* the repeating of phrases and lines from stanza to stanza but with slight changes. The changes enhance suspense by altering the meaning of each stanza.

8. Outline the units of meaning in the poem. That is, indicate where the poet moves from one idea to another. Show how the units of meaning relate to visual structural divisions (such as stanzas), if they do.

9. Describe the imagery of each unit. Show what images dominate each unit. Show differences in imagery from unit to unit. Explain how the images help create the sense of the unit.

10. Some poems, for instance ballads, the songs in Shakespeare's plays, and popular songs, were meant to be sung. For one of these poems, explain the effect of this intention on the poem (choice of words, metrical pattern, rhyme, other sound devices, stanzaic form). If you can, listen to a recording of the song.

11. Some poems, such as George Herbert's "Easter Wings" and many of the poems by e. e. cummings, create an effect by the way they look on the page. Choose one such poem and explain the relationship between how it looks and other elements of the poem, including rhyme scheme, metrical pattern, line length, word choice, and meaning.

Free Verse

One sometimes puzzling form of poetry is *free verse.* It is puzzling because it is hard to see obvious structural elements in it. The first practitioner of free verse in modern times was Walt Whitman (in the 1855 edition of *Leaves of Grass*). Many people, when they saw Whitman's poetry for the first time, wondered if it was really poetry. They asked why any "prose" writings could not be arranged into lines of varying lengths and be called poetry. Since Whitman's time, many poets have written in free verse, and there is one very well-known antecedent to Whitman's free verse: the Bible. Hebrew poetry has its own complicated system of rhythms and sound associations, but when it is translated into English it comes out as free verse. Here is a well-known example (from the 1611 King James translation):

> The Lord is my shepherd; I shall not want.
> He maketh me to lie down in green pastures; he leadeth me
>   beside the still waters.

He restoreth my soul; he leadeth me in the paths of righteousness
for his name's sake.
Yea, though I walk through the valley of the shadow of death, I will
fear no evil, for thou art with me; thy rod and thy staff they
comfort me.
Thou preparest a table before me in the presence of mine enemies;
thou anointest my head with oil; my cup runneth over.
Surely goodness and mercy shall follow me all the days of my life,
and I will dwell in the house of the Lord for ever.

Free verse is "free" in certain ways. It avoids strict adherence to
metrical patterns and to fixed line lengths. But it is not entirely "free,"
for it uses other ways of creating rhythm and sound patterns. First, it
often uses the sound qualities of words to create associations within
words—assonance, alliteration, internal rhyme, and so forth. Second, it
creates rhythm by repeating phrases that have the same syntactical
structure. See the Twenty-third Psalm, for example: "He maketh me,"
"he leadeth me," "he restoreth my soul," "he leadeth me." A more blatant
example is the "out of" phrases in the first section of Whitman's "Out of
the Cradle Endlessly Rocking":

Out of the cradle endlessly rocking,
Out of the mocking-bird's throat, the musical shuttle,
Out of the Ninth-month midnight . . .

Third, free verse can establish rhythms within lines by creating phrases
of about equal length. Finally, free verse can vary lines meaningfully.
Whitman, for example, will sometimes have a series of long lines and
then one very short line that comments pertly on the preceding lines or
resolves a tension within them.

Questions about free verse   Questions about free-verse
poetry, then, should be similar to questions about any poetry. What
structural devices—divisions within the poem, line length, repeated
syntactical units—does the poet use and how do they complement the
poet's meaning? What patterns of imagery—descriptive and figurative—does the poet use? What sound devices does the poet weave into
the poem? Why does the poet choose the words he or she does? Who is
the speaker, and to what situation is the speaker responding?

Thinking on Paper About Free Verse

1. Read the poem aloud. Note the phrases that create the rhythm of the poem.

2. Underline repeated phrases in the poem, as with the "out of the cradle" phrase in Whitman's poem.

3. Mark with double vertical lines the caesuras in each line of the poem.

4. Mark the accents in each line of the poem.

5. Explain why the lines end where they do.

6. Note any variation between short phrases and long phrases. Explain how these variations relate to the sense of the poem.

7. Explain the relationship between the rhythms of the poem and its meaning and purpose.

8. Mark and account for all of the sound qualities of the poem: alliteration, assonance, cacophony, euphony, internal rhyme, and so forth.

SYMBOLISM

Poets frequently use symbolism because, among other reasons, symbols are highly suggestive yet can be established in just a few words. As we said in chapter 4, a symbol is an object—usually a physical object—that represents an abstract idea or ideas. The most powerful symbols are those that do not exactly specify the ideas they represent. An example of a symbol in poetry occurs in the Twenty-third Psalm, shown previously. The poem begins with a metaphor: God is like a shepherd and I (the speaker) am like one of his sheep; just as a shepherd takes care of his sheep, so will God take care of me. But the poem shifts from metaphor to symbol with phrases such as "green pastures," "still waters," and particularly "the valley of the shadow of death." The meanings of "green pastures" (nourishment, security, ease) and "still waters" (peace, sustenance, calm) are fairly easy to ascertain. But the meaning of "the valley of the shadow of death" is more difficult. It does not seem to mean just death, but a life experience—perhaps psychological or spiritual—that is somehow related to death (the "shadow" of death) and that we must journey through (through the "valley"). Perhaps the indefiniteness of this phrase, combined with its ominous overtones, explains the grip it has had on people's imaginations for generations.

Another example of symbol in poetry is William Blake's "The Sick Rose" (1794):

THE SICK ROSE

WILLIAM BLAKE

O Rose, thou art sick
The invisible worm
That flies in the night
In the howling storm

Has found out thy bed
Of crimson joy,
And his dark secret love
Does thy life destroy.

This poem can possibly be read as a literal treatment of a real rose beset by some real insect that preys on roses. But Blake probably means for the rose, the worm, and the action of the worm to be taken symbolically. For one thing, the poem occurs in Blake's collection of poems *Songs of Experience*, suggesting that it represents the ominous aspects of life, particularly human life. For another, much of the poem makes little sense unless it can be taken symbolically: the "howling storm," the bed of "crimson joy," the worm's "dark secret love," for example. What, then, do these things represent? One interpretive approach would be to consider word meanings that Blake, who read widely in symbolic Christian literature, may have had in mind. The archaic meaning of "worm" is dragon, which in Christian romance represented evil and harks back to the devil's appearance to Eve as a snake. Also in Christian romance, the rose represented female beauty and purity, and sometimes it represented the Virgin Mary. Blake seems, then, to be symbolizing the destruction of purity by evil. The poem probably also has sexual implications, since, for example, the worm (a phallic image) comes at "night" to the rose's "bed." In general, the poem may represent the destruction of all earthly health, innocence, and beauty by mysterious forces. The point is that although we get the drift of Blake's meaning, we do not know precisely what the symbolic equivalents are. Yet the symbols are presented so sensuously and the action so dramatically that the poem grips us with a mesmerizing power.

When you read poetry, be alert for symbols, but convince yourself and certainly your reader that the objects you claim to be symbols were intended as such by the author. Remember that not *every* object in a poem is a symbol. What, then, are the symbols in the poem you are reading? Why do you think they are symbols? What do they mean? In answer to this last question, offer reasonable and carefully thought out explanations for your interpretations. Stay close to what the author seems to have intended for the symbols to mean.

Thinking on Paper About Symbolism

1. Circle the symbols in the poem.
2. List the possible meanings of each symbol. Explain what evidence suggests these meanings.
3. Explain what each symbol contributes to the overall meaning of the poem.

FOR FURTHER STUDY

Boulton, Marjorie. *The Anatomy of Poetry.* London: Routledge, 1953.

Fussell, Paul, Jr. *Poetic Meter and Poetic Form.* New York: Random, 1967.

Holman, C. Hugh, and William Harmon. *A Handbook to Literature.* 5th ed. New York: Macmillan, 1986.

MacLeish, Archibald. *Poetry and Experience.* Boston: Houghton, 1961.

Reeves, James. *Understanding Poetry.* New York: Barnes, 1965.

Marjorie Boulton's *The Anatomy of Poetry* and James Reeves's *Understanding Poetry* offer thorough explanations of the elements of poetry. Both attempt the difficult task of defining what poetry is. Paul Fussell, Jr., provides a lucid explanation of metrical patterns and poetic structures and how one uses them to analyze poetry. His book concludes with an inviting bibliography. Archibald MacLeish is a fine American poet who, in *Poetry and Experience,* offers his own view of poetry. Holman and Harmon's *Handbook to Literature* is an encyclopedia of literary terms.

7

How to Generate Topics by Using Specialized Approaches

IN CHAPTERS 3 THROUGH 6 we describe ways of analyzing literature that draw only from the facts provided in the works themselves. Other analytical methods, however, often require specialized knowledge, knowledge that comes from outside the text. Some of these approaches are more accessible than others, but all of them are based on general principles that are provocative and that might suggest topics and ideas for your essays. These approaches not only contain theories of what literature is and how one should study it, they also state or imply philosophical and psychological concepts whose implications extend well beyond the study of literature. This chapter describes some of the best known of these specialized approaches and places them in a historical framework.

HISTORICAL CRITICISM

Two specialized approaches, historical and biographical criticism, emerged in the nineteenth century as a result of the widespread faith in science. Critics felt that they could understand literature best by studying the factual causes of the work: the social and cultural environment from which it came, the author's life, the author's intentions, the sources on which the work was based. They believed that their approach was "scientific" because they were dealing with objective reality—historically verifiable facts—and were using a scientific method for collecting such facts.

Historical criticism attempts to study literature by period and movement. This approach recognizes that literary phenomena— methods of composition, subject matter, and philosophical outlook— characterize various historical periods. Thus, the use of blank verse in plays characterizes the Shakespearean era; the use of heroic couplets the Neoclassical era. An emphasis on free will characterizes the Romantic movement; a philosophy of determinism the Realistic and Naturalistic movements. A focus on hedonistic self-indulgence distinguishes the 1920s; an attention to social conflict the 1930s. The historical approach also assumes that literary periods and movements are dynamic. As one period reaches exhaustion, another period begins.

The historical approach has several goals: to study a work's relationship to its own and other periods, to learn more about a writer's culture, to place the work within an evolving tradition (like the novel, Christian literature, allegory, political fiction, the epic), to compare it with the literature of other countries. But the most important goal of historical criticism is to illuminate the work. We know, for example, that Jack London read the most influential thinkers of his day, Darwin and Spencer; by studying their ideas, we understand better the philosophical implications of London's fiction. T. S. Eliot, like other poets of the early twentieth century, read the French Symbolist poets; by studying their poetry, we understand Eliot's methods better. John Steinbeck depicted the social dislocations of poor people in the 1930s, and by studying their problems and the social theories prominent then, we understand his themes better.

Undergraduate survey courses typically use a historical approach. They present a country's literature chronologically or thematically and show how authors exemplify their periods. The papers you write for survey courses will often focus on the relationship between a work and its historical context. One way to generate paper topics for these courses is to apply definitions of social, intellectual, and literary trends to individual works—definitions of concepts such as romanticism, realism, neoclassicism, symbolism, the Renaissance, modernism, surrealism, Darwinism, imagism, naturalism. The most obvious source of these definitions is your instructor, but you can also find good definitions in dictionaries of literary terms, literary histories, encyclopedias, history books, and other sources of background information. Another source of essay topics is comparisons—comparisons of works from different movements, comparisons of works from the same period. A third source is the cultural traits authors describe or draw upon for their themes. William Faulkner, for example, used the "Southern Myth" in his fiction—a nostalgic, glorified concept of Southern ideals and history that evolved before the Civil War and received acute enlargement afterward. Faulkner never says directly that he focuses on this myth, but by studying Southern history and observing the myth in other works, we can see that he does so, and thus we can understand better the unspoken, implied tensions in his work.

Two comprehensive examples of historical criticism are the *Columbia Literary History of the United States* (New York: Columbia UP, 1988) edited by Emory Elliott and others, and *The Literary History of England*, 2nd ed. (New York: Appleton, 1967), edited by Albert C. Baugh and others. A book that develops a thesis about the relationship between history and literature is Robert E. Spiller's *The Cycle of American Literature: An Essay in Historical Criticism* (New York: The Free Press, 1967). A fine historical treatment of a genre is Walter Allen's *The English Novel: A Short Critical History* (New York: Dutton, 1954).

BIOGRAPHICAL CRITICISM

The *biographical approach* relates the author's life and thought to his or her works. Usually the author's life and thought are reflections of his or her time and are thus important aspects of the historical approach. Sometimes a writer may have been ahead of his or her time, or may even be unclassifiable. Or the writer may have been the predominant figure of the time. Or the writer's life may have been the major source of his or her literary material. For whatever reason, a writer's life may shed light on his or her literature and the literature of the era.

The biographical approach has two major advantages. First, it helps to illuminate elements within a work—words, allusions to local and historical events, conflicts, themes, characters, setting. Learning, for example, that F. Scott Fitzgerald had an ambivalent attitude toward people with great wealth prompts us to look for a similar ambivalence in his works. Second, works often take on an added significance when we see them as expressions of authors' deep concerns and conflicts. The more we empathize with a writer's problems, the more meaningful his or her works may seem to us. The more we know about the full historical and biographical context of a work's themes, the more relevant they may seem to all human experience.

Third, we can discover more about a work's meaning and importance by trying to understand the author's intentions and audience. Authors don't always state their intentions, and even when they do, we may not interpret their works the way they intended them to be interpreted. But knowing something about their intentions and the reactions they wanted to draw from their original audiences gives us at least a starting point for understanding their works. And sometimes we recover understandings of works that time has otherwise erased.

If you use the biographical approach, avoid two mistakes. First, avoid equating the work's contents with the author's life. They are never the same. No matter what the source of a work's material may be, it is a *re*creation of life, a stylization and alteration of it. Literature is "fictional." Some scholars argue that this is even true of nonfictional writings such as memoirs and autobiographies. Second, avoid using unsound sources of information. Many biographies are highly speculative or contain erroneous information. Not until the twentieth century, for example, did we have a biography of Edgar Allan Poe that did not distort, sometimes grossly, the facts about his life.

Three very fine and enjoyable examples of biographical criticism are K. J. Fielding's *Charles Dickens: A Critical Introduction* (Boston: Houghton, 1964), F. W. Dupee's *Henry James: His Life and Writings* (Garden City: Doubleday, 1956), and Arthur Mizener's *The Far Side of Paradise: A Biography of F. Scott Fitzgerald* (Houghton, 1965).

SOCIAL CRITICISM

The economic theories of Karl Marx and the psychological theories of Sigmund Freud gave birth early in the twentieth-century to three critical approaches that were influential before World War II and that, with modifications, continue to be practiced today. They are social criticism, psychological criticism, and archetypal criticism.

Social criticism is similar to historical criticism in recognizing literature as a reflection of its environment. It would focus, for example, on the ways in which Jane Austen's novels depict the emphasis on decorum and etiquette by the English country gentry at the end of the eighteenth century. But in recent times, social criticism has described a particular kind of social reality and sometimes a particular economic and social theory. Social critics were most active in the 1930s during the Great Depression. They applauded literature that depicted the struggles of the poor and downtrodden, especially when they engaged in strikes against oppressive capitalist bosses. Examples of literature with such strong "proletarian" elements are the works of Carl Sandburg, Émile Zola, Maxim Gorky, Nikolai Gogol, Frank Norris, Charles Dickens, Richard Wright, John Steinbeck, Theodore Dreiser, John Dos Passos, and James T. Farrell. The social critics usually approved of a socialist solution to the problems of the oppressed, and they sometimes judged the quality of works solely on the basis of their Marxist orientation. Partly because of this narrowness of focus and rigidity of standards, the social approach, as it was applied in the 1930s, has lost some of its appeal. It showed, however, that many works do reflect society in great detail, that they sometimes attempt to reform society, and that understanding them means in part grappling with the social issues they reflect. A well-known and thoroughgoing work of social criticism is Granville Hicks's *The Great Tradition: An Interpretation of American Literature Since the Civil War* (New York: Macmillan, 1935).

If the social approach seems relevant to works you want to write about, you should first define the social situations the works describe and identify the authors' attitudes toward them. Do the authors, for example, seem to have solutions in mind? Do they feel that society has to be the way they describe it? If you suspect that the authors depict a historical situation and you want to compare their treatment with the actual events, then you will need to seek reliable secondary sources. (Primary and secondary sources are discussed in chapter 9.) And if you want to argue that particular economic or social theories help to explain an author's social concerns in a work, you will need reliable explanations of those theories.

Since World War II, a new generation of Marxist critics has infused social criticism with renewed vigor. An example is the Hungarian critic Georg Lukacs, who argues that literature should reflect the real world. Lukacs does not mean that literature should be a mirror image of society by, for example, giving detailed descriptions of its physical contents or its patterns of behavior. Rather, literature should represent the economic tensions in society as described in Marx's writings. Ironically, for Lukacs, works that give an accurate description of the real world may be less "real" than works that emphasize interpretation over description. Lukacs believes that literature might even have to distort in order to represent the "truth" about society. To show the economic struggles caused by capitalism, for example, an author might have to create character types one would never meet in real life. Lukacs, therefore, prefers the novels of Balzac to those of Flaubert, because even though Balzac's plots and characters are less plausible than Flaubert's, Balzac reveals the economic pitfalls of capitalism as Marx saw them.

A general introduction to Marxist literary criticism is Peter Demetz's *Marx, Engels, and the Poets: Origins of Marxist Literary Criticism* (Chicago: U of Chicago P, 1959). For a brief overview of contemporary Marxist criticism, see David Forgacs's "Marxist Literary Theories" in *Modern Literary Theory: A Comparative Introduction*, edited by Ann Jefferson and David Robey (Totowa, NJ: Barnes and Noble, 1982). A defense of the Marxist approach is Terry Eagleton's *Marxism and Literary Criticism* (Berkeley: U of California P, 1976). Eagleton's *Literary Theory: An Introduction* (Minneapolis: U of Minnesota P, 1983) surveys modern critical theory from a Marxist point of view.

PSYCHOLOGICAL CRITICISM

Psychological criticism attempts to apply modern psychological theories to authors and their works. Because of the predominance of Freudian psychology in the twentieth century, psychological criticism usually relies upon the theories of Sigmund Freud. Freud's ideas are complex and multiple; not all of them relate to literature. But literary critics find three of them very attractive: the dominance of the unconscious mind over the conscious, the expression of the unconscious mind through symbols (most notably in dreams), and the primacy of sexuality as a motivating force in human behavior. These three ideas are related. Freud believed that sexual drives reside in the unconscious, that the conscious mind represses them, and that unconscious symbols usually represent this repressed sexual energy.

The earliest Freudian critics saw literature as a kind of "dream" and thus a source of insight into the authors themselves. Using works of literature as symbolic representations of an author's subconscious, Freudian critics would create a psychological portrait of the author. An example of this kind of psycho-biography is Marie Bonaparte's *The Life and Works of Edgar Allan Poe: A Psychoanalytic Interpretation* (London: Imago Press, 1949). Early Freudian critics also used psychoanalytic principles to analyze characters in works of literature. They looked upon characters as having motivations, conflicts, desires, and inclinations similar to those of real people. They sought psychological clues to the makeup of literary characters, especially the unconscious symbolic expressions found in dreams and repeated patterns of behavior and speech. In Eugene O'Neill's *Long Day's Journey into Night*, for example, whenever Mary Tyrone raises her hands to her hair, she unconsciously expresses anxiety about her wrecked youth, health, and innocence. Many authors purposely incorporated psychological theories in their works. Eugene O'Neill, D. H. Lawrence, Sherwood Anderson, and Tennessee Williams, for example, were familiar with Freudian psychology. Some writers employed structural devices drawn from psychological theories. Examples are the *stream of consciousness* technique, which conforms to William James's ideas about the workings of the conscious mind, and the surrealistic technique, which conforms to Freud's ideas about the undisciplined unconscious. Examples of stream-of-consciousness narration are James Joyce's *Portrait of the Artist as a Young Man* and *Ulysses*, William Faulkner's *The Sound and the Fury*, T. S. Eliot's "The Love Song of J. Alfred Prufrock," Virginia Woolf's *To the Lighthouse*, and O'Neill's *Strange Interlude*. Examples of surrealism are Joyce's *Finnegans Wake* and the fiction of Franz Kafka.

Many other works of literature were also rich fields for early psychological criticism, even though they may not have been directly influenced by psychological theories. Freudian critics were interested in any works that are themselves dreamlike, such as Lewis Carroll's *Alice in Wonderland*, or that contain accounts of characters' dreams, as do some of Dostoevsky's novels. Other works have appealed to psychological critics because of their heavy emphasis on complex or unusual characters.

Recent psychological critics continue to find in Freud's theories a rich source of ideas about literature, but whereas earlier critics focused on author and characters, recent critics have turned their attention to the relationship between text and reader. The critic Norman Holland, for example, argues that the text contains a secret expression of what the reader wants to hear. The reader is not consciously aware of this urge, but it is nonetheless the cause of his enjoyment of the work. The French critic Jacques Lacan holds that the structure and devices of literature make it similar to the unconscious, which Lacan claims is a product of language and is structured like language.

One of the most influential works of early psychological criticism is Ernest Jones's *Hamlet and Oedipus* (New York: Norton, 1949), in which Jones, a psychiatrist, argues that Hamlet's problems stem from

Oedipal conflicts. An anthology of psychological criticism is *Literature and Psychoanalysis* (New York: Columbia UP, 1983), edited by Edith Kurzweil and William Phillips. This collection opens with writings by Freud, it includes a sampling of Freudian critics from early to recent times, and it gives examples of Freudian approaches to individual works of literature, such as *Alice in Wonderland* and Kafka's fiction. *The Purloined Poe: Lacan, Derrida, and Psychoanalytic Reading* (Baltimore: Johns Hopkins UP, 1988), edited by John P. Muller and William J. Richardson, features psychoanalytic readings of Edgar Allen Poe's detective story "The Purloined Letter". It includes an influential essay by Jacques Lacan as well as responses to Lacan's approach by other critics.

ARCHETYPAL CRITICISM

Archetypal criticism emerged from the theories of the Swiss psychologist Carl Jung. Jung accepted Freud's concept of the unconscious mind, but whereas Freud held that each person's unconscious is unique, Jung argued that a part of the unconscious is linked by historical associations and communal "memories" to the unconscious minds of all people. To represent this phenomenon, he coined the phrase "collective unconscious." He believed that certain human products and activities— myth, symbols, ritual, literature—reproduced these memories in the form of "archetypes." Jung defined an *archetype* as any figure or pattern that recurred in works of the imagination from generation to generation.

Archetypal Characters

Although there are many possible archetypes, they fall into three broad categories. The first, characters, contains such figures as the hero, the rake, the scapegoat, the outcast, the hypersensitive youth, the earth mother, the martyr, the *femme fatale*, the rebel, the cruel stepmother, the saint, the "spiritual" woman, the tyrannical father, star-crossed lovers, the ruler. The following are examples of literary treatments of some of these archetypes: the *femme fatale* (Shakespeare's *Antony and Cleopatra*, Prosper Mérimee's *Carmen*, Keats's "La Belle Dame Sans Merci," Zola's *Nana*); the tyrannical father (Rudolph Besier's *The Barretts of Wimpole Street*, Shakespeare's *King Lear*, Longfellow's *Hiawatha*); the hero (Hemingway's *For Whom the Bell Tolls*, Cooper's *The Last of the Mohicans*,

Malory's *Morte d'Arthur*, the anonymous *Sir Gawain and the Green Knight*, Homer's *The Iliad*); the scapegoat (Shirley Jackson's "The Lottery," Melville's *Billy Budd*); the outcast (Dickens's *Great Expectations*, Victor Hugo's *The Hunchback of Notre Dame*, the Book of Job, Coleridge's "The Rime of the Ancient Mariner," Tennyson's "The Lady of Shalott"); the rake (Byron's *Don Juan*, Samuel Richardson's *Clarissa*, Etheridge's *The Man of Mode*, Goldsmith's *She Stoops to Conquer*, Marvell's "To His Coy Mistress," Wycherley's *The Country Wife*); and star-crossed lovers (Marlowe's "Hero and Leander," Shakespeare's *Romeo and Juliet*, Hawthorne's *The Scarlet Letter*).

Archetypal Situations

The second category, situations, includes the quest, the initiation, the journey, the fall, death and rebirth, and the task. Some works, like *Oedipus Rex*, contain more than one archetypal situation. Oedipus makes a "quest" for the truth about King Laius's murderer. He has already performed a task—answering the Sphinx's question—that saved the kingdom. And when he achieves his quest, he suffers a catastrophic fall (from highest in the land to lowest). The quest is usually combined with a journey, as in the search for the Holy Grail of Arthurian legend, and often results in the initiation of a naïve, inexperienced protagonist into the hardship and complexity of life. Examples of works dealing with initiation are Hawthorne's "Young Goodman Brown," Joyce's "Araby," Dickens's *Great Expectations*, Fitzgerald's *The Great Gatsby*, Crane's *The Red Badge of Courage*, and Hardy's *Jude the Obscure*. The death-rebirth archetype appears in myth and fantasy as the literal death and rebirth of a character—Snow White and Sleeping Beauty, for example—but in more realistic literature it often appears in connection with seasonal changes: fall (old age), winter (death), spring (rebirth), summer (life and fruition). In such works, seasonal changes emphasize the metaphorical death and rebirth of a character or place. For example, Émile Zola's *Germinal* concludes with spring, and the renewal of plant and animal life coincides with the end of the workers' strike. The mining town has "died" as an economic entity, but with the end of the strike it is reborn. Spring also represents the germination and growth of ideas that will lead to a better life for the workers. Often allied with the death-rebirth situation is a descent into hell. In some works, like Homer's *The Odyssey*, Virgil's *The Aeneid*, and Dante's *The Divine Comedy*, the protagonist literally descends to hell. But in works that shun fantasy, the journey is metaphorical and equivalent to a traversal of hell-like places (T. S. Eliot's *The Waste Land*) or to psychological states of deep despair. Dostoevsky's Raskolnikov in *Crime and Punishment* emerges at the end from a psychological hell brought on by his cold-blooded murder of an innocent person. Tennessee Williams's play *Orpheus Descending* and Jean Cocteau's film *Orphée*, are conscious meta-phorical uses of the journey-into-hell archetype.

Archetypal Symbols and Associations

The third category of archetypes is symbols and associations, many of which suggest polarities. Examples are light-darkness (light equals knowledge, hope, purity, spirituality; dark equals ignorance, despair, evil, bestiality), water-desert (water equals rebirth, life, creativity; desert equals spiritual and intellectual sterility, death), heights-depths (heights equal achievement, sublimity, heaven, revelation, purity; depths equal dejection, mystery, entrapment, hell, death), and the already mentioned spring-winter. One critic argues that Hemingway's novels utilize the height-depth polarity: When Hemingway's characters occupy high places, things go well for them; when they descend to the lowlands, the fragile order of their world falls apart.

The Appeal of Archetypal Criticism

Jung's theories are controversial among psychologists, but they have attracted literary critics for several reasons. One is that remarkably similar patterns do exist from culture to culture. Early Christian missionaries, for example, encountered myths celebrating a martyred, resurrected hero who promised to return and bring a new, golden age. Such was the case when the Aztecs mistook Cortez for the god Quetzalcoatl. Another reason is Jung's contention that archetypes have a profound emotional and intellectual impact on people, that people unconsciously recognize them as being somehow profoundly meaningful. This theory helps critics to explain, apart from aesthetics, the long-lasting appeal of such works as *Oedipus Rex*, the *Odyssey*, portions of the Bible, the Greek myths, and fairy tales. And the archetypal approach helps to explain the appeal of art forms that lack high aesthetic quality but that are nonetheless very popular, such as American westerns, detective and spy stories, and soap operas. In fact, critics often use the archetypal approach to understand not just the literature of a culture but the culture itself. A culture's recurring emphasis on extensive travel, for example, might suggest restlessness and rootlessness. Or patterns featuring strong, dominant females might suggest a diminished masculine role. Or recurrent violence might indicate a lack of patience to solve complex problems peacefully and lastingly. Archetypal critics have made all of these points about American society.

Perhaps the most practical attraction of archetypal criticism is simply the recognition that patterns in literature do exist and recur, that they often give structure to a work, that many artists have used them in one way or another, and that, for whatever reason, they often deal with profound aspects of human experience. You don't have to believe in Jung's theories to use the archetypal approach to literature. You need only be alert to the possibility of recurring patterns and write about them if you find them meaningful.

Norman Friedman in Chapter 16 of *Form and Meaning in Fiction* (Athens: U of Georgia P, 1975) provides thought-provoking descriptions of frequently used archetypal patterns. A work that thoroughly explores one archetype is Joseph Campbell's *The Hero with a Thousand Faces* (New York: Pantheon, 1949). Two controversial but enjoyable works of archetypal literary criticism by Leslie A. Fiedler are *Love and Death in the American Novel*, revised edition (New York: Stein, 1966) and *No! in Thunder: Essays on Myth and Literature* (New York: Stein, 1972). The most important spokesman for archetypal criticism is Northrop Frye. See especially his *The Educated Imagination* (Bloomington: Indiana UP, 1964) and *Anatomy of Criticism* (Princeton: Princeton UP, 1957).

NEW CRITICISM

In the United States perhaps the most influential movement in literary criticism since World War II has been New Criticism. Although New Criticism began well before World War II with the criticism of T. S. Eliot and I. A. Richards, it received its fullest expression after the war by such critics as John Crowe Ransom, W. K. Wimsatt, Allen Tate, Cleanth Brooks, and Robert Penn Warren. These and other New Critics published best-selling textbooks that established practical and easily understood ways of teaching and studying literature. These ways continue to dominate the study of literature in American higher education.

The term "New Criticism" comes from the title of a book published by John Crowe Ransom in 1941, *The New Criticism* (Norfolk, CN: New Directions). Ransom surveyed the work of recent ("new") critics and thereby made clear some of his own critical principles. Other critics who agreed with Ransom came to be called the New Critics. The New Critics break dramatically with the nineteenth-century emphasis on historical and biographical background. They hold that understanding and appreciating a work of literature need have no connection with the author's intention, with the author's life, or with the social and historical circumstances that may have influenced the author. Everything the reader needs to understand and appreciate a work is in the work itself.

The New Critics see their method as "scientific." The work is a self-contained phenomenon made up of "physical" qualities—language and literary conventions (rhyme, meter, alliteration, plot, point of view, and so forth). These qualities can be studied in the same way a geologist studies a rock formation or a physicist the fragmentation of light particles.

But some New Critics, like Cleanth Brooks, claim that the meaning contained in works of literature cannot be paraphrased, cannot be stated in a straight-forward, "scientific" way. One can state what a work is "about" or summarize a work's themes, but a work's meaning is much more complex than such statements alone. Brooks argues that a work's complexity lies in its "irony" or paradoxes. A paradox is a statement that seems contradictory but is nonetheless true. Statements such as "the first shall be last" or "you must lose your life to gain it" are paradoxes. Brooks claims that good works of literature are filled with paradoxes, with apparently contradictory meanings. In William Wordsworth's poem "It Is a Beauteous Evening," for example, a child seems oblivious to the beauty of nature but is, paradoxically, more aware of it than anyone else. The young lovers in John Donne's poem "The Canonization" paradoxically discover that by rejecting life they capture the intensity of life.

The New Critics use their theories about literature to judge the quality of works of literature. A "good" work, they believe, should contain a network of paradoxes so complex that no mere summary of the work can do them justice. Yet a good work should also have unity. The author achieves this unity by balancing and harmonizing the conflicting ideas in the work. Everything in the work is meaningfully linked together. Because the New Critics favor complex yet unified works, they downgrade works that seem simple or seem to lack unity. They prefer "difficult" works that contain apparently illogical and troubling material. They prefer works that stay away from social and historical subject matter and that deal rather with private, personal, and emotional experience. They prefer indirect representation—symbolism, metaphor, connotation—to realistic representation.

For an overview of New Criticism, see *Modern Literary Theory: A Comparative Introduction* (Totowa, NJ: Barnes and Noble, 1982), edited by Ann Jefferson and David Robey. Two influential New Critical essays are "The Intentional Fallacy" and "The Affective Fallacy," both by W. K. Wimsatt and Monroe Beardsley, contained in Wimsatt's *The Verbal Icon: Studies in the Meaning of Poetry* (Lexington: U of Kentucky P, 1954). A readable and stimulating work of New Criticism is Cleanth Brooks's *The Well Wrought Urn: Studies in the Structure of Poetry* (New York: Harcourt, 1947). See especially chapter 1 ("The Language of Paradox") and chapter 11 ("The Heresy of Paraphrase").

STRUCTURALISM AND POST-STRUCTURALISM

Structuralism

Like New Criticism, *structuralism* denies the value of historical, social, and biographical information and concentrates on identifiable elements in works of literature. But unlike New Criticism, its theory and methodology are grounded in linguistics. Although some nineteenth-century thinkers anticipated structuralist principles, structuralism originated from the work of the Swiss linguist Ferdinand de Saussure (1857–1913). Early in the twentieth century, Saussure gave three innovative courses in linguistics. Because he left no notes on the content of these courses, his students pooled their notes and published a reconstruction of the courses called *Course in General Linguistics* (LaSalle, IL: Open Court, 1986; published originally in 1916). This work is the basis of Saussure's fame and provides the theoretical underpinning of both structuralism and post-structuralism.

Saussure made several points about the nature of language that have provided new pathways for studying literature. First, a language is a complete, self-contained system and deserves to be studied as such. Before Saussure, linguists studied the history of languages (how languages evolved and changed through time) and the differences among languages. For this kind of study Saussure coined the word *diachronic* (literally "through time"). But Saussure argued that a language deserves to be studied as it functions in the present. Linguists should try to understand the parts of the system and their interrelationships. This kind of study Saussure called *synchronic* ("at the same time"). Second, Saussure claimed that a language is a system of signs. Saussure defined a *sign* as consisting of a sound plus the thing the sound represents. He called the sound the *signifier* and the thing represented the *signified*. Third, Saussure said that the sounds that make up a language system are arbitrary. Any sound, it doesn't matter which one, could represent a given thing. The sound for the concept "tree" varies from language to language, yet users of each language know that the sound represents "tree." Fourth, any given language is self-contained. The signs that make up a language have no meaning outside the system of that language. Finally, Saussure distinguished between the whole system, which he called *langue* (French for "language"), and one person's use of the system, which he called *parole* (French for "word" or "speech"). Langue consists of everything that makes the system work—words, grammatical structures, inflections. Parole consists of these same elements but with variations from user to user. Each speaker of a language uses the same system but does so in a slightly different way.

In the 1930s and 1940s, literary critics began applying Saussure's ideas and methods to the study of literature. This application has taken two parallel and often merging paths, literary criticism and cultural criticism. A term that describes both kinds of criticism is *semiotics*, the systematic study of signs. For all practical purposes, the terms *structuralism* and *semiotics* are synonomous.

Structuralist literary critics attempt to show that literature is a form of language or that it functions like language. These critics see the individual work of literature as similar to parole, and literary genres or literature in general as similar to langue. Just as linguists study instances of parole in order to understand langue, literary critics study works of literature in order to understand the system of signs that make up a genre or literature as a whole. They might study a Sherlock Holmes story in order to understand detective fiction, a specific poem in order to understand lyric poetry, a short story in order to understand narrative, a Shakespeare play in order to understand drama, a Louis L'Amour novel in order to understand westerns, a James Bond novel in order to understand spy fiction.

One kind of structuralist literary criticism is *stylistics*, the study of the linguistic form of texts. Stylistics can deal with both prose and poetry, but it has dealt mainly with poetry and particularly with the qualities of language that distinguish poetry from prose. Some stylistic critics claim that the only thing that distinguishes poetry from prose is qualities of language. By analyzing individual poems, these critics attempt to identify those qualities.

Structuralists who study whole cultures attempt to understand a culture's sign systems. The most prominent practitioner of this kind of criticism is the French anthropologist Claude Lévi-Strauss. Lévi-Strauss claims that a culture is bound together by systems of signs and that these systems are like language. He uses Saussurian linguistics as a way of describing the "grammar" of these systems. All aspects of a culture—technology, religion, tools, industry, food, ornaments, rituals—form sign systems. The people of the culture are unaware of these systems, so the structural anthropologist's task is to bring them to light. Lévi-Strauss is perhaps most famous for his study of myth. He examines multiple versions of single myths in order to isolate their essential structural units. Although Lévi-Strauss applies his theories to the study of primitive cultures, other critics, like the Frenchman Roland Barthes, use Lévi-Strauss's approach to "psychoanalyze" modern society. They look for the unconscious sign systems that underlie all aspects of Western culture, including foods, furniture, cars, buildings, clothing fashions, business, advertising, and popular entertainment.

Structuralist analysis of culture and literature often merge, because literature can be considered an artifact of culture. Literature is a system of signs that can be studied for itself or for its place in a given culture. As a result, structuralist critics often shy away from complex and classic works and focus instead on popular literature. The Italian critic Umberto Eco writes essays on spy thrillers and the comic book story of Superman. He has even written a "semiotic" detective novel, *The Name of the Rose* (San Diego: Harcourt, 1983). Structuralist critics also are more interested in fitting a work within a culture or a tradition than in understanding the work itself.

For an introduction to structuralism, see Leonard Orr's *Semiotic and Structuralist Analyses of Fiction: An Introduction and a Survey of Applications* (Troy, NY: Whitston, 1987). Orr describes structuralist theory and then provides an annotated bibliography of important works of structuralist criticism. A clear and readable book-length treatment is Robert Scholes's *Structuralism in Literature: An Introduction* (New Haven: Yale UP, 1974). Tzvetan Todorov's "The Grammar of Narrative" in his *The Poetics of Prose* (Ithaca: Cornell UP, 1977) equates narrative structure to sentence structure. Umberto Eco's *The Role of the Reader: Explorations in the Semiotics of Texts* (Bloomington: Indiana UP, 1979) includes essays on Superman and James Bond. A collection of stylistic studies is *Linguistics and Literary Style*, edited by Donald C.

Freeman (New York: Holt, Rinehart and Winston, 1970). See, for example, J. McH. Sinclair's "Taking a Poem to Pieces."

Post-Structuralism

Post-structuralism evolved from Saussure's theories of language. It accepts Saussure's analysis of language and uses his methodology to examine the language of literary works, but it concerns itself with the relationship between language and meaning. Post-structuralism, in fact, offers a radical theory of reading that rejects the certainty of meaning altogether. The most influential post-structuralist critic is the Frenchman Jacques Derrida.

The basis of Derrida's radical skepticism is Saussure's distinction between signifier and signified. Theorists of language have long maintained that words (signifiers) represent identifiable objects (the signified). The word "tree" represents the object "tree." But Saussure questioned the pervasiveness of such one-to-one correspondences. Words, he said, usually refer not to objects but to "concepts," which are expressed by other words. It seems possible, then, that language, or at least parts of language, may not refer to anything in the sensuously apprehendable world. Saussure said that language is a self-contained system, and that in order to function it does not need to reflect reality. It needs only to reflect itself. Signs gain meaning from other signs in the system, not necessarily from the real world.

Derrida and other post-structuralist critics conclude from Saussure's theories that there is a "gap" between signifier and signified. This gap blurs the meaning of the signifier so that we cannot know exactly what it refers to. The resulting ambiguity is multiplied by the connection of signifier to signifier in an endless chain, no part of which touches the real world. A literary text is equivalent to just such a chain. It is a self-contained system that exists independently of the real world. As we read, we absorb this system with our consciousness, which Derrida maintains is itself made up of language. Reading is the confrontation of one language system (our consciousness) with another (the text). Recovering meaning from texts, then, is impossible, because interpretations of a text never point to the real world but only to more language. Our interaction with the text makes us *think* we are moving toward meaning, but we never get there.

The purpose of post-structuralist criticism is to expose the meaninglessness of texts. Derrida calls his critical method *deconstruction*. To "deconstruct" a work, the critic analyzes the text, especially its language, to show that whatever connection may seem to exist between the text and the real world is an illusion created by the author's clever manipulation of language. The critic attempts to show that whatever the author may intend for the work to mean or whatever a reader may think it means is always undercut by the ambiguity of the work's language. The gap between signifier and signifier is symptomatic of a "space" of emptiness, nothingness, non-meaning that lies at the heart of every text. The presence of this space, the critic tries to show, makes the text an "abyss" of limitless and contradictory meanings.

Post-structuralist criticism is not very reassuring for someone who wants to understand a work better. But it does reveal, through the application of a rigorous and sophisticated method of analysis, the complexity of literature. And its skepticism about meaning points to the mysteriousness of art, the inexplicable something in art that grips our imagination.

A brief explanation of both structuralism and post-structuralism is Ann Jefferson's "Structuralism and Post-Structuralism" in *Modern Literary Theory: A Comparative Introduction* (Totowa, NJ: Barnes and Noble, 1982). More thorough are the chapters on post-structuralism in Art Berman's *From the New Criticism to Deconstruction* (Urbana: U of Illinois P, 1988). A clearly written book-length study is Christopher Norris's *Deconstruction: Theory and Practice* (New York: Methuen, 1982). Norris discusses structuralism, New Criticism, Marxist and psychoanalytic criticism, and philosophical influences on post-structuralism.

READER-RESPONSE AND FEMINIST CRITICISM

Reader-Response Criticism

Reader-response criticism studies the interaction of reader with text. Reader-response critics hold that the text is incomplete until it is read. Each reader brings something to the text that completes it and that makes each reading different. Reader-response critics vary on what that "something" is. Recent psychoanalytic critics, like Jacques Lacan and Norman Holland, say that the something is the unconscious. Post-structuralist critics say that it is the "language" that makes up the conscious mind. Marxist critics say that it is the economic ideology of the dominant culture. And critics interested in the relationship of culture and literature say that it is a whole way of looking at the world, absorbed from the reader's cultural environment. Whatever readers bring to the text, the text has no life of its own without the reader.

Of all the post-World War II movements in literary criticism, reader-response criticism most successfully challenges the dominance of New Criticism in the university classroom. It borrows methodology from New Criticism, structuralism, and post-structuralism, but it rejects their contention that the work must be studied in isolation from its context. Context—historical, biographical, cultural, psychoanalytic—is relevant to the understanding of the text. Reader-response criticism, furthermore, rejects the post-structuralist claim that texts are meaningless. Texts may be incomplete in themselves, but the reading of them makes them potentially reflective of the real world, or at least the reader's experience of the real world.

Some reader-response critics, most notably the German critic Wolfgang Iser, agree with Derrida that works contain "gaps"—not necessarily because of the slippage between signifier and signified but because of the incompleteness of works. Authors always leave something unsaid or unexplained, and they thus invite readers to fill the resulting spaces with their own imaginative constructs. Iser argues, therefore, that many equally valid interpretations of a work are possible. Interpretations of a work will vary from person to person and even from reading to reading. Critics who agree with Iser often attempt to study how readers fill the gaps in works. These critics are more interested in mapping the process of reading than in explaining individual works.

But perhaps the most prominent group of reader-response critics focuses on how biographical and cultural contexts influence the interpretation of texts. These critics argue that reading is a collective enterprise. The American critic Stanley Fish says that a reader's understanding of what "literature" is and what works of literature mean is formed by "interpretive communities"—groups to which the reader belongs. These groups could be very small (a circle of friends) or very large (a region, country, or cultural entity like "Western civilization"). Fish rejects the idea that a text has a core of meaning that everyone in any age would agree on. Rather, any shared understanding of a text's meaning comes from the beliefs of a community of readers, not from the text. Each reader's preconceptions actually "create" the text. If for example, a reader believes that a miscellaneous collection of words is a religious poem, the reader will perceive it as a religious poem. If a reader believes that the work will fit a particular theory, the reader will find facts in the work to support the theory. The theory, in a sense, "creates" the facts.

Feminist Criticism

Feminist criticism has much in common with reader-response criticism, especially with critics who, like Fish, believe that interpretations of literature are influenced by communities of readers. Feminist critics claim that although interpretive communities may have changed over the years, the one thing they have in common is that they have been made up of men. Men have determined the conventions that create "literature." Men have established the criteria for judging the quality of works. Men have written the literary histories, thereby establishing lists of "officially" approved works—the literary canon. The consequence is that works by and about women have been left out of the canon; women authors have been ignored; women characters have been misconstrued; and men have used literature to present a distorted view of women and women's place in society.

Feminist critics attempt to redress these problems in a number of ways. First, they argue that more works by and about women should be included in literary histories and anthologies. Second, by valuing the kinds of writing that women have done, feminist critics broaden the scope of "literature." Women in the past have often lacked access to the means of literary production, such as publishers and theater companies. So they have written diaries, journals, and letters. Feminist critics argue that these kinds of writing are "literature" and belong in the company of more traditional forms of literature, with poems, short stories, novels, and plays.

Third, feminist critics publish and celebrate neglected works by women. The rediscovery of fine works such as Zora Neale Hurston's novel *Their Eyes Were Watching God* (1937), Kate Chopin's novel *The Awakening* (1899), Charlotte Perkins Gilman's short story "The Yellow Wallpaper" (1892) and Rebecca Harding Davis's short novel *Life in the Iron-Mills* (1861) is due in part to the work of feminist critics. All of these works were almost unread until the 1970's. Fourth, feminist critics examine attitudes toward women that are explicit and implicit in all works of literature. They seek to bring to light assumptions about women and to understand how literary conventions, like the "happy ending" (in which hero marries heroine), convey those assumptions. Finally, feminist critics are trying to create a new interpretive community, one informed by female psychology and female values. To do this, they reach out to other disciplines—history, anthropology, psychology, sociology—for an understanding of female culture and a definition of female consciousness.

Because of the influence and provocative nature of reader-response and feminist criticism, writings about them abound. *The Reader in the Text: Essays on Audience and Interpretation*, edited by Susan R. Suleiman and Inge Crosman (Princeton: Princeton UP, 1980) provides an introduction to reader-response criticism plus readings from prominent critics. Stanley Fish's *Is There a Text in This Class?: The Authority of Interpretive Communities* (Cambridge: Harvard UP, 1980) is a collection of lively and sometimes funny essays. *The New Feminist Criticism: Essays on Women, Literature, Theory* (New York: Pantheon, 1985) contains an introduction to feminist criticism by the editor, Elaine Showalter, plus essays by other critics. Sandra Gilbert and Susan Gubar's *The Madwoman in the Attic: The Woman Writer and the Nineteenth-Century Literary Imagination* (New Haven: Yale, 1979) is a radical reinterpretation of nineteenth-century female writing. Jane Tompkins's essay "Sentimental Power: *Uncle Tom's Cabin* and the Politics of Literary History" in her *Sensational Designs: The Cultural Work of American Fiction 1790–1860* (New York: Oxford UP, 1985) is a good example of canon revision.

8

How to Generate Topics by Evaluating the Quality of Literature

EVALUATING THE QUALITY of works is basic to all serious reading of literature. Teachers who create literature courses on whatever level of sophistication choose works because they are "good," and individual readers decide whether works are "good *for them*." It is perhaps inevitable that we rate what we read even on the most superficial level: "Boy, I really enjoyed that play"; "That book was sure boring." In addition to appraising the quality of works you read, you might also want to write essays about their strengths and weaknesses. This chapter provides some criteria and questions to help you do so.

Perhaps the best place to begin is with yourself. Your subjective responses to a work may not be systematic or even logical, but they should help you begin a systematic and logical analysis of the work's successes and failures. The subjective responses of other readers may be useful too.

1. If you like the work, why do you? Is it the characters, the setting, the mood, the humor, the ideas, the action, the sentiment, the language? Why does it succeed?

2. Does the work move you emotionally? Do you care about its ideas, characters, events? If so, why?

3. If you dislike the work, where specifically does it fail for you? Even if you think highly of a work, what do you perceive to be its flaws?

4. If your acquaintances like or dislike the work, do you agree with their reasons?

Literary critics of all ages have developed their own methods of evaluating literature. They do not always agree, and their standards of excellence vary from age to age and person to person. However, their ideas do provide some practical guidelines for judging specific works. In this chapter we will consider some questions that most critics ask when evaluating works of literature.

IS THE WORK UNIFIED AND COHERENT?

Many critics, like the New Critics, claim that unity and coherence are a work's most important aesthetic qualities. If a work is unified and coherent, it is "good." If not, it is "bad." A *unified* work creates a single effect, has a single aim or purpose; a *coherent* work uses all its elements to attain that effect, to contribute to that aim or purpose.

Critics who value unity in works feel that seemingly superfluous elements mar the quality of works. Sir Walter Scott's novel *Ivanhoe*, for example, begins with a heavy emphasis on Ivanhoe's relationship with the Saxon heroine Rowena, as if it and she are to be important parts of the novel, and then inexplicably drops them to concentrate on Ivanhoe's troubled relationships with the more exotic and more interesting Rebecca. Also in *Ivanhoe*, one character "dies" in battle, is mourned at length, and then suddenly sits up and proclaims himself recovered. Scott gives no reason for this remarkable reversal; he just puts it in In fact, Scott often seems to be writing to please the momentary interests of his readers. He wants to tell a good story, not to create unified works of art. Consequently, critics downgrade the quality of *Ivanhoe*. They admit that it is a good "read" the first time through, but conclude that it does not reward more careful attention. O. Henry is another writer whom critics deride, in this case for his contrived endings. In his short stories he creates one set of circumstances only to produce endings that don't follow logically from these circumstances. These endings may pleasantly surprise us by their happy turn of events, but they are inconsistent with what precedes them and thus are ultimately unsatisfying.

It may be that critics overemphasize the importance of unity and coherence in literature. Some forms of literature, namely novels, long narrative poems, and plays, lend themselves to disparateness. Shakespeare and Dickens include extraneous elements in their works, and yet their works are unquestionably "great." Works that benefit most from the demand for unity and coherence are short works, like stories and poems, in which practically every word counts toward a total effect and in which coherence is recognizable almost at a glance. But most good works, including long ones, seem to have an *overall* sense of consistency and order, even if a few elements may not seem to fit the pattern. Careful analysis of the texts should reveal such patterns.

DOES THE WORK GIVE CONTINUAL PLEASURE?

Does the work give pleasure the first time through? Does it give pleasure on subsequent readings? Answers to these questions are obviously subjective and vary from person to person. One way to answer them is to examine a work's history. If a work has survived several generations of readers, then the answer to both questions might be yes. If a work was very popular with one generation but with no others, then the answer to the first question might be yes, and no to the second. But such historical evidence is inadequate. A work might be rediscovered, or it might never have been popular but nonetheless have been read and reread by an elite group. Or it might be too new to have become popular.

The pleasure-giving quality of literature is mysterious. Two criteria for evaluating it may be helpful. First, some critics hold that novelty and surprise are major causes of pleasure. Thus many novels give pleasure by utilizing exotic settings, unusual characters, and suspenseful plots. Publishers call such novels "page turners" because they compel the reader to keep turning the page to find out what will happen next. The novels of Robert Louis Stevenson, Jack London, James Fenimore Cooper, Alexander Dumas, Rafael Sabatini, James Michener, Agatha Christie, Leon Uris, Herman Wouk, Allen Drury, Victoria Holt, and a host of other best-selling writers are examples of page turners. The novelty of the material makes our first-time experience with the work exciting and fun. But good works of art should give pleasure beyond a first-time reading. You should be able to reread them and *continue* to find novelty and to be surprised. The limitation of a suspenseful plot is that once you know "what happens," its chief interest is dissipated. If a work continues to be new to you, then it is "good."

A second criterion for evaluating the pleasure a work provides is the distinction critics make between easy and difficult beauty. Difficult beauty, they maintain, is preferable to easy beauty. Elements that give immediate pleasure, like dramatic plots, simple ideas, heroic characters, euphonious language, glamorous settings, and happy endings do not give as lasting satisfaction as materials that seem at first to discourage enjoyment, like tragic events, plain and troubled characters, dissonant language, threatening landscapes, undramatic happenings, and pessimistic ideas. The reason may be that the difficult materials emerge from aspects of life that deeply affect us emotionally and intellectually, and we take longer-lasting satisfaction in seeing works of art put them in order. The easy materials, in other words, give superficial pleasure; the difficult materials give profound pleasure.

IS THE WORK TRUE?

Critics are divided about the importance of "truth" in literature. Some contend that even though a work may represent great ideas, it still may not be good. Others argue that a work can be very skillfully assembled, but if it has no relation to the real world, then it is less good than works that do. Each reader must resolve this controversy to his or her own satisfaction. Probably, however, the works that people read again and again are those that offer some insight into the nature of the real world. In this section we will discuss some questions that should help you to determine the quality of the "truth" offered in literary works.

Is the Work Meaningful?

Although it is possible to have meaningless works in other media—dance, music, painting, sculpture—it is probably impossible to create a totally meaningless work of literature. The reason is that literature uses an inherently meaningful medium: language. Words are symbols. At least on a practical level, they connect with aspects of reality, and the stringing of words together into phrases makes them coherent. Words become ideas. Also, literature represents real life, at least superficially, or else we could not understand it. If it did not, it would be another art form, either visual (a kind of "painting") or aural (a kind of "music"), but not literature.

However, literature can *avoid* meaning by creating imaginary worlds that have little practical relation to the real world. Usually this literature is "escapist" because it emphasizes the ideal—characters, settings, and events that rarely exist in the real world. In the dissolute court of Charles II (king of England, 1660–85), the most popular works of literature were long French romances depicting impossibly honorable courtiers, impossibly beautiful and chaste heroines, all interacting in an impossibly just court. A modern example is Ian Fleming's James Bond thrillers, whose protagonist possesses incredible skills and tolerances, meets an endless sequence of willing, shapely females, gets caught up in bizarre conspiracies (like voodoo on the Southern Railroad), and clashes with supervillains who gain immense power and yet who stupidly tell Bond all their secrets. Usually such works are enjoyable for a single reading, or they are important for what they reflect of the values and tastes of their reading public. But because they have little relation to the real world, they are quickly forgotten. They are not "good" literature.

Does Your Perception of the Real World Square with the Author's?

One way to assess the meaningfulness of a work is to compare its presentation and interpretation of reality with your own perceptions and experience. Of course, your experience is not the totality of experience. You should consider other readers' experiences and reactions to the work. But we are all limited by time and space. We must base decisions about truth on what we know now, not on what other people know or on what we will know later. Such decisions are valid and important.

Does the Work Present the Probable and the Typical?

Since authors best communicate their interpretations of reality by presenting the probable and typical, your assessment of their ability to do so is crucial to determining a work's meaningfulness. Examples of atypical characters are the flat characters of melodrama: the unmotivated villain, the pure-as-the-driven-snow heroine, the square-jawed hero. Examples of improbable events are the hero's arrival just in time to rescue the heroine from being sawed in half or run over by a train, the corrupt politician's sudden conversion to righteousness, the spendthrift father's avoidance of financial ruin by inheriting a fortune or winning the state lottery.

Does the Work Present a Mature Vision of Reality?

Any work can offer an interpretation of reality, but some interpretations are immature and simpleminded. More valuable are those that reflect qualities that serious, thoughtful people would accept.

These include a recognition of the world's potential for injustice and tragedy, of the ambiguity inherent in moral choices and judgments, of the complexity of human events and decisions, of the three-dimensionality of human nature. The world is filled, for example, with people who do both evil and good. A mature view recognizes that such people are equal to more than just a limited set of actions. The death-row murderer has some admirable (or at least sympathetic) traits. The philanthropist is capable of destructive acts and of cruelty. All people are flawed and all people have redeeming traits.

Does the Work's Interpretation of Reality Deserve Serious Reflection?

Sometimes we may find ourselves in disagreement with a work's worldview. Sinclair Lewis's *Babbitt*, James Joyce's *Ulysses*, Arthur Miller's *The Crucible*, Allen Ginsberg's *Howl*, and D. H. Lawrence's *Lady Chatterley's Lover* present views of the world that have been extremely controversial and that many people still find objectionable. If you object to a work's ideas, you can test their quality by asking if the author has rendered them vividly, has represented his or her position fairly (that is, has kept opposing positions in sight), and has focused on ideas that are worth thinking about. One value of literature is that it compels us, through the force and logic of its imagined worlds, to give serious consideration to important concepts with which we are unfamiliar or with which we disagree. If the artist renders his or her ideas compellingly and if they are important, then that is all he or she can be expected to do. The author's ideas are "good." But just because a work has artistic integrity does not mean we have to agree with the author's world view.

Is the Work Universal?

Does the work transcend the ideology of the author? Does it transcend the narrow concerns, obsessions, and prejudices of one reader, one group, one society, one nation, one generation, one century?

These questions represent one test of a work's quality. The better a work can "live" beyond the interests of a few readers, the better the work. This does not mean that everyone will like the works of Chaucer, Dante, Shakespeare, Spenser, Milton, Wordsworth, Racine, Goethe, Molière, Emily Brontë, Homer, Ovid, Dickens, Emily Dickinson, George Eliot. It means that their works have touched an ever-increasing number of people, that they have universal appeal. It also means that the *ideas* represented in their works are in accord with most people's perception of reality, even though those ideas might emerge from narrow ideological concerns. John Bunyan, for example, was a radical, nonconformist English minister living in a time famous for its fierce struggles between religious groups. He was a mentally wracked, obsessive Calvinist whose narrative *The Pilgrim's Progress* reflects anguish over his immediate condition—he was in jail—and over his state of grace. He meant it as a guide for members of his own sect. And yet even though its protagonist, "Christian," must travel the straight and narrow Puritan road to the "Celestial City," somehow Christian becomes more than a seventeenth-century Puritan. His struggles, temptations, emotions, and interests are those that we all feel as we make our way through life. His companions may have allegorical names—Obstinate, Hopeful, Faithful, Pliable, Mr. Worldly Wiseman, Talkative, Giant Despair—but they embody people that any of us might meet. His places—Vanity Fair, the Slough of Despond, Doubting Castle, the Valley of the Shadow of Death—have a psychological and even a physical reality that has meaning for all readers. The basic theme of the book—that life threatens and tests our emotional and moral integrity with ambiguous situations—is one that we all recognize as true. Christian could as well be called "Everyman," for his pilgrimage is real to all people, no matter of what faith, nationality, or century.

Are the Ideas of the Work Consistent with One Another and with the Form of the Work?

A work's ideas must emerge convincingly from its form, not be imposed on that form. One should be able to induce the work's ideas from its materials. No one, including the author, should have to tell us what a work means. Furthermore, if all the elements of a work are logically related to one another and to an overriding purpose, then the work's ideas will also be consistent with one another. A work should not, for example, show us that one thing is true in one part and that a contradictory thing is true in another part. Henry David Thoreau seems to do this in *Walden*, where throughout he praises the "indescribable innocence and beneficence of Nature" and then in the chapter called "Higher Laws" says that "Nature" (the "animal" part of humanity) is evil and must be suppressed; nature is "hard to be overcome, but she must be overcome."

IS THE LANGUAGE OF THE WORK APPEALING?

The appeal of an author's use of language, especially if it is prose rather than poetry, may be hard to define. The writer may be especially adept at imitating the rhythms of spoken speech, at using internal rhyme, at choosing apt and delightful words, at building suspenseful sentences, at making witty or striking analogies. Emerson and Thoreau are famous, for example, for their pithy, rhetorical phrasing. We expect the language of poetry to be appealing, but one test of the quality of any work is the ability of its language to grip us. The stories and novels of F. Scott Fitzgerald may sometimes seem trivial but they are wonderfully, charmingly written. The attractiveness of a work's language helps make it "good."

DOES THE AUTHOR PRESENT HIS OR HER WORLD VIVIDLY AND INTENSELY?

This quality, like compelling language, is difficult to define, but some authors have the ability to imprint their worlds so vividly on our imaginations that no matter how ridiculous those worlds may be, we delight in the mere rendering of them. Poe and Dickens describe scenes that are utter nonsense (Dickens has one of his villains, whose name is "Krook," die of spontaneous combustion) but are so graphic that we enjoy them nonetheless. The energy and virtuosity of a work may give pleasure no matter what the materials.

HOW WELL DOES THE WORK USE GENERIC ELEMENTS?

Are the characters believable? Is the plot plausible? Are the symbols appropriate? These are but a few questions dealing with specific elements in a work. For more detailed discussions of these questions, see chapters 4, 5, and 6.

9
How To Draft Your Essay: Content and Organization

S O FAR, WE HAVE DEALT with the prewriting stage of the writing process. For essays about literature, prewriting means studying works of literature and developing ideas about them. The next stage of the writing process is drafting the essay. Drafting means developing ideas into an essay. Drafting may seem like a formidable task: How do you get started? What form should the essay take? How do you make your ideas convincing? How do you organize the essay? This chapter offers some answers to these questions.

READ SAMPLE ESSAYS

When you want to do a particular kind of writing, studying models of that kind of writing may be helpful. Use the student essays in chapter 10 (on documentation) and chapter 13 to give you a sense of the form of essays about literature. Note the kinds of topics they discuss, how and where they state their theses, how they use facts to support their claims, how they are reasoned, and how they are organized.

156

KEEP EARLY DRAFTS INFORMAL

Most writers go through several drafts of an essay before producing a final draft. The very first draft might be miscellaneous jottings; the next draft a more connected list that serves as a rough outline; the third draft a series of paragraphs; the fourth draft a more thorough outline; the fifth draft a genuine essay that incorporates the paragraphs and follows the latest outline. These drafts are usually very informal. No one need see them but the writer. Think of the earliest drafts as being like free writing, a means of getting ideas and facts on paper to expand on, support, explain more clearly, rearrange, even discard later. At the beginning of the drafting process, the most important thing is to get started writing. Writing generates thoughts, not only about what to say about the work but also about how to arrange your ideas.

REMEMBER YOUR AUDIENCE

Think of your audience and its needs while you write the drafts of your essay. As we noted in chapter 2, you will write better essays if you write for an audience that includes not just your instructor but anyone who enjoys literature and has ideas about it. Your goal is to convince readers that your ideas have merit. Imagine yourself in conversation with your audience members. In order to follow your line of thought, they will need to know certain things, they will have questions that need to be answered, and they will want complex points clarified. Try to anticipate and supply their needs, just as you would if you were talking with them in person.

One of their needs is for clarity. They need a full and clear explanation of the points you are making. Your readers—including your instructor—cannot read your mind. Assume that they have already read the work or can read it; this means that you need only summarize and paraphrase those parts of the work that illustrate your points. But if you do not spell out your ideas, your readers may miss them altogether. In being fully clear, you may feel that you are being childishly obvious, but better to be obvious than to risk having your readers miss your points.

Your readers also need to be convinced. Assume that your readers want to learn from you, but don't expect them to surrender their views of the work just because you tell them to. Think of them as constantly asking, Why should we believe what you say? Your task is to explain and to show them why. To help you do this, we now turn to the very heart of any argument—its reasoning.

REASON CONVINCINGLY

To understand how to use reasoning in an essay about literature, consider how you arrive at the thesis of your essay. Any work of literature consists of "facts": words, structural devices, sound patterns, plot elements, information about characters, details of setting, and so forth. The first thing you do is acquaint yourself with these facts by reading the work. Gradually, after studying and thinking about the work, you single out some of these facts for special consideration. In your mind, they are linked together because you have an idea about them. You have, in short, moved from a confrontation with all of the facts to an idea about some of the facts. The following diagram represents this process:

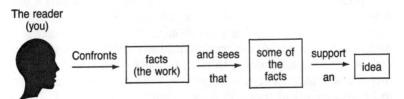

Once you have your idea, you decide to tell someone about it. Before you can do that you have to formulate the idea as a proposition. A *proposition* is a statement that can be affirmed or denied: Abraham Lincoln was a melancholy person; gothic cathedrals were built in France during the thirteenth-century; William Wordsworth lived a long time. For the sake of illustration, we will say that your proposition is as follows: In his novel *The Sea Wolf,* Jack London shows human beings to be animalistic. Imagine that over coffee in the snack shop you state this proposition to a friend. Your friend says, "That's interesting. What makes you think so?" And you respond by stating the facts that have led you to this proposition. In short, *you reverse the process of your reading experience*:

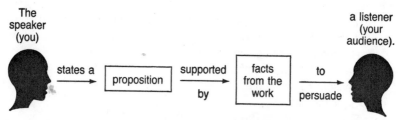

When you write essays, you reproduce the structure of this conversation. The essay is, of course, more sophisticated and complex than a conversation over coffee. It is more thorough, more carefully reasoned, and more controlled by persuasive strategies. But the structure of the oral exchange is generally the same as the structure of an essay. Your idea—the proposition—becomes the thesis of the essay. Your presentation of the facts becomes the body of the essay. In the actual essay, you may choose to state your thesis at the end rather than in the beginning. But this is merely a strategy of persuasion. *You* know what your thesis is and you present facts to support it. The thesis comes first, the facts second.

A general and unavoidable principle of sound reasoning, then, is that an essay must have a clear thesis and this thesis must be supported by facts. In essays about literature, the thesis is a proposition about the work and the facts come from the work.

Another principle of reasoning rests on how you present the facts. Later in this chapter we suggest ways to organize facts so your readers can group them easily and understand how they relate to your thesis. But here we need to say that facts are grouped around the propositions that support the thesis. Few theses are supported with just bare facts. Rather, theses are supported with "good reasons"—propositions or claims about the facts. *To make your reasoning convincing, you must state these propositions clearly and you must relate your facts to them.* The outline of your reasoning will look something like this:

Thesis (a proposition, supported by reasons)
Reason #1 (a proposition, supported by facts)
Reason #2 (a proposition, supported by facts)
Reason #3 (a proposition, supported by facts)
Reason #4 (a proposition, supported by facts), and so forth.

An essay with the Jack London thesis would have an outline similar to the following:

> Thesis: In his novel *The Sea Wolf*, Jack London shows human beings to be animalistic.
> Reason #1: Wolf Larsen, the ship's captain, is animalistic.
> Reason #2: The members of the crew are animalistic.
> Reason #3: Humphrey Van Weyden, the protagonist, is animalistic.
> Reason #4: Maud Brewster, Humphrey's love interest, is animalistic.

USE SOUND LOGIC

Another aspect of reasoning is logic. Logic is too complex a subject for us to discuss thoroughly here, but a few principles of logic should help make your reasoning convincing.

Define the Key Terms in Your Thesis

Logic is largely a matter of placing items within categories. A thesis statement always names the categories. When you define these categories, you accomplish several purposes. One is that you establish a common ground with your audience. Your readers, of course, are always free to disagree with your definitions, but they are unlikely to do so if you rely on reputable sources for your definitions. Another is that you enable readers to understand your thesis. If you use vague terms or unexplained terms, your readers will fail to understand what you are trying to prove.

There are several strategies to follow for defining key terms in a thesis. First, you could offer a formal definition near the beginning of the essay. A formal definition is like a dictionary definition. You would follow this strategy if the term is especially controversial or ambiguous and if you know your readers would want a forthright definition before considering any of your reasoning. Second, you could define the term as you move from section to section of your paper. You would use this strategy if the term represents a concept with a number of different parts. You would explain each part as you come to it in the essay.

Finally, you could define the term simply by using it consistently. The meaning of many terms is commonly agreed upon. They do not really need formal definition. Throughout your paper, you would use the term according to its widely accepted meaning. If you depart from that meaning, you would need to say so and explain why.

The following thesis statements illustrate the importance of definition in all thesis statements:

> Thesis #1: In Edith Wharton's novel *The Age of Innocence*, Newland Archer is torn between two women who represent opposing qualities. Ellen Olenska represents freedom, and May Welland represents entrapment.

This thesis has two parts. The first part puts Newland Archer into the category *torn between two women*. But you hardly need to prove this claim or define this category, since both are obvious to anyone who reads the novel even casually. Much more important is the second part of the thesis, which puts Ellen Olenska into the category *freedom* and May Welland into the category *entrapment*. You do not need a formal definition of these terms. Nearly everyone has a general idea of what they mean. They are, however, vague terms. You must make them specific by naming the qualities of freedom or entrapment that each character exhibits.

> Thesis #2: In his novel *The Sea Wolf*, Jack London shows human beings to be animalistic.

The key term in this thesis is *animalistic*. You are putting human beings into the category of animalistic beings. This term is more problematic than the terms *freedom* and *entrapment*. Your readers are less likely to be sure what it means and especially what it means to you. Still, you probably do not need a formal definition at the beginning of the essay. The definition of the term would emerge as you name and illustrate the traits that characterize this category.

> Thesis #3: Theodore Dreiser's novel *Sister Carrie* is Naturalistic.

The key term here is *Naturalistic*. Because it is a specialized term, you almost certainly need a formal definition of it at the beginning of the essay.

> Thesis #4: In Jane Austen's *Pride and Prejudice,* Elizabeth changes her mind about Mr. Darcy when she visits his estate, Pemberley.

You might wonder what the key terms are in this thesis statement. The fact is, there aren't any, at least as the thesis is stated here. But if you think about this statement, you should see that the thesis isn't complete. The thesis is a cause-and-effect proposition, and it gives the effect but not the cause, at least not in precise terms. The cause, of course, is Elizabeth's visit to Pemberley, but what about her visit? What qualities in her visit cause her to change her mind? If you identify those qualities, you will have the terms that need definition. A complete statement of the thesis would be as follows:

> Thesis #4 (revised): In Jane Austen's *Pride and Prejudice,* Elizabeth changes her mind about Mr. Darcy when she visits his estate, Pemberley. Pemberley "speaks" for Mr. Darcy in a way that he could not speak for himself. It represents his good qualities: kindness, good taste, responsibility, love of nature, and family affection.

The key terms are in the phrase "kindness, good taste, responsibility, love of nature, and family affection." Since they are commonly understood terms, you would not need formal definitions. You would illustrate them as you take them up in your essay.

This fourth thesis statement illustrates a method of presenting a thesis that writers sometimes use. They may choose to present part of the thesis at the beginning of the essay and the rest in the body of the essay. Here, for example, they might start the essay with everything but the final sentence, the list of qualities, and then state and illustrate the qualities in the rest of the essay. When you use this method, it is easy to lose sight of the key terms of the thesis and to forget to define them. But a complete statement of the thesis will always bring them to light.

Define the Key Terms in the Reasons That Support Your Thesis

As we say above, in most essays, theses are supported not with facts alone but with reasons. These supporting reasons are propositions, with key terms of their own. You need to define these terms.

Follow the same strategies for defining them as for defining terms in a thesis.

Support Your Reasons with Facts

The claims that support your thesis must themselves be supported with facts. Each claim is a proposition about the facts. You must show how the facts led you to your proposition. If you claim, for example, that Wolf Larsen (in Jack London's *The Sea Wolf*) is animalistic, you must provide facts from the novel to show that your claim is true.

Two kinds of facts are relevant for essays about literature: facts from primary sources and facts from secondary sources. Almost always, facts from primary sources are more valuable and persuasive than facts from secondary sources. *Primary sources* are the works of literature themselves. If your essay is about *The Sea Wolf*, then *The Sea Wolf* is your primary source. If you are writing about all of Jack London's short stories, then all of them comprise your primary source. Anything in your primary source is a "fact." Facts can be quotations, words, incidents, details of setting, descriptions of characters, conflicts within the plot, word sounds, punctuation—anything in the work. Quoting from the work is one way of presenting facts from the work. The following quotation from *The Sea Wolf*, for example, supports the claim that Wolf Larsen is animalistic:

> [Larsen had] a sinewy, knotty strength, of the kind we ascribe to lean and wiry men, but which, in him, because of his heavy build, partook more of the enlarged gorilla order. . . . It was a strength we are wont to associate with things primitive, with wild animals, and the creatures we imagine our tree-dwelling proto-types to have been—a strength savage, ferocious, alive in it-self, the essence of life in that it is the potency of motion, the elemental stuff itself out of which the many forms of life have been molded; in short, that which writhes in the body of a snake when the head is cut off, and the snake, as a snake, is dead, or which lingers in a shapeless lump of turtlemeat and recoils and quivers from the prod of a finger.

But quotations are not the only way to present facts from the work. Sometimes your reasoning is more convincing when you summarize facts in your own words. Summarizing allows you to feature those details that are most relevant to your claim, something that is hard to do in long quotations. To show that Wolf Larsen is animalistic you could simply say that London compares his strength to that of a gorilla or a snake with its head cut off. You could describe Larsen's animalistic actions: his brutality, his enormous strength, his amorality, his egotism, his inability to reason clearly, his failure to love. You could describe how Larsen's fate at the end of the novel draws a comparison between himself as an "animal" and the more "human" characters, Humphrey and Maud. You could effectively present all of these facts without quoting from the novel at all.

Facts from *secondary sources* come from places other than the work. Facts concerning the author's life, the period in which the author lived, the author's philosophy, literary history, other authors, the audience, the work's influence, similarities to other works—these come from secondary sources. Secondary sources are valuable for what they teach us about the work. They give information that helps us form our own opinions. When we study Hawthorne's fiction, our perception of his themes sharpens when we learn that he was deeply ashamed of his Puritan ancestors' dire deeds. When we learn that Jane Austen used an actual calendar to plot the events of *Pride and Prejudice,* we appreciate the care with which she crafted her fiction. When we compare Shakespeare's sources with his plays, we see his genius for deepening characterization and creating complex philosophical themes.

Use secondary sources, then, to learn as much as you can about a work. Use reliable secondary sources—accurate histories, biographies, autobiographies, memoirs, interviews. When you include facts from secondary sources in your essay, cite them and your sources for them. But keep in mind that secondary sources are no substitute for facts from primary sources. Even when you use secondary sources, you should draw most of your conclusive facts from primary sources. Chapter 10 (on documentation) explains how to incorporate secondary sources into your essays.

Give Enough Facts to Support Your Reasons

You need not report every fact in the work, but your reader should feel that you have given a thorough account of the work or the parts you discuss. Support your claims with facts that are representative of all the relevant facts rather than with facts that are isolated and atypical. Use important rather than trivial facts. Account for facts that contradict your thesis. If some facts fly in the face of your thesis, explain why they don't nullify it. Often when you deal with negative examples of your reasons, you make your overall argument more subtle and convincing. You discover profundities in the work that your readers—and you as well—may not have expected to be there.

Understand and Accurately Represent Key Words in the Work

If you misconstrue words in the work, then you cannot draw logical conclusions. You will misapply the facts and fail to convince your readers. The need to understand words in the text is especially strong for poetry and earlier authors, such as Shakespeare and Chaucer. Be sensitive to word usage, and look up puzzling words in an up-to-date and scholarly dictionary.

Use Certain Kinds of Secondary Sources with Caution

Authors sometimes comment on their own work, but such interpretations are far from infallible. Mark Twain and William Faulkner, for example, spoke about their own work but were forgetful about what they had actually written and were not above pulling the legs of their audiences. Faulkner's comments are fascinating and are in a way extensions of his novels. But to consider them the only correct interpretations of his characters is to limit severely the complexity and meaning of his fiction. Other authors, such as Henry James, are more careful when discussing their own work and are thus more reliable. But even here you must beware of making the "intentional fallacy," the assumption that the only valid interpretations of a work are those the author intended. Sometimes an author doesn't entirely know what he or she intends. Sometimes he or she intends one thing but creates something very different. Sometimes the author forgets what he or she originally intended and later claims another "intention" for the work. Authors do not have total conscious control of their art, and once they create a work, they are as much outside it as any sensitive critic. Although authors' comments on their own work should not be ignored, they should not be taken as the last word.

Information from biographies can also be misapplied. Biographies are rich and thought-provoking repositories of information, but they do not necessarily provide a one-to-one relationship between facts about an author and the author's works. Edgar Allan Poe had, without question, serious problems with alcohol, but that does not in itself mean that his nightmarish fiction was a product of alcoholic dreams.

Avoid Non Sequiturs

The Latin term *non sequitur* means, "It does not follow." *Non sequiturs* result from improper categorization. Either the terms describing the categories are improperly defined or the facts do not support placing certain things in the categories. The use of facts about Poe's alcoholism, mentioned above, is an example of a *non sequitur.* Another example is the following proposition: Because Sinclair Lewis satirized American business practices in his fiction, he hated America. The key term in this proposition is *haters of America.* Most people would disagree with the implicit assumption here, that the category *haters of America* includes all people who satirize American business practices.

ORGANIZE THE ESSAY ACCORDING TO ESSAY FORM

The *essay* is a form of literature that over the centuries has been written in many different ways. But although people still take a variety of approaches to the essay, the form of the essay has become fairly standardized. When you write an essay about literature, especially for university courses, your readers will expect certain things.

The *topic* is the issue the essay addresses, the problem the essay tries to solve. You should be able to state the topic in the form of a question. (In the essay itself you do not *have* to state the topic as a question, but you should be able to for yourself.)

The *thesis* is the one proposition that unifies the whole essay. Everything in the essay exists to establish the validity of the thesis. State the thesis in the introduction or conclusion or make it implicit in the essay as a whole.

The *title* tells enough about the topic of the essay to interest the readers and let them know the focus of the essay. It is usually helpful to include the author's name and the title of the work you are discussing, as in the following example:

The Jungle as Symbol in Joseph Conrad's *Heart of Darkness.*

The introduction consists of one paragraph or at most several paragraphs. It states the topic of the essay, it grabs the reader's attention, and it may (but need not) state the thesis of the essay.

The body consists of a series of paragraphs that develop the topic. These paragraphs contain facts and interpretations that support the thesis of the essay.

The conclusion consists of one or at most several paragraphs. It signals to the reader that the essay has come to an end. It states or restates the thesis.

ORGANIZE YOUR FACTS INTO LOGICAL GROUPS

Your most important organizational task is to find a plan for presenting the claims and facts that support your thesis. When you start to draft your essay, your claims and facts may be jumbled up in your mind. Or you may have plenty of facts but few clear claims. Or you may even have facts and claims but no thesis. Don't despair. Most people have the experience of being intrigued by a group of facts but of not knowing quite what the facts add up to. Such people have, as it were, facts in search of a thesis. Or if they have a thesis, they may not know exactly how those facts lead to the thesis. One way to work yourself out of this bind is to think about how to arrange your facts into groups and how to spot those qualities that link the facts together. These groups of facts constitute the claims that support your thesis.

You can use various strategies to group facts, but two strategies are especially helpful: Look for logical groups in the facts themselves, and analyze the key terms of your thesis.

Look for Groups in the Facts Themselves

As we say near the beginning of this chapter, when you read you confront all of the facts in a work. But thinking about the work causes you to select *some* of the facts for special consideration. You may not know why at first, but something about those facts causes you to link them together. Your job is to discover what that something is.

Consider, for example, how you might think about grouping the facts in London's *The Sea Wolf.* After thinking about the novel, you realize that something intrigues you about the characters, but what? Then you realize that part of Wolf Larsen's forcefulness lies in the "animal" qualities that London blatantly assigns him. Are the other characters animalistic? Yes, you decide; in different degrees and ways, they are. You now have the one thing that for you links these characters together, their animalism. You also have your thesis (that London shows people to be animalistic) and a way to group your facts (around each of the characters).

Look for Groups in the Key Terms of the Thesis

The key terms of a thesis stand for concepts, and most concepts are complex enough to contain many elements. One method of grouping facts, then, is to group them around at least some of the elements of each key term.

The term *animalistic*, for example, is a concept that includes a number of different qualities. Rather than group your facts around each important character, as in the above example, you could group them around the qualities of "animalism." Each group of facts would support a separate claim:

Thesis: In his novel *The Sea Wolf*, Jack London shows human beings to be animalistic.
Reason #1: His characters look like animals.
Reason #2: They are brutal and vicious.
Reason #3: They lack the ability to think clearly.
Reason #4: Their moral code is based solely on physical strength.
Reason #5: Most are unable to love.

Another example is a thesis in which you claim that a work criticizes high society. The key term in this thesis is *high society*, and you could group the facts around typical negative aspects of high society life: snobbery, exclusivity, extravagant displays of wealth, lack of concern for the needy, narrow-mindedness, hypocrisy, obsession with silly rules of decorum. If, on the other hand, you looked for a method of grouping the facts from the facts themselves, you might group them quite differently. You might show how four important scenes in the work represent negative aspects of high society, or several different households, or six different characters.

ORGANIZE YOUR CLAIMS AND FACTS ACCORDING TO AN EASY-TO-FOLLOW PLAN

Once you arrive at the claims that support your thesis, you need to organize the body of your essay in a way that is interesting and easy to follow. Although patterns of organization vary from essay to essay, three frequently used patterns may at least help you think about how to organize your material.

1. *Spatial organization* presents the facts as they appear in the work, from beginning to end.

2. *Chronological organization* takes up the facts in the order in which they occur in time. Often spatial order is the same as chronological, but not always. Many works employ devices such as stream of consciousness and flashbacks that make spatial sequence different from chronological. Detective fiction, which depends on a gradual revelation of past events, is a good example. One advantage of either organization is that you give the reader the sense that you are covering all the important details of the work. The essay on "Young Goodman Brown" in chapter 13 is an example of spatial and chronological organization.

3. *Organization by ascending order of importance* moves from the least important facts or claims to the most important. The primary advantage of this method is that it gives your essay an element of suspense by moving your readers toward a climax. Organizing from least controversial claims to most controversial is a variation on this plan.

USE PARAGRAPHS TO REPRESENT THE MAJOR UNITS OF YOUR ESSAY

Paragraphs are a visual way of representing units of thought. The indentation at the beginning of a paragraph signals that a new idea is about to be stated, explained, and supported with facts. Paragraphs are essential to each section of your essay.

The *introduction* consists usually of one paragraph, but no more than about three. The typical introductory paragraph begins with general information about the work and ends either with a specific statement of the topic (the problem to be solved) or the thesis (the solution to the problem).

The *body* consists of a series of linked paragraphs. The units of thought that make up the *body* of an essay consist of claims and facts that support the claims. In shorter essays, each paragraph typically corresponds to one of these units. In longer essays, it may take more than one paragraph to represent a unit of thought. When that happens, each paragraph of the unit represents a subcategory of the claim. If you claim, for example, that there are two ways in which Wolf Larsen is animalistic, you might use two paragraphs, one for each way.

All of the paragraphs of your middle need topic sentences and transitions. A *topic sentence* states the main idea of the paragraph. Usually you put the topic sentence at the beginning of the paragraph. *Transitions* are statements that move readers smoothly from one unit of thought to another. Topic sentences often serve as transitions, but not always.

The *conclusion* should be short, about one paragraph long. It should remind the reader of the problem you have addressed in the essay and your solution to it.

For extended examples of how essays about literature are organized and paragraphed, see the sample essays in chapter 13. The marginal comments indicate strategies of organization and point to topic sentences and transitions.

ORGANIZE YOUR ESSAY ACCORDING TO TRADITIONAL PATTERNS OF THINKING

As we said in chapter 2 (p. 21), traditional patterns of thinking (*topoi*) can provide you with both ideas for your essays and ways to organize them. We will explain how you can use several of the most common.

Definition

Definition is unavoidable in arguments, because the thesis contains terms that must be defined. Quite often, the terms of the thesis are not controversial or ambiguous and therefore need no formal definitions. But when you have controversial terms, you must define them, and you must use all key terms in such a way that your readers know what you mean by them.

Apart from the necessity of defining terms in your thesis, definition can be useful in two other ways. First, your claims about the facts may rest on the definition of a particular word within the work. The student essays in chapter 13 on Emily Dickinson and E. A. Robinson both contain such claims. Second, you may want to focus your whole essay on a definition. You might, for example, show that "imagination" is Isabel Archer's most admirable trait in Henry James's novel *The Portrait of a Lady*. Your whole essay would attempt to explain what James means by the term. Or you might argue that Jane Austen in *Pride and Prejudice* distinguishes between "good pride" and "bad pride." And again, you would discuss the novel in order to define these terms. Finally, you might claim that Emily Brontë uses "gothic" elements in *Wuthering Heights*. You would need a reliable definition of *gothic* to make your case convincing, and you would need to apply all parts of the definition to the work, showing which ones fit and which do not. Hugh Holman and William Harmon's *A Handbook to Literature* and the articles in *The Encyclopaedia Britannica* are helpful starting points for finding definitions of literary and philosophical concepts.

One way to organize an essay based on a definition is to take up each element of the term, devoting about a paragraph to each. You would explain what these elements are. And you would show, one at a time, how the novel uses them.

Structural Analysis

Structural analysis identifies the parts of a "structure." A structure is something that has a definite pattern of organization. Works of literature always have a structure, sometimes more than one structure. Some works conform to established structures, like the sonnet form. Many other works establish their own structures. Your purpose in writing about a work's structure is to identify the structure and explain its relationship to other elements, such as theme and characterization. You might, for example, claim that the passage of the seasons provides the structure of William Wordsworth's poem "The Ruined Cottage"; or that the rhyme scheme of his "I Wandered Lonely as a Cloud" emphasizes the narrator's shift from feeling isolated to feeling connected to nature. The less obvious the structure or its effect on the work, the

172 HOW TO DRAFT YOUR ESSAY: CONTENT AND ORGANIZATION

more revealing your essay would be. You might even argue that the work has several structures—an obvious structure and one or more less obvious structures. The organization of your essay would usually be spatial. You would take up each part of the structure as it appears in the work.

Process Analysis

Process analysis identifies the stages in which things change—characters, states of mind, societies, settings, situations, conditions. Since literature often represents events occurring in time, it lends itself to process analysis: Characters change from weak to strong, societies from coherent to incoherent, settings from beautiful to ugly. The sample essay on Hawthorne's "Young Goodman Brown" in chapter 13 is a process analysis of Brown's emotional state, from integration to disintegration.

When making a process analysis, be careful that you do not simply retell the plot. You should explain and illustrate clear *steps* in the overall process. The pattern of organization would almost always be chronological; you would explain the steps in the order in which they occur in time. Each step would be a unit—probably a paragraph—of your paper. The claim of each unit would be your proposition about what characterizes the step.

Cause-and-Effect Analysis

Cause-and-effect analysis helps you investigate the causes and effects of events. When you investigate *causes*, you are always dealing with events in the past. Why does Goodman Brown go into the forest? Why does Hedda Gabler act the way she does? What causes Pip to change? Two kinds of causes are relevant, the immediate or surface cause and the remote or deep cause. If someone has been murdered, the immediate cause is the murderer. But the remote cause would be those forces—childhood experiences, parental models, heredity, financial situation, psychological state—that may have led the murderer to commit the crime. When you investigate *effects*, you may deal with events in the past or the future. In Faulkner's fiction, you could examine the effect of slavery on Southern society and on his characters. These effects are part of the historical past in his work. But you could also try to predict what the South will be like in the future, given the way he depicts it. The student essay in chapter 13 on "The Lottery" is a cause-and-effect analysis. It tries to predict what the villagers will do in the future by examining the causes of their actions in the past and present. Because literature often deals with the actions of complex characters, cause-and-effect analysis is a fruitful source of topics for essays. We constantly wonder why characters do what they do and what effects their actions have had or will have. Remember that just as in real life, causes and effects in works of literature can be complex and subtle. The more you investigate this complexity and subtlety, the more interesting—and controversial—your essay is likely to be.

You can organize cause-and-effect analyses in various ways. One way would be to discuss the causes or effects in order of importance, moving from least important to most important. You would devote the most attention to the more important items.

Comparison

Comparison means indicating both similarities and differences between two or more subjects. One use of comparison is to establish the value of something. You might argue that one of Shakespeare's comedies is less good than the others, because it lacks some of the qualities the others have. To establish this judgment, you would compare the play to the other comedies. Another use of comparison is to reveal the elements of a work, such as theme, characterization, point of view, and setting. You could compare one character to another, or one set of circumstances to another, or one setting to another in order to expose the nature of these things. A comparison of the two sets of lovers in Tolstoy's *Anna Karenina,* for example, helps us to understand his distinction between sacred and profane love. Comparisons of one work to another are also revealing. Sir Walter Raleigh's poem "The Nymph's Reply to the Shepherd" is a response to Christopher Marlowe's poem "The Passionate Shepherd to His Love." Raleigh not only disagrees in general with the premise of Marlowe's poem, but he makes nearly every line of the poem a response to the parallel line in Marlowe's poem. A line-by-line comparison of the two poems helps make clear Raleigh's themes and methods.

Comparison is revealing also when the author of a work makes allusions. An *allusion* is a reference to another work, a historical event, a myth, or an author. An allusion is always an invitation to compare the work at hand to the thing alluded to. Wordsworth, for example, in his long autobiographical poem *The Prelude* often alludes to Milton's *Paradise Lost*. You could write a comparison of *The Prelude* and *Paradise Lost* to clarify Wordsworth's methods and themes.

When you use comparison, you may want simply to make brief comparisons to support specific points in your essay, but when you make extended comparisons, follow certain guidelines about organizing the comparison. First, cover the *same aspects* of all the things compared. For example, if you compare two works and talk about metaphor, symbolism, and imagery in one work, you need to talk about these same things in the other work. Second, discuss the aspects *in the same order* for each thing compared. If you talk about metaphor, symbolism, and imagery in one work, keep this same order when you discuss the other work: metaphor first, symbolism second, imagery last. The outline for such a comparison would look like this:

Work #1
  Metaphor
  Symbolism
  Imagery
Work #2
  Metaphor
  Symbolism
  Imagery.

For comparisons of more than two things or for long, complex comparisons, another method of organization may be easier to follow:

Metaphor
  Work #1
  Work #2
  Work #3
Symbolism
  Work #1
  Work #2
  Work #3
Imagery
  Work #1
  Work #2
  Work #3.

There are other ways to organize a comparison as well as these. You could, for example, discuss all the similarities in one place and all the differences in another. But the general rule is to make the comparison thorough and orderly so the reader can clearly see all the lines of similarity and difference.

FOR FURTHER STUDY

A thorough explanation of the use of reasoning in arguments is Robert J. Fogelin's *Understanding Arguments: An Introduction to Information Logic* (San Diego: Harcourt, 1987). Fogelin discusses not only logic but different kinds of argumentation as well, such as legal, moral, scientific, and philosophical argumentation. For definitions of terms, the two most authoritative dictionaries are *The Oxford English Dictionary*, Second Edition, prepared by J. A. Simpson and E. S. C. Weiner, 20 volumes (Oxford: Oxford UP, 1989), and *Webster's Third New International Dictionary of the English Language*, unabridged, edited by Philip Babcock Gove (Springfield: Merriam, 1966). *The Oxford English Dictionary* (*OED*) is based on "historical principles"; it describes and gives examples of a word's use over the years. If you want to know what a word meant to Shakespeare or Chaucer, look it up in the *OED*. The Merriam *Webster's Third International* is a "descriptive" dictionary; it describes how the word is used and spelled today. The college edition of the Merriam, abridged from the *Third New International*, is adequate for nearly all your needs, as are most hardcover "desk" dictionaries on the market. For definitions of specialized literary terms, like *gothic* and *Naturalism*, see C. Hugh Holman and William Harmon's *A Handbook to Literature*, 5th ed. (New York: Macmillan, 1986).

10

How to Document Sources

DOCUMENTATION, or "giving credit," means identifying the sources you consult when you prepare your essays. When you write essays about literature, you must use at least one source: the primary source, the work of literature itself. You may also want to use secondary sources. (For a full discussion of primary and secondary sources, see chapter 9, the section on supporting your ideas with evidence, beginning on page 163.)

TESTIMONY

In Chapter Nine we discuss how essays about literature, like all arguments, must support their theses with reasoning and facts. A third kind of support is testimony. *Testimony* is commentary by experts. For essays about literature, testimony is an expert's interpretation of works of literature.

Of the three kinds of support in arguments, testimony is the least important. Sound reasoning and supporting facts are necessary to the believability of an argument; testimony usually is not. But testimony can add to the persuasive power of your essays. You can use testimony to show that experts agree with you. The reader may more readily accept your reasoning if you demonstrate that certain literary critics also agree with you. Furthermore, you can use testimony to show that your argument is part of an ongoing debate about the work. You let your reader know that you are aware of the debate and therefore of the different solutions already proposed to the problem you are discussing. You would explain the other solutions, identify the one that seems most reasonable, or offer a new solution of your own.

Use testimony, then, as a complement to your reasoning and facts, not as a substitute. If a critic makes an especially good point or gives an especially good analysis, summarize his or her ideas and include particularly apt or telling quotations from his or her essay. Think of testimony as witnesses on your behalf.

RESEARCH PAPERS AND THE USE OF SECONDARY SOURCES

The place to find both testimony and facts about literature is secondary sources. Most people associate the use of secondary sources with "research" and "research papers," so a word is appropriate here about what research papers are. In literary studies, there are essentially two kinds of research papers. The first kind is the informational paper, discussed briefly in chapter 1. The informational research paper reports on background, publication, or biographical information that illuminates works of literature. When you write an informational research paper, you assume your reader wants to know the facts in your paper and will probably use them to interpret and to understand the works better. Otherwise you would have no reason to write the paper. Perhaps the most valuable informational research papers are those that present new facts, facts that you have turned up in your research and that no one else knows. Sometimes, however, instructors assign informational research papers to give you practice in writing them. For whatever reason, if you write an informational research paper your job will be to gather the facts, to give order to them, and to report them accurately. You will also need a framing generalization—something like a thesis— to give focus to your material. This generalization will probably identify a reason for presenting the information, perhaps a problem of interpretation that the information will help solve. An example of such a paper might be one on a work's critical reception or on an event in an author's life, such as the financial crisis that struck Mark Twain late in his career and that helped cause the increased bitterness of his writing.

The second kind of research paper does more than simply present information; it offers an interpretation of a literary work or works. The writer searches through secondary sources in order to find facts and opinions that will help establish a reasonable interpretation, or perhaps even a new one. Some research papers try to represent as many different views on a work as possible. Others use only a few secondary sources, either as support and illustration for their own ideas or as springboards for alternative interpretations. The sample essay on E. A. Robinson's "Richard Cory" in chapter 13, for example, takes issue with one critic's opinion in order to present another view.

The most important point to remember about this second kind of research paper is that, for all its use of sources, it is still an *argumentative essay*. Here the terms *research paper* and *research essay* become synonymous. Like all arguments, a research essay presents opinions about a subject. A research essay, then, should be a synthesis of *your* discoveries about a topic and *your* evaluation of those discoveries. The reader should hear *your* voice speaking throughout the paper, should be constantly aware of *your* intelligence and consciousness shaping the essay. The paper should not be a mere anthology of other people's ideas or of facts. It should have what all good argumentative essays have: a unifying idea expressed directly and emphatically in a thesis; an introduction and a conclusion; and paragraphs that relate to the essay's thesis and that follow a logical plan. The sample essay at the end of this chapter exemplifies these traits.

GUIDELINES FOR FINDING INFORMATION AND OPINIONS ABOUT LITERATURE

Your research needs will vary from writing project to writing project. Some projects will require minimal research, others more elaborate research. Let us say, however, that you have to write an essay about a particular work. Your instructor requires only that you use the primary source, but you want to do some outside reading to get yourself thinking about the work. Go to the *card catalog* of your college library, find where the author's works are in *the stacks,* and browse among the books in that section. A good library will have many books about well-known authors. So choose a few of the books that look promising for your needs. In the indexes, look up the work you will be writing about, and read what each book has to say about the work. If, for example, you are interested in an important poem by Browning, a book that surveys all of Browning's works will have several pages on your poem. It should take you only a few minutes to read through what you find.

Your purpose in doing this kind of exploratory and casual reading is to familiarize yourself with critics' assessment of the characteristics and themes of the work. This knowledge should stimulate your thoughts and get you started on your essay. Sometimes, no matter how carefully you have read the work, you may be at a loss for a topic. Doing this kind of introductory reading should help you find one. If it turns out that you want to incorporate some of this material in your essay or that your teacher does in fact require you to use a few secondary sources, then you should read carefully in these books, take notes, and, in your essay, give credit for your sources.

However, what if there is very little in the stacks on your author, or what if your teacher asks you to do a full-fledged research paper? It may be that you will be lucky enough to find plenty of material in the stacks—biography, background information, criticism—but you will probably need to supplement that material with what you turn up in a second place in the library, the *reference room*. The reference room is especially helpful when books are missing from the stacks (lost or checked out) or when your library's collection on a particular author is small.

The reference room of a college library typically provides several kinds of materials. First, it contains books with background information. These include encyclopedias, literary histories, books containing brief biographies, books that describe and illustrate critical reactions to authors, handbooks to literary terms, surveys of contemporary authors and their works, guides to works by ethnic minorities. The "Oxford Companion" series published by the Oxford University Press (the *Oxford Companion to American Literature,* the *Oxford Companion to English Literature,* the *Oxford Companion to the Theatre,* and so forth) is an example of this kind of book. So, too, is the *Encyclopaedia Britannica,* which contains fine essays on authors and literary movements. Second, the reference room contains books that give specific and specialized information about primary sources. These include concordances and indexes to standard authors like Tennyson, Milton, and Shakespeare as well as books dealing with specialized qualities of works, such as their use of allusions, Greek mythology, or the Bible.

A third kind of material typical of reference rooms is bibliographies.[1] With these, you can make your research systematic and thorough. Three bibliographies should be very useful to you and should probably be the first you consult:

> *Literary History of the United States.* Ed. Robert E. Spiller et al. 4th ed. rev. New York: Macmillan, 1974. Vol. 2. (Vol. 1 is the literary history; Vol. 2 is the bibliography.)
>
> *MLA International Bibliography of Books and Articles on the Modern Languages and Literatures.* New York: MLA, 1922–.
>
> *The New Cambridge Bibliography of English Literature.* Ed. George Watson. 5 vols. Cambridge: Cambridge UP, 1969–1977.

Between them, the *LHUS* and the *New CBEL* bibliographies cover all of English and American literature up through the modern period. They cover movements, historical periods, and authors. They are "selective" bibliographies in that they list the most important writings by and about authors. In other words, they save you time by weeding out unimportant and repetitive books and essays. The *MLA International Bibliography* is published annually and covers everything published each year on "modern languages, literature, folklore, and linguistics." To find what you need in the *MLA International Bibliography*, look up your author's country and the period in which he or she has written. Authors are listed alphabetically within periods; works are listed alphabetically under authors.

Probably you will find all you need in the *New CBEL* and the *LHUS* bibliographies, but like all bibliographies, these are dated. That is, they cover what has been written up to their dates of publication. To cover work done after these dates, consult the *MLA International Bibliography*.

In addition to these three bibliographies, you might find some others helpful. There are individual bibliographies for almost every major author, and in contrast to the *New CBEL* and the *LHUS* bibliographies, these usually list everything written by and about an author. Also, the *Readers' Guide to Periodical Literature* and the *Book Review Digest* list articles and reviews in newspapers and popular journals.

---

[1] The bibliographic references provided here are given with the names of the works first for easy comparison and use. However, in the "Works Cited" section of your papers, use the author-first style suggested in the upcoming section on the guidelines and form for the "Works Cited" list.

Finally, there are the bibliographies of broad categories of literature, such as the novel, the short story, and drama. These bibliographies point you to the major criticism on specific works. To use these bibliographies, look up the work in the appropriate bibliography; there you will find a list of critical essays on the work you are studying. These bibliographies undergo constant revision, so check for supplements that bring them up to date. You can bring them up to date yourself with the *MLA International Bibliography*. A few examples are as follows:

The Contemporary Novel: A Checklist of Critical Literature on the British and American Novel since 1945. Comp. Irving Adelman and Rita Dworkin. Metuchen: Scarecrow, 1972.

The Continental Novel: A Checklist of Criticism in English 1900–1966. Comp. E. I. Kearney and L. S. Fitzgerald. Metuchen: Scarecrow, 1968.

The Continental Novel: A Checklist of Criticism in English 1967–1980. Comp. E. I. Kearney and L. S. Fitzgerald. Metuchen: Scarecrow, 1983.

Dramatic Criticism Index: A Bibliography of Commentaries on Playwrights from Ibsen to the Avant-Garde. Comp. Paul F. Breed and Florence M. Sniderman. Detroit: Gale, 1972.

English Novel Explication: Criticism to 1972. Comp. Helen H. Palmer and Anne Jane Dyson. Hamden: Shoe String, 1973. *Supplement 1* (1976). *Supplement 3* (1986).

European Drama Criticism: 1900 to 1975. Comp. Helen H. Palmer. 2nd ed. Hamden: Shoe String, 1977.

Greek and Roman Authors: A Checklist of Criticism. Comp. Thomas Gwinup and Fidelia Dickinson. 2nd ed. Metuchen: Scarecrow, 1982.

A Guide to Critical Reviews: Part I: American Drama, 1909–82. Comp. James Salem. 3rd ed. Metuchen: Scarecrow, 1984.

Poetry Explication: A Checklist of Interpretation since 1925 of British and American Poems Past and Present. Comp. Joseph Kuntz and Nancy Martinez. 3rd ed. Boston: Hall, 1980.

Twentieth-Century Short Story Explication: Interpretations 1900–1975, of Short Fiction since 1800. Comp. Warren S. Walker. 3rd ed. Hamden: Shoe String, 1977. *Supplement 1* (1980). *Supplement 2* (1984).

One other specialized bibliography may also be helpful: *The Essay and General Literature Index*. This bibliography indexes essays that appear in books. The card catalog of your library and the *MLA International Bibliography* do not do this. Someone, for example, might have written an essay on Wordsworth for an anthology of essays called *Twenty Different Views of Nature*. If you were doing a paper on Wordsworth, you (and most bibliographies) would be likely to overlook this essay because it is "hidden" by the title of the book. *The Essay and General Literature Index*, however, would have it. This bibliography comes out every year and is easy to use. Just look up the author or subject you are interested in (listed alphabetically). After each will be titles and locations of essays about them.

By consulting these bibliographies, you can draw up a thorough list of books and journal articles about an author. But you probably won't have time to read all of these books and articles, so unless your instructor wants a comprehensive list, list only those items that seem most interesting and most relevant to your topic. Then check to see if your library has the books on your list. If not, or if the books are checked out, move on to the journal articles. One advantage of journal articles is that if your library subscribes to the journals, almost certainly they cannot be checked out. In other words, they should be available for your use. To find the article, you need to go to a third place in the library, the *periodicals room*. Ask the periodicals librarian to help you find the journal you need. These will usually be bound and located in the stacks or they will be on microfilm. You can also check the "serials holding catalog" to see whether your library subscribes to the journal and to discover its call number and thus its location.

The information provided here about finding information about works of literature is basic and should serve almost all of your research needs while you are in college. If you want more thorough guidance on a particular project, or if you are interested in learning more about the methods of literary research, you might consult the following excellent book:

> *Selective Bibliography for the Study of English and American Literature*. Ed. Richard Altick and Andrew H. Wright. 6th ed. New York: Macmillan, 1979.

But perhaps the most valuable resource for doing research is the reference librarian. Reference librarians are experts on locating sources of information and opinion. They are usually eager to help. And they can save you time.

GIVING CREDIT TO SOURCES

Why Should You Give Credit?

There are several reasons for giving credit to your sources. One is to give readers information that allows them to find and read the same material you read. They may also want to check the reliability of your sources or your ability to use them fairly and accurately. Giving credit, to put it positively, is one more means of arguing. The more careful and honest you are in giving credit, the stronger your argument will be. Another reason for giving credit is to distinguish your ideas from those of others. The purpose of the essay, after all, is to express your ideas, to argue your position. You may use facts, ideas, and words from other sources to clarify and support your ideas, but readers are interested, finally, in knowing what you think. That is why they are reading your paper. By giving credit, both in your text and in footnotes, you show them exactly where your ideas begin and where other writers' ideas leave off.

The most obvious reason for giving credit is to adhere to an ethical standard. Student honor policies stress this reason heavily. But although the ethical principle is obvious, it is not always simple. The usual definition of *plagiarism* is "the presentation of someone else's ideas, work, or facts as your own." The moral judgment that follows is, "Plagiarism is stealing and therefore wrong." These judgments are adequate when applied to blatant plagiarism, cases in which someone copies, verbatim or almost verbatim, the work of someone else and claims it as his or her own. Most cases of student palgiarism, however, are not so obvious or so consciously criminal. The issue of plagiarism is clouded with some uncertainties. Everything you know, for example, comes from a "source." When is what you know "yours" and not someone else's? Another uncertainty is that when you summarize someone else's ideas, you will probably use some of that writer's words. How many and what kind of words can you use without plagiarizing? A third uncertainty is the nature of facts. Some facts, even when they appear in a source, do not need documentation. But which ones? Because of uncertainties like these, most students who "plagiarize" do so unconsciously. The following are principles and guidelines that anyone using sources in essays about literature should obey. They should help you to use sources usefully, clearly, and ethically.

When Should You Give Credit?

1. Give credit for primary sources. Whenever you make a specific reference to an incident or words in a work and whenever you quote from a work, you need to give credit to the source from which you obtained the information. This is as true for primary as for secondary sources. You must do this for several reasons. Works of literature, especially famous ones, often go through many editions and even different publishing houses. Readers need to know which edition you are using so they can refer to the parts of the work you discuss. You document your primary source, then, for their convenience. But another reason is that the edition you use may affect the validity of your argument. If the edition is unscholarly and contains misprints or omissions, then your interpretations will be suspect. A well-known example is Emily Dickinson's poetry. After the poet's death in 1886, Thomas Wentworth Higginson and Mabel Loomis Todd edited her poetry for publication. They published it (or some of it) in four volumes throughout the 1890s. But instead of printing it as Dickinson had written it, they "regularized" it for the tastes of nineteenth-century readers. They changed the meter to make it more conventional, changed words to make them rhyme, normalized punctuation, and altered metaphors that seemed illogical. Not until Thomas H. Johnson published his edition of her poems in 1955 did we have versions of Emily Dickinson's poetry as she wrote it. If you write an essay about Emily Dickinson's poetry, your readers will want to know that you used Johnson's edition (or reprints therefrom). By giving full information about the editions you use, you enhance the reliability of your essay.

Often the nature of a college course allows you to omit complete citations for primary sources. You may be writing about a work that appears in one of your course textbooks. If so, the number of the page on which each quotation or specific reference occurs is usually all the documentation you need. Give the quotation or reference and then follow it with the page number or numbers in parentheses, placing your final mark of punctuation after the closing parenthesis.

> EXAMPLE (a quote): Lawrence says that when she is with her children she feels "the center of her heart go hard" (125).

EXAMPLE (a specific reference but not a quote): When she returns home from the party, she finds Paul riding the rocking horse. Lawrence contrasts her elegant, even icy dress with Paul's frenzied and exhausted state (134–35).

More formal usage, however, requires that you give a complete citation for the edition you are using. This practice is always necessary when you use a book that is not a basic text in your course.

2. Give credit for facts that are not common knowledge. "Common knowledge" facts are those the average well-read person would be likely to know. You assume that such persons have some familiarity with your subject, even though they may not. Common knowledge facts include very basic facts about history (say, that Woodrow Wilson was president of the United States during World War I, that the United States entered the war several years after it began), birth and death dates, occupations, publication dates, basic biographical facts about famous people (that Ernest Hemingway began his writing career as a newspaper reporter, that he entered World War I as an ambulance driver, that in 1929 he published a famous novel, *A Farewell to Arms*, based on his wartime experiences, that just before the outbreak of World War II he published a novel, *For Whom the Bell Tolls*, about the Spanish Civil War). Facts that are not common knowledge have to come from sources (what Hemingway's parents thought of his newspaper career, where he saw action during the war, how he was wounded, the identity of the nurse he fell in love with while recuperating, his attitude toward his home town when he returned from the war, what he actually said to people about the war), and those sources must be cited. Also, facts that are in any way controversial need to be documented. If you claim that Theodore Roosevelt was a secret Marxist, or had an affair with Emma Goldman, or conspired to assassinate President McKinley, you must give sources (assuming there are any!) for these assertions; otherwise your reader will write you off as a crank.

3. Give credit for all direct quotes. This kind of documentation is crucial, whether you quote from primary or secondary sources.

4. Give credit for summaries or paraphrases of someone else's ideas. Even when you don't quote directly from the work, you must provide documentation for the sources of your summaries or paraphrases of someone else's ideas. This includes ideas that are held by other writers, by your instructor, or even by other students. It also

includes ideas that you arrive at on your own and then find expressed in print.

5. Give credit for ideas not "assimilated" by you. Once you have absorbed someone's ideas, thought about them over a period of time, added thoughts of your own or of others, you can assume that these ideas are now "yours." If, however, your memory is so good that these ideas remain in your mind exactly as they were when you read and heard them, then you must give credit to the original author.

A final word about when to give credit: the dividing line between facts that are common knowledge and those that are not is sometimes frustratingly vague. So too is the line between ideas that are assimilated by you and those that are not. When in doubt about where that line is, give credit. Doing so takes a little extra trouble, a little extra time; but the trouble and time are worth it to protect yourself against charges of plagiarism or simply to provide the curious reader with enough information to check your facts and ideas.

CORRECT DOCUMENTARY FORM

Documentary form varies from discipline to discipline. For people writing about literature, the authoritative guide to documentary form has been the *MLA Handbook for Writers of Research Papers, Theses, and Dissertations*. (*MLA* stands for Modern Language Association, the preeminent scholarly organization devoted to the study of modern languages and literature.) In 1984 the MLA created a new documentary format, one that resembles the formats of the social and natural sciences. The MLA has published a revised edition of its handbook:

> *The MLA Handbook for Writers of Research Papers.* Joseph Gibaldi and Walter S. Achtert. 3rd ed. New York: MLA, 1989.

The guidelines in this chapter are from the current MLA documentary format.

Where Should You Give Credit?

1. Give credit by introducing your source in your text. When you use the ideas and specialized or controversial facts of another person,

introduce them *in your own text*, not just in parenthetical references. To do this, use introductory phrases like the following:

As Lionel Trilling says, "The ground for complaint . . ."

One critic has called attention to "the absurdity of Huck's shore experience."

Robert E. Spiller suggests . . .

Tuchman's second point is . . .

Leo Marx's theory about technology in America is . . .

All of these introduce paraphrases, summaries, and short quotations. The following example introduces an indented or blocked quotation (that is, a long quotation set back ten spaces from the established margin).

EXAMPLE: Friedman's definition of plot focuses on the changes the protagonist undergoes:

> The end of plot, then, is to represent some completed process of change in the protagonist . . .

Acknowledgments for facts are necessary, too,when the facts are very specialized or controversial. For example, details about F. Scott Fitzgerald's love life in Hollywood during his last years can come from only a few people. You must mention such people *in your text* when you use them:

Sheilah Graham claims that . . .

Budd Schulberg saw that Fitzgerald was . . .

Nathanael West said that at the party Fitzgerald concentrated his attention on . . .

Note, however, that facts available from many sources do not need textual acknowledgment. Details about English history, for example, are available in many textbooks and are not associated with any one person or group. You do, however, need to provide parenthetical references for such information.

2. Give credit in a list of "Works Cited" at the end of your essay. In this list, include only those works that you actually use in your essay.
3. Give credit in the text of your essay by making parenthetical references to the works contained on your "Works Cited" list. (These references take the place of most numbered footnotes or endnotes in the old MLA style.)

Guidelines and form for parenthetical references

1. Make a parenthetical reference

   a. whenever you refer directly to a particular part of a source,
   b. Whenever you use facts that are not common knowledge,
   c. whenever you use direct quotations,
   d. Whenever you summarize or paraphrase someone else's ideas.

2. Give enough information for the reader to do two things: identify the work on the "Works Cited" list and find exactly where your reference is in the work itself.
3. To do this, usually it is enough to give the author's last name and the page number or numbers of the reference:

   (Mast 116–17)

   The author's name points you to the work in the "Works Cited" list, and the page number points you to the reference in the work itself.
4. Give more information when necessary to eliminate ambiguity. If you use several works by the same author, give the author's last name, a portion of the title, and the page number.

   (Mast, *A Short History* 116–17)

   If you have several authors with the same last name, give initials or the whole name to distinguish among them:

   (H. Jones 58–60)

5. You can leave out the author's last name if you use it in your text. All you need to include in parentheses is the page number or numbers.

EXAMPLE: Gerald Mast says that D. W. Griffith's *The Birth of a Nation* is racist in its social attitudes but brilliant in its cinematic technique (80–81).

This usage is especially helpful when you cite primary sources.

EXAMPLE: In Shirley Jackson's "The Lottery" the people are at first reluctant to participate in the lottery. The men standing around waiting are subdued: "Their jokes were quiet and they smiled rather than laughed" (219). The children, when called, come "reluctantly, having to be called four or five times" (220). Once the black box is brought out, the villagers keep "their distance" from it (221).

If, however, you use more than one work by the same author, be sure the reader knows which work you are discussing. Make this clear by introducing the references properly or by giving adequate information in the parenthetical references.

EXAMPLE: Lawrence describes the two mothers differently. Elizabeth Bates is "a tall woman of imperious mien, handsome, with definite black eyebrows" ("Odour of Chrysanthemums" 248), whereas Paul's mother is simply "a woman who was beautiful" ("The Rocking-Horse Winner" 271).

Or,

EXAMPLE: Lawrence describes the two mothers differently. Elizabeth Bates in "Odour of Chrysanthemums" is "a tall woman of imperious mien, handsome, with definite black eyebrows" (248), whereas Paul's mother in "The Rocking-Horse Winner" is simply "a woman who was beautiful" (271).

6. You may leave out the author's name and the page numbers if you refer in your text to the whole work.

EXAMPLE: E. M. W. Tillyard devotes a short book to explaining how the Elizabethans saw the structure of the cosmos.

If readers are interested in Tillyard's book, they can find it in the "Works Cited" list.

7. When referring to primary sources, use page numbers for prose works; line numbers and division numbers for long poems (more than about twenty lines); and act, scene, and line numbers for verse drama.

> EXAMPLE: In *Hamlet* the queen bids farewell to Ophelia by saying, "I hoped thou shouldst have been my Hamlet's wife" (V.i.211).

Here the reference is to act five, scene one, line 211. If your instructor prefers, you may use arabic numbers instead of roman numerals to cite acts and scenes.

> EXAMPLE: In *Hamlet* the queen bids farewell to Ophelia by saying, "I hoped thou shouldst have been my Hamlet's wife" (5.1.211).

The following is an example of a quotation from a long poem:

> EXAMPLE: In commenting on our growing distance from heaven, Wordsworth says in "Intimations of Immortality,"
>
>> Heaven lies about us in our infancy!
>> Shades of the prison-house begin to close
>> Upon the growing Boy. (66–68)

For references to the Bible, use arabic numbers separated by periods to indicate chapters and verses:

(Isaiah 29.3–15).

8. Use hyphens between line or page numbers to indicate a continuous sequence, or the pages within which your material is included, such as a section of the work (231–33). Use commas between line or page numbers to indicate interruptions in sequence (200, 219). Use colons to separate volume and page numbers (*Clarissa* 3: 451). (Leave a space between the colon and the page number.)
9. If your reference is to a work with more than one volume, indicate in your parenthetical reference which volume you are referring to.

> EXAMPLE: Even on the point of death, Clarissa writes to her father asking his forgiveness. She begs him "on her knees" to forgive her for

"all her faults and follies," especially "that fatal error which threw her out of [his] protection" (4: 359).

Here the reference is to the fourth volume, page 359. If you use only one volume from a multivolume work, do not give the volume number in the parenthetical reference; include it instead in the "Works Cited" listing.

10. If the author of a work is anonymous, give the whole title or the first few words of the title, plus the page number (Anonymous works are alphabetized by title in the "Works Cited" list.)

> EXAMPLE: Unlike the pilgrims, the Puritans remained members of the Anglican church. But like the Pilgrims, they adhered to a Calvinistic theology ("Early American Literature" 2).

11. You may refer to more than one work in a single parenthetical reference by separating the works with semicolons.

> EXAMPLE: At least two critics have seen the similarity between Voltaire's character Candide and the young Benjamin Franklin in the *Autobiography* (Orkney 13; Scott 151–52).

If, however, you want to refer to more than two or three works, use a footnote or endnotes instead of a parenthetical reference. (See the discussion of footnotes and endnotes coming up.)

12. When referring to a work with two or three authors, give all their names in the text or in the reference.

> EXAMPLE: One work makes the useful distinction between "representational" and "illustrative" narrative (Scholes and Kellogg 84).

Or,

> EXAMPLE: Scholes and Kellogg make the useful distinction between "representational" and "illustrative" narrative (84).

13. When referring to a work with more than two authors, you may give all their names or, more simply, give the first name and "et al." (abbreviation for Latin *et alii*, "and others").

EXAMPLE: The trickster has been a traditional folk hero not just of American "Yankee" narrative but of American Indian and Afro-American narrative as well (Spiller et al. 729).

14. If you find an author or someone else quoted in a book or article but cannot find the original source for the quotation, rather than abandon the quotation, cite the place where you found it. To do so, use "qtd in" ("quoted in").

EXAMPLE: When Dreiser was a magazine editor, he would write on rejection slips, "We like realism, but it must be tinged with sufficient idealism to make it all a truly uplifting character" (qtd in Fiedler 46).

15. Follow these guidelines for placing parenthetical references. Place the reference immediately after the material that needs referencing. Usually this is at the end of a sentence or paragraph, but sometimes it can be within a sentence as well. Put the reference before the closing punctuation of the phrase or sentence (comma, period, semicolon, colon, exclamation point):

EXAMPLE: James Joyce, as Arnold Kettle notes, was consistent about employing his artistic principles (301), but that does not mean his works are all the same.

The exception to this puncutation rule occurs when a quotation is indented. Then the reference goes outside the closing punctuation.

EXAMPLE: At a crucial point in the story, Hawthorne admonishes Wakefield for cutting himself off from the warmth of human affection and companionship:

> Go quietly to thy bed, foolish man; and, on the morrow, if thou wilt be wise, get thee home to good Mrs. Wakefield, and tell her the truth. Remove not thyself, even for a little week, from thy place in her chaste bosom. Were she, for a single moment, to deem thee dead, or lost, or lastingly divided from her, thou wouldst be woefully conscious of a change in thy true wife, forever after. It is perilous to make a chasm in human affections; not that they gape so long and wide—but so quickly close again! (932)

Guidelines for Using Footnotes and Endnotes

1. Use footnotes or endnotes for citing several sources (more than two or three) all at once.

   TEXT: A host of critics agree that Swift does not share Gulliver's extreme condemnation of human beings and approval of Houyhnhnms at the end of *Gulliver's Travels*.[1]

   NOTE: [1]Abrams 23–28; Converse 55–70; Portnoy 150–65; Clore and Barchester 300–05; Kellerman 83; Soles 15–20.

2. Use footnotes or endnotes for further comments or information relating to something in your text. These comments or facts are not necessary to your line of thought but possibly they are interesting to your readers nonetheless.

   TEXT: Irving adopts the stance of the ironic narrator in his comic masterpiece "The Legend of Sleepy Hollow."[2]

   NOTE: [2]The ironic narrator was a common fictional device in eighteenth-century English fiction and was most notably present in one of Irving's favorite authors, Henry Fielding.

3. In a footnote or endnote, a number immediately follows the reference in the text and is raised slightly above the line. A corresponding number appears, indented five spaces, immediately before the note; it is also raised slightly above the line. The rest of the note goes all the way to the margins. Number all notes sequentially throughout the paper, not for each page. If the note appears at the bottom of the page (footnote), separate it from your text by three lines (that is, begin the note on the fourth line below the last line of text) and single-space the note. Double-space between notes. If the notes appear at the end of your paper (endnotes), put them on a separate sheet of paper between your text and the "Works Cited" list. Double-space each endnote and triple-space between notes.

Guidelines and Form for the "Works Cited" List: General Rules

1. Arrange entries alphabetically by author. If the author is anonymous, list the entry by its title.
2. Do not number entries.
3. In each entry, put the author's last name first. (The author's name is printed last name first because the list is in alphabetical order.) If there is more than one author in an entry, put the last name first for the first author but not the others, and keep the authors in the order in which they were listed on the work's title page.
4. Put the first line flush with the left margin. Indent the rest of the entry five spaces from the left hand margin.
5. Include without exception every source—primary or secondary—cited in your paper.
6. When you include more than one work by an author, substitute three hyphens for the author's name after the first citation:

> Jewett, Sarah Orne. *A Country Doctor.* New York: Garrett, 1970.
> —. *A White Heron and Other Stories.* Boston: Houghton, 1886.

7. Divide your entries into three main sections:

   a. author's name,
   b. the name of the article or book,
   c. information about publication.

   Sometimes more sections are necessary—for information about editors, about volume numbers, or about reprinted editions. But these three divisions are essential for all entries.
8. Put the "Works Cited" list at the end of your paper, on sheets separate from your text. Double-space each entry and triple-space between entries.

Sample Entries for Books

1. Book with one author.

> Hoffman, Daniel. *Poe Poe Poe Poe Poe Poe Poe.* Garden City: Doubleday, 1972.

2. A book with two authors.

> Berry, Lester V., and Melvin Van den Bark. *The American Thesaurus of Slang: With Supplement.* New York: Crowell, 1947.

3. A translation.

> Cervantes, Saavedra, Miguel de. *The Adventures of Don Quixote.* Trans. J. M. Cohen. Baltimore: Penguin, 1950.

4. A book that has three authors or more, has gone through several editions, and is one of several volumes in a set.

> Spiller, Robert E., et al. *Literary History of the United States.* 4th ed. rev. 2 vols. New York: Macmillan, 1974. Vol. 1.

5. A work in more than one volume.

> Richardson, Samuel. *Clarissa; or, the History of a Young Lady.* 4 vols. London: Everyman, 1932.

6. An introduction to a primary source.

> Charvat, William. Introduction. *The Last of the Mohicans.* By James Fenimore Cooper. Boston: Riverside, 1958.

7. An edition of an author's work.

> Trollope, Anthony. *The Last Chronicle of Barset.* Ed. Arthur Mizener. Boston: Riverside, 1964.

8. An anonymous introduction in an anthology of literature.

> "The Middle Ages (to 1485)." *Norton Anthology of English Literature* Ed. M. H. Abrams et al. Rev. 2 vols. New York: Norton, 1968. 1: 1–25.

Here the reference is to the first volume, pages 1—25. Separate volume numbers from page numbers with a colon. (Use arabic numerals for both.) Note that when you cite sections of books, you usually give numbers for the whole section. An exception is the introduction to an entire book, as in example six above. The abbreviation "ed." after the titles in 7 and 8 above means "edited by," so you do not add an "s" to the abbreviation if the book is edited by more than one person.

9. A work from an anthology.

> Chekhov, Anton. "The Lady with the Dog." *Norton Introduction to Literature.* Ed. Carl E. Bain et al. 3rd ed. New York: Norton, 1981. 55–70.

10. A book with an editor.

> Stevick, Philip, ed. *The Theory of the Novel.* New York: The Free Press, 1967.

Sample Entry for Articles in Scholarly Journals

> Hoffman, Daniel G. "Irving's Use of American Folklore in 'The Legend of Sleepy Hollow.'" *PMLA* 68 (1958): 425–35.

In this entry, *PMLA* is the journal (the initials stand for "Publications of the Modern Language Association," but the title of the journal is *PMLA*), 68 is the volume number, 1958 is the year of publication, and 425–35 are the page numbers. Note that you give page numbers not just for the pages you cite but for the entire article.

Sample Entries for Articles in Popular Publications

1. A weekly magazine.

> Troy, Judy. "In One Place." *New Yorker* 10 Sept. 1984: 42–43.

2. A monthly magazine.

> Malone, Michael. "Books in Brief." *Harper's* June 1977: 82–84.

3. A book review in a weekly magazine.

> Blake, Patricia. "Gingerly Removing the Veil." Rev. of *Josephine Herbst*, by Elinor Langer. *Newsweek* 3 Sept. 1984: 80.

4. An article in a newspaper.

> Coneroy, Herman. "*David Copperfield* Revisited." *New York Times* 19 Aug. 1962, F23.

SAMPLE RESEARCH PAPER

The following sample student research paper illustrates the use of the new MLA documentary style as well as the principles of the argumentative research essay. As in this paper, the first page of your paper should have your name and course information in the upper left corner, the title centered just below this information, and the text just below the title. *The MLA Handbook* says that you do not need a title page, but you might ask your instructor for his or her preference. Usually, you do not need a title page. If you have endnotes, put them right after your text, beginning on a new page. Put your "Works Cited" list after the endnotes, beginning on a new page. For more detailed instructions on the format of your paper, see chapter 11.

```
Joanna Briscoe
Professor Teleman
English 252-04
February 24, 1989
```

```
                 The Forsaken Sister:
  Roderick's Failure to Rescue Madeline in Edgar Allan
          Poe's "The Fall of the House of Usher"
```

```
     Perhaps the most obviously strange aspect of Edgar
Allan Poe's "The Fall of the House of Usher" is the
setting. The bleak landscape, dim tarn, crumbling
```

mansion, and miasmic atmosphere are nightmarish and
inexplicable. They defy norms. But equally strange is
Roderick's behavior toward his sister, Madeline. He
claims to love her, and he grieves when she "dies."
But when he hears her trying to escape from her tomb,
he merely listens and waits. Why doesn't he rescue
her?

 The critical interpretations of the story are
often as bizarre as the story. They range from incest,
to vampirism, to madness.[1] But the interpretation that
most meaningfully accounts for Roderick's treatment of
his sister is the symbolic. This view holds that the
story is symbolic of one person's deeply troubled
mind. Richard Wilbur, for example, contends that the
"typical Poe story occurs <u>within</u> the mind of a poet;
and its characters are not independent personalities,
but allegorical figures representing the warring
principles of the poet's divided nature" (274–75).
"The Fall of the House of Usher," he says, is a
"journey into the depths of the self . . . a dream of
the narrator's, in which he leaves behind him the
waking, physical world and journeys inward toward his
<u>moi intérieur</u>, toward his inner and spiritual self.
That inner and spiritual self is Roderick Usher"
(265). Roderick and Madeline, then, are symbolic of
states of mind. Daniel Hoffman agrees with Wilbur and
sees the story as "a terrifying tale of the
protagonist's journey into the darkest, most hidden
regions of himself" (302). Hoffman argues that the
story is the narrator's dream (307).

 Edward H. Davidson offers a lucid explanation of
what this dream may represent. Like Wilbur and
Hoffman, Davidson sees the tale as an allegory of one
person's mental disintegration. And like them he sees
the disintegration as caused by two warring sides of
the same mind. Roderick, he says, "represents the mind
or intellectual aspect" of the person. Madeline
represents "the sensual or physical side" of this
same person (197). Roderick "suffers from the
diseased mind which has too long abstracted itself
from physical reality; in fact, the physical world,

and even the physical side of himself, fills him with
such repugnance that he can maintain his unique world
or self of the mind only by destroying his twin sister
or physical side of himself" (197). He tries to bury
her "in a place as far remote as possible from the
place of aesthetic delight wherein the mind of
Roderick lives" (197). But he cannot kill her, and
she returns to kill both mind and body (198). The
collapse of the house represents the collapse of "the
total being of this complex body-mind relation which
Poe had studied in the symbolic guise of a brother and
sister relationship" (198).

Davidson does not discuss the story specifically,
but a careful examination of it supports his theory.
Not only does the story have, as Hoffman says, "the
fixated, tableau-like rigidity, the inexorability, of
a dream" (307), but Poe hints that the story might
be a dream. The narrator looks upon the house for the
first time as if he were experiencing "the after-
dream of the reveller upon opium" (Poe 397). As he
examines the atmosphere enveloping the house, he tries
to shake off from his sprit "what must have been a
dream" (400). For several days after he first sees
Madeline, the narrator listens to Roderick's "wild
improvisations" on the guitar "as if in a dream"
(404). And the climax of the story occurs in the
middle of the night during a tempestuous storm, when
the narrator cannot sleep and when his "fancy"
becomes increasingly "excited" (414).

As a "dream," the story projects psychological
phenomena; the characters, setting, and events
represent aspects of the mind. One key detail that
supports this interpretation is "The Haunted Palace,"
the poem that Roderick sings to the narrator during a
moment of "the highest artificial excitement" and
that represents "the tottering of his [Roderick's]
lofty reason upon her throne" (406). "The Haunted
Palace," as Wilbur points out, is the allegory of a
man who goes mad. It represents two states of mind
(263). In the first half of the poem, the palace is
described as a "head" inhabited by the "monarch,"

"Thought." It is topped by "banners yellow, glorious, golden" (hair). It has "two luminous windows" (eyes). Out of its "fair palace door" (mouth) come sounds (speech) that represent the "beauty," "wit," and "wisdom" (artistic productions, sane and noble ideas) of the "king." But all changes in the second half, when "evil things" assail the "monarch's high estate." The windows become "red." Inside, "vast forms" move "fantastically / To discordant melody," and out of the "pale door" rushes "a hideous throng" that "laugh--but smile no more" (406-07).

A comparison of this allegorical house with the narrator's description of the Usher mansion, Wilbur says, leads to the realization that the Usher mansion "is, in allegorical fact, the physical body of Roderick Usher, and its dim interior is, in fact, Roderick Usher's visionary mind" (264). Details from the story support this claim. When the narrator sees the mansion for the first time, he describes it as having "vacant eye-like windows" (397-98), which make the mansion look like a head. He also thinks that "a mere different arrangement of the particulars of the scene, of the details of the picture, would be sufficient to modify, or perhaps to annihilate its capacity for sorrowful impression" (398), as if the house has the flexible quality of the mind, the capacity for rearrangement and thus for sounder mental health. The narrator then says the house is indeed symbolical; local peasants see it as an equivalent to the family. And the interior of the house, with its "many dark and intricate passages," its "feeble gleams of encrimsoned light," its rooms containing dark angles and recesses (400-01), resembles the complexity and mysteriousness of the mind.

The most important psychological phenomenon represented by the story is a mind at war with itself. Madeline is Roderick's twin, his mirror image: "her figure, her air, her features--all, in their very minutest development were those--were identically . . . those of the Roderick Usher who sat beside me" (404). As such, she seems to represent one aspect of

the mind contained within the house, an aspect that
Roderick wants to suppress and destroy. But what does
she represent?

An analysis of Roderick supports Davidson's claim
that within the symbolic "house" two forces are at
war. The character "Roderick" represents a desire
to retreat from reality, whereas the character
"Madeline" represents those qualities that make up
reality—the physical, the sensuous, the bodily.
Roderick's disease, for example, manifests itself as
an extreme aversion to sensuous experiences—tasting,
touching, smelling, seeing, hearing; that is, to all
the ways the mind (through the body) receives and
reacts to the physical world (403). It is as if the
intellect is retreating from the body. Roderick seems,
furthermore, to have a morbid fear of the physical,
especially as it is embodied by the house. He
confesses to a conflict between his "spirit" and "the
physique of the gray walls and turrets, and of the dim
tarn into which they all looked down" (408). His
artistic products are further evidence of his escape
from the physical world, from reality. Rather than
paint real scenes, Roderick paints ideas, "pure
abstractions," and "phantasmagoric conceptions"
(405). Rather than sing about real people and
situations, he composes songs that are "fantastic,"
"fervid," "wild fantasies," and "artificial" (406).

Roderick's apparently innate preference for the
ideal over the real has led him to a practice that is
the probable cause of his disease. He has increasingly
isolated himself from the world outside his mind.
The narrator traces the beginning of this process to
Roderick's childhood, when his "reserve had been
always excessive and habitual." Now the process is
complete, for the narrator is his "best and indeed
his only personal friend" (398). But the disease
represents a further extension of Roderick's isolation
from the exterior world. Roderick has reached the
point where he wants to isolate himself from
everything physical, and that means especially from
his body. The result is that Roderick's body, although

still whole, is near the point of disintegration, a
fact symbolized by the "barely perceptible fissure"
that goes from top to bottom of the mansion (400).

A logical extension of Roderick's tendency toward
isolation is his obsession with death, the ultimate
alienation from reality. When he plays his guitar and
sings, he improvises dirges, most memorable of which
is "a certain singular perversion and amplification
of the wild air of the last waltz of Von Weber"
(405), a piece of music that Von Weber was reputed to
have composed on his deathbed (405n9). When among his
books, Roderick's "chief delight" is perusing a "rare
and curious" book detailing the last rites for the
dead (409). His most memorable painting seems to
represent total and final isolation. It is of a "vault
or tunnel" at "an exceeding depth" with "no outlet"
and no natural sources of light (405–06).

Roderick's treatment of Madeline, the nature of
her disease, and her subsequent behavior seem to
indicate that she represents the physical, bodily
world from which he is trying to escape. Her disease
links her directly to the bodily, for it consists of
"a gradual wasting away of the person" (404). And
after her first appearance, Roderick's own bodily
strength diminishes: "a far more than ordinary wanness
had overspread the emaciated fingers through which
trickled many passionate tears" (404). After he
announces her "death," Roderick buries her in a vault
that corresponds not only to the vault in his painting
but to the oppressive atmosphere surrounding the Usher
mansion. It is "small, damp, and entirely without
means of admission for light." It lies at a "great
depth." It seems impregnable and inescapable because
of its "massive iron" door and archway "sheathed with
copper." Its oxygenless "oppressive atmosphere" half
smothers the torches so that the light is lurid and
dim (409).

All of these details suggest Roderick's obsessive,
final attempt to isolate his bodily self, to separate
it from his intellectual self. He even carries the
entombment process further by putting Madeline in a
casket, screwing down the lid, and locking the iron

door. But one detail suggests that he will fail.
Even though Madeline seems "dead," she retains a
surprising physical vitality. She displays "the
mockery of a faint blush upon the bosom and the face,
and [a] suspiciously lingering smile upon the lip"
(410). When she finally emerges from her tomb, her
incredible physical strength is but a final detail
linking her to the physical and the bodily. Her
resurrection seems to show that repressing the
physical side of the self results inevitably in its
overwhelming and powerful reassertion at a later time.

Throughout the story, Roderick is pitiable. He
seems to recognize that he is in deep trouble. As a
last attempt to help himself, he reaches out to his
only remaining contact with the outside world, the
narrator. He also seems to recognize the importance
of physical health and the tie of normal sensuous
experience to mental health. He loves Madeline, and in
the first half of "The Haunted Palace," he describes
a healthy balance between the sensuous and the
intellectual. But by the time we see him, he has
carried the process of isolation too far to stop it.
Against his better judgment, he acts out allegorically
the final severing of mind and body. He buries
Madeline, believing that she—the body—is finally
dead. When he realizes that she is still alive, he
refuses to rescue her because he wants her dead. His
mistake from the beginning was to think that the
mind can operate independently from the body, the
intellectual from the physical, the ideal from the
real. In the end, he pays for his mistake with his
sanity and his life.

Notes

[1]Lawrence (84–85) and Spitzer (58) argue for the
incest theory. A supporter of the vampire theory is
Kendall (99–104). Hill (396–402) and Walker (585–92)
claim that Madeline really dies and that both the
narrator and Roderick go mad and hallucinate her
resurrection.

Works Cited

Davidson, Edward H. Poe: A Critical Study. Cambridge:
    Harvard UP, 1957.
Hill, John S. "The Dual Hallucination in 'The Fall of
    the House of Usher.'" Southwest Review 48 (1963):
    396–402.
Hoffman, Daniel. Poe Poe Poe Poe Poe Poe. Garden City:
    Doubleday, 1972.
Kendall, Lyle H. "The Vampire Motif in 'The Fall of
    the House of Usher.'" Twentieth-Century
    Interpretations of "The Fall of the House of
    Usher." Ed. Thomas Woodson. Englewood Cliffs:
    Prentice, 1969. 99–104.
Lawrence, D. H. Studies in Classic American
    Literature. New York: Penguin, 1977.
Poe, Edgar Allan. "The Fall of the House of Usher."
    Collected Works of Edgar Allan Poe. Ed. Thomas
    Ollive Mabbott. Cambridge: Harvard UP, 1978. 2:
    392–422.
Spitzer, Leo. "A Reinterpretation of 'The Fall of the
    House of Usher.'" Twentieth-Century
    Interpretations of "The Fall of the House of
    Usher." Ed. Thomas Woodson. Englewood Cliffs:
    Prentice, 1969. 56–70.
Walker, I. M. "The 'Legitimate Sources' of Terror in
    'The Fall of the House of Usher.'" Modern
    Language Review 61 (1966): 585–92.
Wilbur, Richard. "The House of Poe." The Recognition
    of Edgar Allan Poe: Selected Criticism since 1829.
    Ed. Eric W. Carlson. Ann Arbor: U of Michigan P,
    1966. 255–77.

Analysis of the Sample Research Paper

Notice the way this paper begins. The writer raises a question about the story. She states that question in the first paragraph, or introduction. In the rest of the essay, the writer argues in favor of a certain answer to the question. The paper, in short, is an argumentative essay. It has a narrowly focused topic, a thesis, and a structure like other essays about literature. Its purpose is to enlighten and convince the reader. It is a "research paper" because it uses research as a tool to solve a problem, but it is nonetheless an argumentative essay.

In the second paragraph, the writer introduces the research part of the essay. After explaining that she surveyed literary criticism of the story, the writer passes quickly over interpretations that are not helpful to the thesis and lights upon one that is: the symbolic interpretation. The writer then accurately and fully explains that approach in the second and third paragraphs. These paragraphs contain the bulk of the references to research material. But the critical theory does not in itself answer the writer's question. It merely shows how the question might be answered. The writer proceeds to answer the question in the rest of the essay by analyzing the story in detail, using the critical theory as a guide. The transition sentence of the fourth paragraph ("Davidson does not discuss the story specifically, but a careful explanation of it supports his theory") signals the beginning of this part of the essay. In the last paragraph of the essay, the writer answers the question and, in so doing, states her thesis.

Not all research essays will be structured like this one, but this essay has a simple and functional organization that you might find useful when structuring your own research essays. First, it states the problem (question) in an introductory paragraph. Second, it surveys the pertinent literary criticism and fully explains what the writer believes is the most relevant approach. Third, it examines the work in light of this approach. This third part of the essay is the longest and most important. It represents the writer's use of the critical approach to solve the problem. In this section you might continue to draw upon secondary sources, as this essay does. But otherwise, you are on your own. Fourth, in a concluding paragraph, the writer states a solution to the problem, an answer to the question. This answer is the essay's thesis.

FREQUENTLY USED ABBREVIATIONS

When you read essays and books about literature, you will often run into abbreviations. When you write your own essays, you may want to resort to some of the more well known and space-saving of these abbreviations. Here, then, is a list of them. Many pertain to essays that use secondary sources.

adapt.	adapted by
app.	appendix
c., ca.	*circa*, "about" (Usually used with dates when the exact date is not certain—for example, ca. 1594)

cf.	*confer,* "compare" (not the equivalent of "see")
ch., chs.	chapter, chapters
d.	died
ed., eds.	edited by, editor, editors
esp.	especially
e.g.	*exempli gratia,* "for example"
et al.	*et alii,* "and others"
etc.	*et cetera,* "and so forth"
i.e.	*id est,* "that is"
l., ll.	line, lines,
ms., mss.	manuscript, manuscripts
NB	*nota bene,* "note well"
p., pp.	page, pages
pt.	part
rev.	revised by, revision; review or reviewed by (for reviews, use *review* where *rev.* might be confused with *revision* or *revised by*)
U, UP	university, university press (in documentation)
vol., vols.	volume, volumes

11

How to Revise and Edit Your Essay: Style, Mechanics, and Format

REVISE THROUGHOUT THE WRITING PROCESS

THE THIRD STAGE of the writing process is revision. The term *revision* means "to see again." Revision takes place throughout the writing process, not just near the end. You constantly see your work anew, and you act upon that fresh understanding by rewriting.

For this reason, you not only produce better essays but you feel more comfortable if you create the conditions that allow you to revise as you go. Assume that you will make several drafts of the essay, from scribbled lists to finished product—say, three to five drafts. Give yourself time—several weeks—to write the essay. You may be able to pull off a one-night-stand every now and then, but few people can do so consistently. Work concentratedly for awhile, then put your work away; let the ideas gestate, then come back to the essay fresh. Use plenty of paper.

REVISE FOR THE FINAL DRAFT

Some people could go on revising forever, but you cannot do that. When you are ready to turn the essay in, you need to produce a final draft. The final draft is different from the earlier drafts, because other people will see it. To help yourself prepare the final draft, think about

what these other people will want from it. They will, of course, want
the qualities of a good argument we have discussed so far—an interesting topic, sound logic, thorough discussion of the works, good organization. These qualities are valuable to your readers because they want
to learn from you. But they want something else as well. They want to
think well of you. They want to feel that your writing is worth reading,
that you are competent to talk about your topic, that you can teach
them something. Rhetoricians call this personal quality *ethos*. Ethos is
the image the writer projects of herself or himself. Ethos is unavoidable;
you can't help projecting an image of yourself. Create an ethos, therefore, that is as persuasive as possible.

The content and organization of the essay are the most important
ingredients of ethos. By reasoning well and especially by presenting
plenty of facts to support your reasoning, you make readers feel that
you are conscientious and intellectually sound. But other aspects of the
final draft also help create a persuasive ethos. They are prose style, rules
of usage, and format (the appearance of the essay).

WRITE A CLEAR AND READABLE PROSE STYLE

Style is the way writers put words together in units of thought—
sentences—and blend sentences together to make larger units—
paragraphs, essays, books. Closely related to style is tone. *Tone* is a
writer's attitude toward the material and the readers. You convey tone
through style.

You should adjust your style and tone to fit occasion and audience. Sometimes the occasion and audience call for informal and hu-
morous writing, like speeches made at parties or essays written for
satirical magazines. At other times, they call for gravity and formality,
like newspaper editorials and letters of application. The occasion and
audience for essays about literature almost always require a measure of
formality. Your audience is intelligent, literate, and serious. They are
taking the trouble to read your essay because they want to learn. They
wouldn't mind some levity, some lightheartedness, but mostly they
want you to get down to business and not waste their time. They want
to learn from you economically; they want to get through your essay
with as little trouble as possible.

Your style for this audience, then, should meet these needs. Make
your style clear, interesting, and readable: vary sentence structure, avoid
the passive voice, emphasize active and concrete verbs, eliminate wordi-

ness and unnecessary repetition, use words with precision, base syntax on the natural rhythms of spoken English. Give your tone seriousness of purpose but avoid stiff formality: stay away from incomprehensible words and long, complex sentences. Since essays about literature involve personal judgment, feel free to use "I," especially when you need to distinguish your ideas from those of others and when you want to stress the individuality of your views. But don't overuse "I"; otherwise, you will give the impression of being subjective and egotistical.

Many rhetoric books offer thorough and practical methods for making style clear and readable. Three widely used ones are Strunk and White's *The Elements of Style*, Sheridan Baker's *The Practical Stylist*, and Brooks and Warren's *Modern Rhetoric*.

EDIT THE FINAL DRAFT

The last stage of the writing process is editing the final draft. You complete this stage by bringing the paper into conformity with rules of usage and by putting it into an approved format.

Rules of Usage

Usage here means the way educated speakers and writers in the United States use English on formal and semiformal occasions. Although some rules of usage are arbitrary and seem to serve no purpose other than convention, most serve several important purposes. First, they often aid clarity. Punctuation, for example, represents parts of the sentence—pauses and inflections—that words do not. Marks of punctuation can be as important as the words. Misplace a comma, and you can change the meaning of a sentence. Second, rules of usage help communicate your ethos. Rules of usage are a form of etiquette; educated people are expected to follow them. By doing so, you communicate an image of competence and respect for your readers.

If you are not familiar with the basic rules of usage, they might at first seem bewildering. But they are not hard to learn. Study and practice using them, and you will learn them quickly. Get yourself a handbook of usage, and use it as a reference when you write. A standard handbook of usage is *The Harbrace College Handbook*; another is the *MLA Handbook for Writers of Research Papers*.

Although all rules of usage are important for your writing, in this book we concentrate on ones common to essays about literature. One set of such rules governs documentary procedure (discussed in Chapter 10). Rules for handling documentation vary from discipline to discipline, but their purpose is the same: to help your readers find your sources and to let your readers know that you have a solid knowledge of your subject matter. Another area of usage unavoidable in essays about literature is quotations. And there are a few miscellaneous rules of usage that frequently apply to essays about literature.

Quotations

Quotations are a frequent and essential part of most essays about literature. They serve two key purposes: they help to exemplify claims that the writer of the essay makes, and they represent directly the felicitous or characteristic language of a source.

1. <u>Introduce your quotations.</u>

   a. For primary sources, identify the author, the work, and the context of quotations

   <u>WRONG</u>: The woman tells her lover that the world "isn't ours anymore."

   <u>RIGHT</u>: Near the climax of the lovers' conversation in Hemingway's "Hills Like White Elephants," the woman tells the man that the world "isn't ours anymore."

   The reason for this rule is that quotations take on significance because of what surrounds them. Often, as in the above example, the quotation is meaningless unless the reader knows where it occurs in the story.

   b. Introduce quotations from secondary sources by giving the author's name or claim to authority:

   <u>WRONG</u>: "A fully articulated pastoral idea of America did not emerge until the end of the eighteenth century."

   <u>RIGHT</u>: Leo Marx claims that a "fully articulated pastoral idea of America did not emerge until the end of the eighteenth century."

   <u>RIGHT</u>: A prominent American critic claims that a "fully articulate. . . ."

There are several reasons for this rule. One is that giving the critic's name or claim to authority clearly distinguishes your ideas from the other writer's. Quotation marks help to make this distinction, of course, but introducing the quote by author makes the distinction emphatic. A second reason is that when readers see quotation marks, they are naturally curious about who said the quoted passage. And as they read your essay, they may want to keep track of the different approaches of the critics you are using. A third reason is that by giving the author's name, you distinguish between secondary and primary sources. The distinction may not be clear just from the quotation itself. A final reason is that it is a matter of courtesy to give credit in your text to the words and ideas of other people. It is as if you are standing before an audience making a speech, and for support of your argument you bring forth real people to speak on your behalf. In such a situation, you would always introduce them by name to your audience before they spoke. You are not just giving them credit; in a way, you are thanking them.

  c. Introduce quotations with the correct mark of punctuation. Use a comma for brief, informal, grammatically incomplete introductions.

> WRONG: Prufrock thinks "I am no prophet—and here's no great matter."

> RIGHT: Prufrock thinks, "I am no prophet—and here's no great matter."

Use a colon to separate your own grammatically complete introductions or statements (complete sentences) from quotations.

> WRONG: Edith Hamilton describes Hera perfectly, "She was the protector of marriage, and married women were her peculiar care. There is very little that is attractive in the portrait the poets draw of her."

> RIGHT: Edith Hamilton describes Hera perfectly: "She was the protector. . . ."

The rules of usage here are to a degree arbitrary, and you may find that they vary from handbook to handbook. But their main function is to separate your thoughts from those of the quotation—that is, to eliminate ambiguity. Thus, the first examples above mean two different things. Without the comma, the reader might see the whole sentence as one complete thought: "Prufrock thinks [that] "I am no prophet—and here's no great matter." With the comma, the reader sees that "Prufrock thinks" is merely the introduction to the quotation; the quotation is the complete thought.

2. Intregrate quotations into your own sentences.

> EXAMPLE: Because of this increasing darkness, Brown cannot be quite sure of what he does or hears. The devil's walking stick, for example, seems to turn into a snake, but this may be "an ocular deception, assisted by the uncertain light" (76). He thinks he hears the voices of Deacon Gookin and the minister, but "owing doubtless to the depth of the gloom of that particular spot, neither the travellers nor their steeds were visible" (81).

Once you have properly introduced your source, you may want to integrate short quotations—words or phrases—from it into your own sentences, as in the above example. The quotations, then, become part of your own thoughts rather than thoughts totally separate from yours. This technique is most useful when you want to summarize a source concisely and yet retain something of the language and authenticity of the source. If you use this method, you should obey several rules.

a. Keep all tenses the same. Change the tenses in the quotation to correspond to your tenses, putting your words in brackets. When writing about fictional events, for example, change quoted verbs to the present tense.

> WRONG: While the legislators cringe at the sudden darkness, "all eyes were turned to Abraham Davenport."

> RIGHT: While the legislators cringe at the sudden darkness, "all eyes [turn] to Abraham Davenport."

b. Make sure that sentences are complete.

> WRONG: Yeats asks if "before the indifferent beak." [Incomplete sentence; makes no sense.]

> RIGHT: Yeats asks if Leda "put on [the swan's] knowledge" before his "indifferent beak could let her drop."

c. Clarify pronouns that have no clear antecedents.

WRONG: Captain Wentworth says, "It had been my doing—solely mine. She would not have been obstinate if I had not been weak." [This quotation is wrongly handled if the antecedent of "she" is unclear.]

RIGHT: Captain Wentworth says, "It had been my doing—solely mine. [Louisa] would not have been obstinate if I had not been weak."

d. Make sure that subject and verb agree.

WRONG: Wilfred Owen says that the only prayer said for those who die in battle is war's noise, which "patter out their hasty orisons." [Subject: "noise"; verb: "patter." The subject is singular, the verb plural.]

RIGHT: Wilfred Owen says that the only prayer said for those who die in battle is the "rapid rattle" of guns, which "patter out their hasty orisons." [Subject: "guns"; verb: "patter." Both subject and verb are now plural.]

In short, when you integrate a quotation into your sentence, it becomes a grammatical part of the sentence. You need to make the whole sentence, including the quotation, conform to all the rules of usage that you would normally obey when writing any other sentence. See section 4 below for methods of altering (interpolating) quotations to align them with your sentences.

3. Quote accurately. Copy exactly what the author has written.
4. Make editorial changes in quotations correctly. You may legitimately change the quotation in two ways:

a. By using an *ellipsis*. The ellipsis (spaced periods) indicates material omitted. You may want to do this for brevity's sake. To indicate omitted material *within* a sentence, use three periods, with a space before and after each period.

EXAMPLE: As one critic says, "Oedipus is guilty for two reasons: because of the deeds he actually committed . . . and because of his desire to commit them."

To indicate omitted material at the end of your sentence, put a period with no space in front (the period that signals the end of the sentence) and then three spaced periods (the periods that signal the ellipsis). As in the above example, the spaced periods here indicate that you have left something out of the original sentence.

EXAMPLE: In certain moods, Wordsworth confessed, he "was often unable to think of external things as having external existence. . . ."

If, however, you make a parenthetical reference after the ellipsis at the end of your sentence, put the three spaced periods (the ellipsis) first, then the parenthetical reference, and then the sentence period. Note this revision of the above example:

EXAMPLE: In certain moods, Wordsworth confessed, he "was often unable to think of external things as having external existence . . ." (175).

In addition to using ellipses to indicate the omission of part of a sentence, you can use four periods to indicate the omission of whole sentences, a paragraph, or several paragraphs. The following example omits part of a long paragraph.

EXAMPLE: Ruskin gives two reasons for his belief that to demand perfection of art is to misunderstand it: "The first, that no great man ever stops working till he has reached his point of failure. . . . The second reason is that imperfection is in some sort essential to all that we know of life."

b. By using *brackets*. Brackets indicate editorial changes that *you*, not the author, make to clarify the quotation or to make it fit the grammatical structure of your sentence. Do not use parentheses to indicate such changes; otherwise, your reader will see them as part of the original quote.

WRONG: Alceste says that "sins which cause the blood to freeze / Look innocent beside (Célimène's) treacheries."

RIGHT: "She looked carefully for the place where [Elizabeth] had entered the garden."

RIGHT: Flaubert says that "she [has] an excess of energy."

If your typewriter or word processor does not have keys for brackets, either draw the brackets in by hand, or type them in with slant-line key and the underscore key.

5. Indent long quotations. A *long quotation* is one that is more than three lines of poetry or four lines of prose. Usually, your introduction to a long quotation will be a complete sentence. Conclude your sentence, then, with a *colon* (not a comma or a period). Double-space from your text. Indent ten spaces from the left margin. *Do not* put indented quotations in quotation marks. Double-space the quote.

> EXAMPLE: The duke is chagrined that his own name and presence were not the sole sources of her joy:
>
> She had
>
> A heart—how shall I say?—too soon made glad,
> Too easily impressed; she like whate'er
> She looked on, and her looks went everywhere.
> Sir, 'twas all one! My favour at her breast,
> The dropping of the daylight in the West,
> The bough of cherries some officious fool
> Broke in the orchard for her, the white mule
> She rode with round the terrace—all and each
> Would draw from her alike the approving speech,
> Or blush, at least.

As in this example, keep the first words of a quoted poem exactly where they come in the line. For prose quotations, do not indicate paragraph indentations unless you are quoting more than one paragraph.

6. Punctuate quotations correctly.

a. Use *double quotation* marks ("") for quotations. For quotations within quotations, use double quotation marks for the main quote and single quotation marks (the apostrophe mark on the typewriter) for the inner quote.

> EXAMPLE: After his interview with Hester, Dimmesdale sinks into self-doubt: "'Have I then sold myself,' thought the minister, 'to the fiend whom, if men say true, this yellow-starched and velveted old hag has chosen for her prince and master!'"

b. Always put *periods and commas* inside quotation marks.

EXAMPLE: After performing her "duties to God," as she called them, she was ready for her "duty to man."

c. Always put *colons and semicolons* outside of quotation marks.

EXAMPLE: She had the "exquisite pleasure of art"; her husband had only envy and hatred.

d. Put *other marks of punctuation* (question marks, dashes, exclamation points) inside quotation marks when they are part of the quoted material, outside when they are not.

EXAMPLE: As one critic put it, "Could the Pearl Poet really be the author of *Sir Gawain and the Green Knight?*"

EXAMPLE: But can it be, as one critic claims, that "the Pearl Poet really [is] the author of *Sir Gawain and the Green Knight*"?

e. *When quoting a line of poetry or part of a line,* make the quotation part of your sentence. Use a slash mark, with a space before and after the mark, to indicate line divisions.

EXAMPLE: Hopkins describes God's grandeur as gathering "to a greatness, like the ooze of oil / crushed."

When quoting more than two or three lines of poetry, indent the quotation ten spaces from the left margin. For indented quotations of poetry, do not use slashes to indicate line divisions and do not enclose the quotation in quotation marks. Type the lines and words in exactly the same position as in the original.

Other Rules of Usage Related to Essays About Literature

Essays about literature obey the same rules of usage as other essays, but several rules deserve special mention.

1. <u>Tense</u>. Describe fictional events, whether in drama, poetry, or prose fiction, in the present tense.
2. <u>Auhors' names</u>. Use either the full name (Charles Dickens) or the last name (Dickens). Some exceptions are Lord Byron, Mrs. Browning, and Dr. Johnson.
3. <u>Titles</u>.

   a. Capitalize the first letter of all words in a title except articles, short prepositions, and conjunctions. And capitalize the first word of a title and the first word after a colon.

   EXAMPLE: "How I Won the World but Lost My Soul to the Devil's Wiles"

   EXAMPLE: "Exile's Return: A Narrative of Ideas"

   b. Use quotation marks when you give the titles of works included within larger works. This includes short stories, short poems, songs, chapter titles, articles in journals, magazines and newspapers, and unpublished works such as dissertations and master's theses.
   c. Underline the titles of works published independently, such as books, plays, long poems published as books, periodicals, pamphlets, novels, movies, works of art, works of music, and radio and television programs. An exception is sacred writings such as the Bible, books of the Bible, the Koran, and the Talmud.
   d. Do not underline or put in quotation marks the titles of your own essays.
   e. Many instructors prefer that your essay titles include full names of authors and works.

   WRONG: The Four Stages of Knowledge in Twain's *Huck Finn*

   RIGHT: The Four Stages of Knowledge in Mark Twain's *The Adventures of Huckleberry Finn*

   f. If your instructor approves, in the text of your essay you may use shortened titles for works you frequently cite: "Prufrock" for "The Love Song of J. Alfred Prufrock" or *Huck Finn* for *The Adventures of Huckleberry Finn*.

Format

As with rules of usage, the appearance of your essay also affects your argument. Your readers want an essay that is easy to read, pleasant to hold, and attractive to see. The more care you take with the appearance of the essay, the more competent your readers will think you are. Although your instructor may have specific preferences, the following are standard guidelines. Most of them come from the *MLA Handbook for Writers of Research Papers.*

1. Typewritten and handwritten essays. Some instructors may prefer that you type all your work, but usually you may either type or handwrite college essays. Whether you handwrite or type your essay, use only one side of the page. For *handwritten* essays, use black or blue ink (which, unlike pencil, will not smear or rub off). Use lined paper. Write on every other line if the lines are closely spaced. Above all, write legibly. If you *type* your essays, double-space. Use a good typewriter ribbon. Clean your type.
2. Paper. Use standard-size paper (8½-by 11-inch), not legal-pad size or notepad size. Use a sturdy weight of paper. Never use onionskin paper except for carbon copies. Avoid "erasable" paper; it does not take correction in ink well and it is sticky. In a warm place it is very unpleasant to handle. Don't hand in essays written on pages that have been ripped out of a spiral-bound notebook.
3. Pagination. Number *all* pages, beginning with the first page. Number pages consecutively, including pages for endnotes and works cited. Put the page numbers in the upper right-hand corner of each page. If you think a page might get misplaced, put your last name before each page number (with a space between the two).

   EXAMPLE: Caraway 16.

4. Margins. For typewritten essays, leave one-inch margins at top, bottom, and sides. This gives the page a "frame" and a place for the instructor's comments. For handwritten essays, leave margins at top, bottom, and left side.
5. First page. One inch from the top of the first page, on the left-hand side put your name, the instructor's name, the course title, and the date, each on a separate line. Double-space between the lines. After the last line (the date), double-space again and center your title. If

your title has more than one line, double-space between lines. Between the title and the first line of text, double-space twice.

Title pages for college essays, even research essays, are usually unnecessary, but if your instructor expects a title page, check with him or her for its content and form, or consult a handbook of usage.

6. Corrections. You may write corrections on final copies of essays if the corrections are few and fairly inconspicuous. In typed essays, erase incorrect letters and write or type in the correct letters. Draw a vertical line through an incorrect letter in a handwritten essay and write the correct letter just *above* the line. Separate run-together words with vertical lines (for example, made|a|mistake). To delete words, phrases, and clauses, draw a single horizontal line through them. Add words, phrases, and clauses by writing them in above the line. Use a caret ($\wedge$) to show where inserted material should go.

7. Putting the essay pages together. Use a paper clip to combine the pages of your essay unless your instructor specifies some other method.

8. Copies. Make a photocopy or carbon copy of your essay. If your instructor should lose your essay, you can immediately present him or her with the copy of your finished essay. Or if your instructor keeps your essay indefinitely, you will have the copy for your files. When you turn in the essay the first time, however, turn in the original, not the copy.

9. To fold or not to fold. Leave your essay unfolded unless your instructor specifies otherwise.

12

How to Take Essay Tests

SO FAR, THIS BOOK has dealt with essays written outside the classroom. Tests and examinations, however, are work that you do in class, usually within a given time. When your instructor tests you, he or she wants to know two things: how familiar you are with the course material (the literature, the instructor's lectures, the secondary material you may be required to read) and how creatively you can think about this material. Tests fall into two categories, factual and essay. Sometimes the instructor may include questions, or assignments, from both categories on the same test.

Factual tests ask you to account for, explain, and identify details about the course material. Essay tests ask you to state your ideas about literary works and to support those ideas with facts. Some essay tests call for short, one-paragraph essays; some call for long essays. But the same methods for writing out-of-class essays apply to test essays, short or long. Your test essays are arguments. They should have a thesis. They should try to convince an audience of the validity of that thesis. They should use sound logic and apt illustrations. Most of all, because of time limits, they need good organization. Perhaps the most important general consideration to keep in mind is that your grade will depend on how well you *perform* on a particular assignment, not simply on how much you know. You may know the material very well, but if you do not perform well, your grade will not reflect the abundance or quality of your knowledge. The following guidelines should help you perform well on essay tests.

GUIDELINES FOR TAKING AN ESSAY TEST

1. <u>Prepare thoroughly.</u>

    a. First, learn the facts of the material—of the work or works on which you are being tested. Know who the characters are, what they do and what happens to them, the specifics of setting, and so forth. When you are taking the test, you should know the details so well that they emerge from your memory almost automatically. This subliminal knowledge saves your creative energy for dealing with the interpretive problems the instructor gives you. If you have to dredge up facts from your memory slowly, you waste valuable test time.

    b. Systematically review the key problems or subjects relevant to the works, literary periods, or genres covered by the test. A good way to do this is to ask questions, as you would for finding essay topics. Here, however, you try to cover all the important questions. A knowledge of the elements of literature is especially useful for systematic questioning. How does the author handle setting? characterization? structure? theme? point of view? and so forth.

    c. Review class notes. But do so *along with* a review of the literary works. Reviewing your notes on the instructor's class comments will help you pinpoint important aspects of the works and should help you anticipate test questions. Remember, however, that memorizing class notes is no substitute for reviewing the works themselves. The two should be done together.

2. <u>Understand the assignment.</u> When you get the test, read all of the assignments carefully before you begin writing. If you do not understand some of them, ask the instructor to explain more fully. Sometimes instructors unintentionally write ambiguous assignments. You have a right to know exactly what you are supposed to do.

3. <u>Plan your answer.</u>

    a. Take a few minutes to make a short, topical outline. One advantage of making an outline is that it frees you while you write from worrying about being relevant or complete. Instead, you can devote your whole attention to a creative development of each main point. If you have fifty minutes to write an essay, ten minutes making an outline will be time well spent.

b. Exclude irrelevant topics.
c. Arrange the remaining topics in a logical order. It may be that descending order of importance will be the most practical order for your answer. That way, if you run out of time, you will still have covered your most important points.

4. <u>Address yourself to the assignment.</u> Anything irrelevant to the assignment wastes words and time.
5. <u>Give a direct response to the assignment.</u> One or two sentences somewhere in your answer should do the job. This way the instructor will know that you have kept the assignment in mind and that you have tried to deal with it. Your direct response to the assignment is the thesis of your essay and therefore usually should come near the beginning or end of your essay. Note the following example:

ASSIGNMENT: Huck tricks Jim into believing that he dreamed they were separated in the fog. But Jim finally sees the trick for what it is. What does Huck learn from Jim's reaction?

DIRECT RESPONSE: Huck learns that Jim has feelings and dignity just as white people do.

The complete answer, of course, would explain and illustrate this point fully, but the direct response connects the whole answer firmly to the assignment. Without a direct response, your answer may seem irrelevant.

6. <u>Write in a clear, simple, and correct style.</u> The limited time and the pressure of the occasion make some mechanical slips likely, but you should be able to avoid most of them. Be especially careful to avoid serious errors such as sentence fragments, comma splices, ambiguous pronoun references, and subject-verb disagreement. If your handwriting is normally difficult to read, take care to make it legible.
7. <u>Develop your answer thoroughly.</u>

a. Make claims that respond directly to the assignment. Often, these claims will serve as topic sentences for paragraphs.
b. Offer specific details from the works that support and illustrate your claims.
c. Represent the work or works adequately. The more thoroughly and aptly you relate the work to your claims (and thus to the assignment), the better your answer will be.

d. Your answer is an argument. You must back up your claims with evidence. Therefore, do not just tell your readers, show them.

8. Be creative. Some instructors want no more from you on a test than a perfect reproduction of what they have said in class. Studying for their tests, then, is simple. You just memorize what the instructor has said and paraphrase it on the test. The more perfect your reproduction is, the better your grade will be. But other instructors want more, and they design their tests to get more. They want *your* thinking, not just their own. They want your creativity. But how can you be creative on tests? The answer is—think for yourself! Here are some ways to do so.

a. Use the instructor's points but provide your own examples from the works. This shows the instructor that you are doing more than just memorizing lectures. It shows that you have thought through and applied the instructor's ideas on your own.

b. Find your own points. Although instructors try to cover the most important aspects of a work, limited class time makes it impossible for them to cover every aspect, even all the important ones. There are usually plenty of other points to be made. Study the work yourself and come up with your own points. Read what others have said about the work, and discover points that way. You should not neglect the points made by the instructor when you write test answers, but you can display your own thinking by making other points as well.

c. Address yourself to controversies inherent in works of literature and take a stand. Often the instructor will discuss such controversies in class. In addition, controversies about works become apparent when you read literary criticism on them. Understanding these controversies will sharpen your perception of the work. Showing your awareness of them and taking a stand on them will demonstrate your creative involvement with the work.

d. Disagree with the instructor. This is risky but certainly creative. If you are brave enough to do this, have plenty of facts and logic at hand. Be diplomatic. Some instructors invite disagreement and thus encourage a critical dialogue between themselves and their students.

e. Be detailed in your support and illustration of points. The more details you provide, the clearer your creative involvement becomes, especially if some of the details are those you have noticed on your own.

SAMPLE TEST ESSAYS

All of the following essays respond to the assignment below. The writers had about twenty minutes to write their essays.

ASSIGNMENT: Many stories contain objects that take on symbolic value. These objects represent ideas that emerge from the characters and events in the stories. Explain the possible symbolic importance of the rocking horse in D. H. Lawrence's "The Rocking-Horse Winner."

Essay 1

Paul seems desperately to want his mother to love him. He senses that somehow she disapproves of him, that he stands in her way of achieving happiness. He seeks solace in the rocking horse. She has told him that "luck" means having money, so he rides the horse to get money. He hopes that by giving his mother money, he can buy his way into her heart. But, unfortunately, when he gives her an enormous sum of money, she is even more unhappy than before. Paul returns to the rocking horse to get more money for her. He frantically rides the horse one last time. But although he wins the jackpot, he dies from overexcitement and exhaustion.

Analysis of Essay 1

This is a mediocre essay because it does not directly address the assignment. It describes the action of the story accurately. It is clearly written. Its organization is easy to follow. It seems to have the assignment vaguely in mind. But nowhere does it say what the rocking horse symbolizes. The instructor can guess what the writer has in mind, but he or she cannot know for sure. Possibly because of this lack of focus, the essay omits important details. The writer does not say, for example, how Paul uses the horse to win money. The instructor may wonder whether the writer has read the story carefully.

Essay 2

Paul's mother claims that she is "unlucky," and she explains to Paul that being unlucky means having no money. But the details of the story suggest that Paul's family does have money, because they live very well.

The family has the trappings of wealth—a nurse, a large house, comfortable furnishings, and a gardener. The mother, then, isn't really poor but is obsessed with money. Her children sense this obsession. Most sensitive of all is Paul, who hears voices saying, "There must be more money." As a result, Paul sets out to win his mother's love by being "lucky." His means of achieving luck and thus his mother's love is the rocking horse. He finds that by riding the horse hard enough, he can predict winners of horse races. The rocking horse, then, symbolizes the love his mother has withheld from him. He even experiences something like the ecstasy of love when riding the horse to a winner. But his plan fails when his gift of 5,000 pounds only makes his mother's greed greater. He then becomes so desperate for love that he rides the rocking horse to his death.

Analysis of Essay 2

This is a good essay. It not only accurately recounts details from the story but directly responds to the assignment, and it relates all the details cited from the story to that response. In other words, the details become "evidence." Because it deals directly with the assignment, it treats the story more specifically and thoroughly than does essay 1.

Essay 3

The rocking horse symbolizes many things in "The Rocking-Horse Winner." Paul's mother complains that she has no money, and she tells Paul that to be "lucky" is to have money. Paul is very impressed by what she says and decides to prove to her that he is lucky. He wants also to stop the voices in the house that incessantly demand more money. He feels that the rocking horse can take him where luck is. And, sure enough, when he rides the rocking horse and it takes him "there," he can predict the winners of horse races and make a great deal of money. So one thing the rocking horse symbolizes is luck, which, in turn, means money.

But the rocking horse also seems to represent a second idea. Paul's uncle says after Paul dies that he is better off being dead than living in a world where he had to ride a rocking horse to find a winner. The implication is that Paul was using the rocking horse to get what his mother never gave him: her love. So the rocking horse also symbolizes Paul's need for love and his parents' failure to give him affection.

Finally, the rocking horse symbolizes success. When Paul rides the rocking horse far enough, it brings him financial success. But this success is only ironic, for it never brings him the "success" he desperately wants—his mother's love—and in the end it brings him death. Lawrence seems to suggest that some kinds of success are better than others; it is better to be loved than to be rich.

Analysis of Essay 3

This is an excellent answer. Like essay 2, the essay directly responds to the assignment, and it plausibly and logically connects details of the story to its points. But it is more detailed and creative than essay 2. The writer makes a strong case for the complexity of the rocking horse as symbol and, by so doing, uncovers the multiple meanings and richness of the story. Whereas essay 2 sees only one possible meaning of the rocking horse, essay 3 sees three, all of which the writer explains convincingly.

13

Sample Essays About Literature

THIS CHAPTER CONTAINS six sample essays. Two are about fiction, two about poetry, and two about drama. All literary essays, of course, are different; problems are different and writers have different methods of solving them. These essays, then, are not models to be slavishly imitated. But they do embody the main points of this book: that essays about literature are arguments, that their topics contain implicit questions, that their theses are answers to these questions, that they should convincingly support their theses, and that they should speak to a general audience of interested readers.

The Future of Lotteries in Shirley Jackson's "The Lottery"

Shirley Jackson seems to want us to feel shocked and horrified at the conclusion of her chilling story "The Lottery." We see a group of human beings doing one of the worst deeds imaginable—cold-bloodedly murdering a defenseless person whom they all know and love. We wonder, Will the villagers ever stop doing such a terrible thing?

This is the central question of the essay.

The next sentence indicates the writer's *method* of answering the question.

The answer to this question seems to lie in the resolution of an important conflict—a conflict between the villagers' reluctance to participate in the lottery and their eagerness to participate.

Topic sentence. This paragraph deals with the first half of the conflict.

First reference to the primary source (page number in parentheses).

Their reluctance to participate is evident from the beginning. The men standing around waiting are subdued: "Their jokes were quiet and they smiled rather than laughed" (205). The children, when called, come "reluctantly, having to be called four or five times" (205). Once the black box is brought out, the villagers keep "their distance" from it (205). The fact that people have made no attempt to repair the old black box suggests that when the box wears out, perhaps they will let the custom die. The

A specific reference that is not a quotation but that needs a page citation.

ritual surrounding the lottery has also been neglected, so that only fragments are remembered and practiced (206). Once Mr. Summers begins the formal proceedings, Mrs. Dunbar is uneasy that her sixteen-year-old boy might even be thought eligible to stand in for his father (207). When Mr. Adams's name, the first name, is called, he and Mr. Summers grin at each other "humorlessly and nervously" (207).

Quotation introduced with a comma.

Mrs. Delacroix says to Mrs. Summers, "Seems like there's no time at all between lotteries any more" (207), as if the people find the lotteries unpleasant and put them out of mind as soon as they are over. She holds her breath as her husband goes forward to draw a name (208). We learn that there is some restiveness outside the village

Quotation introduced with a colon.

over lotteries: "over in the north village they're talking of giving up the lottery''; ''some places have already quit lotteries'' (208). The most obvious example of reluctance is Mrs. Hutchinson, who, as soon as her family is chosen, questions the fairness of the draw. She does not, it should be noted, question the fairness of lotteries, just of the particular draw: ''You didn't give him [her husband] time enough to take any paper he wanted. I saw you. It wasn't fair'' (209). Her reluctance to participate grows, of course, and reaches its apex at the very end, just before her death.

Throughout the village, then, people are generally reluctant to participate in the lottery. But their attitude toward the lottery is ambivalent, for they seem eager to participate as well. This eagerness emerges early in the story. Some of the children are apparently the most eager. They are on the scene first. Bobby Martin has ''already stuffed his pockets full of stones,'' and the other boys soon do likewise; some even make piles of stones (205). Ironically, at first Mrs. Hutchinson is the most eager adult. She rushes disheveled to the square and tells Mrs. Delacroix that she ''clean forgot what day it was'' until she noticed her children were gone. Then ''I remembered it was the twenty-seventh and came a-running'' (206). Mrs. Delacroix assures her that she is ''in time'' since ''they're still talking away up there'' (206). Once the drawing begins, Mrs. Dunbar tells her son to ''get ready to run tell Dad'' (208). Mrs. Delac. ix picks up the largest stone she can find and tells Mrs. Dunbar, ''Come on.   . Hurry up''

An interpolation (put in brackets).

Transition sentence.

Topic sentence. This paragraph deals with the second half of the conflict mentioned in the last sentence of the first paragraph.

(210). Mrs. Dunbar has stones in both hands and, "gasping for breath," claims that she "can't run at all"; she will have to catch up. The children already have stones, and someone gives little Davy Hutchinson a few. Old Man Warner says, "Come on, come on, everyone" as they all close in on Mrs. Hutchinson for the kill (211).

Topic sentence. The writer reminds readers of the essay's purpose by asking which side will win.

Which of these two conflicting attitudes toward the lottery will become dominant? The villagers' reluctance to participate and the discontinuance of lotteries elsewhere suggest that the villagers want to stop having lotteries. But there is a weakness in the villagers' reluctance to participate. Their reluctance is purely self-interested. No one objects to the lottery on behalf of someone else. Only the victim is critical of it. It is true that some people exhibit uneasiness when loved ones and children might be victims. Perhaps the villagers are moving toward the belief that everyone's life is good in itself and must not be wantonly destroyed. But not until then will they be able to abolish the lottery as a communal evil. In contrast, the villagers' eagerness to participate is very strong. The lottery, we learn, is irrational. Only Mr. Warner, the oldest of the villagers, has an inkling of why lotteries are held at all: "Lottery in June, corn be heavy soon" (208). No one else remembers why they have lotteries. What everyone does remember is how to kill. The murder, which for the reader is the most horrible part of the lottery, is for the villagers the most important part, the part they most enjoy. So eager are they to kill that they risk being chosen themselves just to be there.

As the story draws to a close, Shirley Jackson seems to offer her own opinion about how the conflict will be resolved. The two people leading the attack on Mrs. Hutchinson are Mr. Adams and Mrs. Graves (211). The name "Adams" suggests the first sinner, Adam. The rural setting and the opening paragraph suggest an idyllic place like the Garden of Eden. The name "Graves" alludes to a result of Adam's sin, Cain's murder of Abel. If Shirley Jackson intended these connections, the lottery may be symbolic of Original Sin, which, according to Christian dogma, is ineradicable and universal. All people——women, men, children, the youngest and the oldest, even Christians (Mrs. Delacroix's name means "of the cross")——are tainted by Adam's fall. Thus, the villagers may give up lotteries in the form they now take, but Jackson implies that "lotteries" will always exist in some form or other and that human beings will always do evil just as eagerly as they do in this story.

Topic sentence.

Throughout the essay, the writer builds toward a conclusion while at the same time revealing details of plot. In this way the writer lends suspense to the argument. This paragraph reveals the writer's thesis and is the climax of that suspense. It also brings in an "expert" to resolve the conflict. Since the writer's conclusions are clearly conjectural, she uses qualifying words such as "may," "if," "suggests," and "implies."

Thesis

Start a new page for the "Works Cited" section.

Work Cited

Jackson, Shirley. "The Lottery." Structure, Sound, and Sense. Ed. Laurence Perrine and Thomas R. Arp. 4th ed. New York: Harcourt, 1983. 204–11.

The Psychological Landscape of
Nathaniel Hawthorne's
"Young Goodman Brown"

The forest in Hawthorne's story
"Young Goodman Brown" seems to
represent sin. At least, the farther
Goodman Brown journeys into the forest,
the more he learns about the nature of
sin and the more he suspects its
presence in his village. But the forest
also represents something else: Brown's
psychological state during each stage
of his journey.

When Brown takes his guilty
leave of Faith ("What a wretch am I,
to leave her on such an errand!"
[75]), the forest has three main
characteristics. First, it is dark;
the road Brown has taken is "dreary"
and "darkened by all the gloomiest
trees of the forest" (75). Second, it
is hard to penetrate; the path is
"narrow" and nearly obstructed by
trees (75). Finally, it causes fear;
Brown feels that something threatening
"may be concealed by the innumerable
trunks and the thick boughs
overhead"—perhaps an Indian or "the
devil himself" (75). The forest here
represents Brown's recognition that
he is entering the domain of evil
(darkness is a traditional symbol of
evil), that he cannot predict what will
happen (he cannot see what lies ahead
on the path), and that the consequences
of his journey may be destructive (he
is afraid).

Once Brown has entered the forest,
the devil joins him and initiates him
into the knowledge of evil. One by one,
the devil implicates individuals whom

Thesis. The implicit question answered by this thesis is, What does the forest represent?

Transition sentence. It announces the first stage of Brown's journey.

Topic sentence. It announces what the forest represents during the first stage of Brown's journey.

Transition sentence. It announces the next stage of Brown's journey.

Topic sentence. It states what the forest represents.

Brown particularly reveres: his grandfather, his father, Goody Cloyse, the minister, and Deacon Gookin. During this part of the story, Brown is confused about what really is true. The forest represents this confusion by its obscurity. It is sunset when Brown enters the forest, but when the devil appears, it has become ''deep dusk'' (76), and when Goody Cloyse appears it is ''nightfall'' (78). Because of this increasing darkness, Brown cannot be quite sure of what he sees or hears. The devil's walking stick, for example, seems to turn into a snake, but this may be ''an ocular deception, assisted by the uncertain light'' (76). Brown thinks he hears the voices of Deacon Gookin and the minister, but ''owning doubtless to the depth of the gloom of that particular spot, neither the travellers nor their steeds were visible'' (81). And he seems to hear ''a confused and doubtful sound of voices,'' among whom are those of his fellow townspeople, ''both pious and ungodly'' (83), when the next minute ''he doubted whether he had heard aught but the murmur of the old forest, whispering without a wind'' (83).

Transition and topic sentence.

Throughout the essay, the organization of the writer's evidence is spatial. Plot details are given in the order in which they occur in the story, and thus the essay has a measure of suspense. It builds toward a climax. All of the evidence, however, directly relates to the writer's thesis. The essay does not merely give a plot summary for its own sake.

After the deacon and the minister leave, the forest represents Brown's next psychological state: disbelief. The part of the forest into which the deacon and the minister travel is ''the heathen wilderness'' where ''no church had ever been gathered or solitary Christian prayed'' (82). Brown is on the verge of taking this road—''he looked up to the sky, doubting whether there really was a heaven above him'' (82)—but resolves to go no farther.

Suddenly he suspects that Faith herself, the person he most reveres, may be engulfed by this forest of evil. He fancies that he hears her voice, and he finds a pink ribbon that might be hers. On this faint evidence, he commits himself irrevocably to the forest: "My Faith is gone," he cries, and rushes headlong into the interior (82).

Topic sentence.

Because of his disbelief Brown now enters into a state of despair and insanity that the forest mirrors perfectly:

A long blocked quotation, introduced by a colon, indented and double spaced.

> The road grew wilder and drearier and more faintly traced, and vanished at length, leaving him in the heart of the dark wilderness, still rushing onward with the instinct that guides mortal man to evil. The whole forest was peopled with frightful sounds—the creaking of the trees, the howling of wild beasts, and the yell of Indians; while sometimes the wind tolled like a distant church bell, and sometimes gave a broad roar around the traveller, as if all Nature were laughing him to scorn. But he was himself the chief horror of the scene, and shrank not from its other horrors. (84)

As he runs, Brown becomes a "demoniac" who brandishes his staff with "frenzied gestures" (84). His cries are in "unison" with the cry of the forest (85). It echoes his "horrid blasphemy" and is a "tempest' that drives him onward (84).

Transition and topic sentence. The climax of the essay coincides with the climax of the story.

.At the climax of his frenzy, Brown sees the next and final step in his journey: complete alienation. Before him is a weird scene that represents the rejection of all belief in the goodness of human beings: a pulpitlike rock surrounded by four pine trees whose tops are on fire. Surrounding the pulpit is a "congregation" of all the inhabitants, past and present, of his village. The devil emerges to complete Brown's initiation. The devil has Faith brought in, and he asks the couple to accept the existence of evil in everyone's soul: "Evil is the nature of mankind. Evil must be your only happiness. Welcome, again, my children, to the communion of your race" (88). But Brown balks at this final step. He tells Faith to "look up to Heaven, and resist the Wicked One" (89). Immediately the forest changes. His frenzy has disappeared and so has the wild blaze of the forest.

Transition sentence. It relates to the experience described in the preceding paragraph and also to the whole experience of Brown's journey.

Topic sentence. It summarizes the total effect of the journey on Brown's mental state.

The writer makes one final point about Brown's mental state and the forest, saying that even here, in the last stage of the journey, the forest represents Brown's attitude.

Hawthorne leaves us with a question of whether Brown's experience was a dream: "Had Goodman Brown fallen asleep in the forest and only dreamed a wild dream of a witch-meeting?" (90). But the question is probably irrelevant, since the effect on Brown is the same as if his experience had really happened. Brown is a changed man. He has, it seems, in fact taken the final step urged upon him by the devil. He sees all people as hypocrites who pretend to be good but secretly worship and follow the devil. He even shrinks "from the bosom of Faith," scowling and muttering when he sees her at prayer. He has become a cold man,

just as the forest when he awakens is
"chill and damp" and "besprinkled
. . . with the coldest dew" (89).

Work Cited

Hawthorne, Nathaniel. "Young Goodman
Brown." The Portable Hawthorne.
Ed. Malcolm Cowley. New York:
Viking, 1948.

Point of View in
Edwin Arlington Robinson's
"Richard Cory"

The writer uses a critic's opinion as a point of departure. One question the essay addresses is, Is Winters right in his interpretation of the poem?

Yvor Winters, a leading American critic, condemns Edwin Arlington Robinson's poem "Richard Cory" for containing "a superficially neat portrait of the elegant man of mystery" and for having a "very cheap surprise ending" (52). It is true that because Richard Cory fits the stereotype of "the man who has everything," his suicide at the end is surprising, even shocking. But the poet's handling of point of view makes the portrait of Richard Cory only apparently superficial and the ending only apparently "cheap."

Thesis.

Topic sentence. This sentence connects with the thesis statement above because it establishes the poem's point of view—a first-person narrative by a citizen of the town.

In the second line of the poem, we learn that the speaker is not Robinson himself (the omniscient narrator), but someone with a limited view of things. He is one of the "people" of the town (38). It is as if he has cornered a visitor on a sidewalk somewhere and is telling him about a fellow townsman whose suicide has puzzled and troubled him. He cannot understand it, so he talks about it. Throughout this speaker's narration, we learn a lot about him and his peers and how they regarded Richard Cory.

Topic sentence. With the point of view firmly established, the writer now states the attitude of the narrator.

Clearly they saw him as something special. The imagery of kings and nobility ("crown," "imperially slim" and "richer than a king") permeates their conception of Richard Cory. To them he had the bearing and trappings of royalty. He was a "gentleman," a word that suggests courtliness as well

Since the poem is quite short, line numbers are not necessary to document quotations.

as nobility. He had good taste ("he was always quietly arrayed"). He was wealthy. He had good breeding (he was "admirably schooled in every grace"). He "glittered when he walked," suggesting, perhaps, that he wore jewelry and walked with confidence. Because of this attitude, the speaker and his peers placed themselves in an almost feudal relationship to Cory. They saw themselves as "people on the pavement," as if they walked on the ground and Richard Cory somehow walked above them. Even if he did not literally walk above them, they saw him as "above" them socially. They seemed

The writer interprets a key word to support the essay's argument. Such interpretations are often necessary in analyzing poetry, since the weight of a poem's meaning often rests on the nuances of words.

to think it unusual that he was "human when he talked." The word "human" suggests several things. One is that the people saw Cory as somehow exempt from the problems and restrictions of being a human being (thus "human") but that when he talked, he stepped out of character. Another is that he, who was so much above them, could be kind, warm, and thoughtful (another meaning of "human"). They were so astonished by this latter quality that when he did such a simple and obvious thing as say "Good-morning," he "fluttered pulses."

Transition and topic sentence.

In the final stanza, the speaker brings out the most important differences between the people and Richard Cory. Most obvious is that he was rich and they were poor; they "went without the meat, and cursed the bread." But another difference is

Interpretation of a key word.

suggested by the word "light": "So on we worked, and waited for the light."

"Light" in this context most apparently means a time when things will be better, as in the expression "the light at the end of the tunnel." But another meaning of "light" is revelation. Light has traditionally symbolized knowledge and truth, and it may be that this is the meaning the speaker—or at least Robinson—has in mind. If so, another difference that the people saw between Richard Cory and themselves was that Cory had knowledge and understanding and they did not. After all, they had no time to pursue knowledge; they needed all their time just to survive. But Richard Cory did have the time. He was a man of leisure who had been "schooled." If anyone would have had the "light"—a right understanding of things—then Richard Cory would have been that person.

Although Robinson does not tell us why Richard Cory killed himself, he leaves several hints. One of these is the assumptions about Richard Cory held by the narrator and the "people." Cory may have been a victim of their attitude. The poem gives no evidence that he sought to be treated like a king or that he had pretensions to nobility. He seems, in fact, to have been democratic enough. Although rich, well-mannered, and tastefully dressed, he nonetheless came to town, spoke with kindness to the people, and greeted them as if they deserved his respect. Could he even have wanted their friendship? But the people s attitude may have isolated Richard Cory. Every time he came to town, they stared at

Transition and topic sentence.

The line reference is necessary here because there is no easy-to-find quotation, but rather a reference to an event in the poem. Without the line reference, readers might find it difficult to spot the specific place in the poem that the writer has in mind.

The writer concludes by returning to the central issue raised at the beginning of the essay, bringing the critic's interpretation back into the essay.

him as if he were a freak in a sideshow (lines 1–2). In their imagination, furthermore, they created an ideal of him that was probably false and, if taken seriously by Richard Cory, would have been very difficult to live up to. Cory did not, at least, have the "light" that the people thought he had. His suicide attests to that. He was, in short, as "human" as they; but, unlike them, he lacked the consolation of fellowship. Ironically, then, the people's very admiration of Richard Cory, which set him apart as more than human and isolated him from human companionship, may have been the cause of his death.

Had Robinson told Cory's story as an omniscient narrator, Winters' complaint about the poem would be justified. The poem would seem to be an attempt to shock us with a melodramatic and too-obvious irony. But Robinson has deepened the poem's meaning by having one of Cory's fellow townspeople tell his story. This presentation of Cory's character, his relationship to the townspeople, and his motives for suicide open the poem up to interpretation in a way that Winters does not acknowledge or explore.

Works Cited

Robinson, Edwin Arlington. Tilbury Town: Selected Poems of Edwin Arlington Robinson. New York: Macmillan, 1951. 38.

Winters, Yvor. Edwin Arlington Robinson. Norfolk: New Directions, 1946.

Tone in Emily Dickinson's
''Because I Could Not Stop for
Death''

Like the "Richard Cory"
essay, this essay uses
someone else's ideas
as a starting point.

Thesis.

Topic sentence. The wirter
keeps the opposite position
in view and represents it
fairly and fully.

This poem is a little longer
than "Richard Cory." Line
numbers, even for
quotations, may thus be
helpful. Use "line" for the
first citation, line numbers
only for subsequent
citations.

One of the questions raised in class about Emily Dickinson's ''Because I Could Not Stop for Death'' was whether or not its tone is optimistic. My feeling is that it is partly pessimistic and that Dickinson communicates that pessimism in the poem's imagery, its structure, its diction, and, in one crucial place, its rhythm.

The tone of the first half of the poem (the first three stanzas) seems optimistic. As was suggested in class, the speaker seems to feel a special and warm relationship to Death, perhaps even to the point of seeing Death as a groom. He comes in a carriage, "kindly" stops for her, rides with only her inside, and takes his time. She in turn seems to be putting away the things of childhood (her "labor" and "leisure") in response to his "Civility" (lines 7–8). She makes a symbolic journey through life with him, just as she would with a husband. Her carriage passes children at school (youth), "Fields of Gazing Grain" (maturity), and the "Setting Sun" (old age) (9–12). Her light, probably white, clothing (a gossamer gown and tulle scarf, mentioned in lines 15–16) further suggests the marriage relationship. Altogether, in the first three stanzas, the narrator seems to feel cozy in her relationship with Death. She feels that Death is a

friendly and kind companion. She
is optimistic about where Death is
taking her.

The tone shifts, however, with the
first line of the fourth stanza (the
beginning of the second half of the
poem): "Or rather--he passed Us--"
(13). Several signals suggest this
shift. One is the narrator's loss
of momentum. She is now acted upon.
The sun passes her. Since the sun
traditionally represents life and the
sunset death, I take this to mean that
she has now died. Another signal is the
change in rhythm. Up to this point, the
rhythm has been a very regular iambic
beat, almost a singsong. But the first
line in the fourth stanza completely
distorts that pattern, almost as if the
regular beating of the heart has been
jerkily disrupted. In the last part of
the line, Dickinson substitutes one
spondee (a foot with two accented
syllables) for the two iambic feet that
one would expect to be there. The
result is that the last three words,
which she isolates with dashes, all
have about the same stress: "Or
rather--He passed Us--." For me, the
effect is as if something has come

suddenly to a halt. No longer is she
certain of where she is going.

It seems logical to associate this
halt with the narrator's death, but I
associate it also with her change of
tone. Immediately after this line, she
feels chilly. The sun has gone down
(she is dead) and her clothes, which
formerly were appropriate as wedding
clothes, seem no longer adequate to

warm her. her gown is "only" gossamer,
her tippet "only" tulle (15–16). The
chill of death is further underscored
by her current place of residence, her
grave:

> We passed before a House that
> seemed
> A Swelling of the Ground—.
> (17–18)

Transition sentence.

In the final stanza, the narrator
tells us that although "Centuries"
have passed, it

> Feels shorter than the Day
> I first surmised the Horses Heads
> Were toward Eternity—. (22–24)

The writer continues to represent the opposition.

Several people in class concluded
that the tone of this final stanza is
optimistic because the narrator is in
"Eternity" and that time in an earthly

Topic sentence.

sense passes very quickly for her. But
this stanza may well have an ironic
twist that suggests a pessimistic tone.
At the end of the first stanza she says
that the carriage held herself, Death,
and "Immortality." But in the last

Interpretation of key words in the poem.

stanza she says that she "surmises"
the horses were headed "toward
Eternity." It seems possible that
the narrator sees a difference
between the concepts "Immortality"

Use of a reference work to bolster the argument.

and "Eternity." The Oxford English
Dictionary defines "immortal" as
meaning "deathless, undying," "living
for ever," and as "pertaining to
immortal beings or immortality."
Almost all the historical quotations

that follow these definitions in the OED associate "immortal" with life after death, particularly life in "heaven." The word "eternal," however, does not necessarily include this idea. Eternity is simply "infinite in past and future duration; without beginning or end." Eternity can exist even though one is dead. The word can also express weariness or disgust over something "that seems to be going on for ever." Thus "immortality" is a more optimistic concept than "eternity." Another nuance of the last stanza is provided by the word "surmised." The OED says that "surmise" means "to form a notion that the thing in question may be so, on slight grounds or without proof; to infer conjecturally." Thus the narrator does not know for certain where she is; she could (and can) only guess. The final stanza may be saying, then, that after her death, the narrator guessed ("surmised") that Death was taking her not to Immortality but only to Eternity. So traumatic was this discovery that although centuries have passed since then, they have not seemed as long as that day seemed.

By the end of the poem, we have learned from the narrator's tone that she is left in a bad way. Whereas before her death she thought that Death was kind, she is now cold and without adequate clothing. She is alone. And she is filled with doubt and uncertainty. She may in time gain "immortality," but it is also possible that she has only gained the bleak, cold wasteland of "Eternity."

Interpretation of another key word.

A summary of the writer's interpretation of the final stanza--put, appropriately, at the end of the paragraph.

The writer concludes by looking at the whole poem in light of the points established in the essay. The writer not only restates the thesis but offers an interpretation of the whole poem based on that thesis.

Works Cited

Dickinson, Emily. "Because I Could Not
Stop for Death." The Poems of
Emily Dickinson. Ed. Thomas H.
Johnson. 3 vols. Cambridge:
Belknap-Harvard UP, 1955. 2: 546.

"Eternal." The Oxford English
Dictionary. 1933.

"Immortal." OED. 1933.

"Surmise." OED. 1933.

Oedipus's Responsibility in Sophocles's
Oedipus Rex

The writer identifies a problem of interpretation in the play.

One of the most puzzling aspects of Sophocles's play Oedipus Rex is that Oedipus at the end accepts full responsibility for what he has done. After horribly maiming himself by gouging out his eyes, he proclaims to the Choragos:

> This punishment
> That I have laid upon myself is just.
> If I had eyes,
> I do not know how I could bear the sight
> Of my father, when I came to the house of Death,
> Or my mother: for I have sinned against them both
> So vilely that I could not make my peace
> By strangling my own life. (Exodos 140–47)

The method of documentation for classic verse plays is to identify the play's division, and its act, scene, and line numbers, when the play has them. The "Exodos" is the concluding section of the play.

The writer summarizes the meaning of the quote in his own words.

In other words, he declares himself a ''sinner'' and accepts full responsibility for what he has done by inflicting the worst punishment upon himself that he can imagine, even worse than death. Yet throughout the play it seems as if Oedipus was fated to do these things and actually did them in spite of his efforts to avoid doing them. How, then, can Oedipus justifiably accuse himself of wrongdoing? Why doesn't he simply excuse himself by saying that he had done his best but fate was against him, that he had no control over what happened and therefore cannot be

The writer raises a specific question about the play.

Thesis. The thesis is the writer's answer to the question.

blamed? The answer to this question, I believe, is that although Oedipus may have been fated to do these actions, he nonetheless does them on purpose. It may even be that the oracle's pronouncements are more like forecasts or conjectures than prophecies. Knowing somethinᵣ about Oedipus's temperament would enable us to predict at least some of the things he did.

Transition and topic sentence.

We learn a lot about Oedipus's temperament in the first part of the play. In the opening scenes he appears as a proud and intemperate man. He enters treating his subjects as inferiors (he calls them "children") whom he, the one with the "famous name," will save (Prologue 8). He anticipates the moment when he can play the hero, just as he did when he solved the riddle of the Sphinx. To this end, he has sent Creon to the Delphic Oracle to learn "what act or pledge of mine may save the city" (Prologue 74). When Creon returns to say that the murderer of Laios, the previous king, must be found, Oedipus places an extremely harsh edict against the murderer; he must be "driven from every house," not spoken to, and his life "consumed in evil and wretchedness" (1.20–31). Teiresias, the blind seer, calls attention to Oedipus's intemperate nature (1.109), and Oedipus suddenly and irrationally accuses Teiresias of planning Laios's murder:

> You planned it, you had it done, you all but
> Killed him with your own hands.
> (1.128–29)

He rails at Teiresias—"You sightless, witless, senseless, mad old man!" (1.153)—and boasts that he is a better exorcist than Teiresias. Oedipus compounds his rash behavior by accusing Creon of the murder as well. Creon quite reasonably requests that Oedipus should at least present evidence against him, but Oedipus ignores him and says, "It is your death I want" (2.106). Throughout the first part of the play, in short, Oedipus overreacts passionately, even violently, to events, especially when they challenge his pride or authority.

It is possible to see Oedipus overreacting in the same passionate and violent way when he kills his father. When he tells Iocasta why he left Corinth, there is at least a hint that he had been coddled, perhaps spoiled as a child. He was adopted (he learns later in the play) by the king and queen, a childless couple who did everything in their power to protect him from the truth about his origins. And he says that he "grew up chief among the men of Corinth" (2.248). After he left Corinth (to escape the oracle's prediction), he came upon King Laios traveling with five attendants. The groom forced Oedipus off the road at Laios's command. At this point Oedipus became very angry and in his "rage" struck the groom back. Laios then hit Oedipus with his "double goad." With his club, Oedipus knocked Laios out of the chariot and onto the ground (2.275–87). Up to this point, Oedipus had acted as any spoiled, egocentric, and spirited person might

The writer summarizes the meaning of the evidence presented in this rather long paragraph.

Transition and topic sentence.

The writer draws inferences from the sketchy evidence in the play, indicating the speculative quality of these inferences with phrases like "there is at least a hint."

act. He paid back in kind what he had received by way of insult. He might have behaved more humbly and temperately, but he at least gave back only slightly more than he had received. But what he did next was completely out of line with what had gone before. After saying that Laios "rolled on the ground," Oedipus says: "I killed him / I killed them all" (2.288). Assuming that Laios had not been killed by the blow that knocked him from the chariot, what Oedipus did was terrible. First he attacked an old man lying defenseless on the ground and killed him. Then he attacked all the rest, killing all he could (one, a "household servant," escaped). Because of Oedipus's pride—his sense of personal injury—he inflicted punishment on these people far in excess of what they deserved. And although Oedipus did not premeditatedly kill his father, he did so without just cause. He is guilty of murder. And he is close to doing the same thing at the beginning of the play, when he demands the death penalty for the innocent Creon.

Oedipus's high-handed way of meting out punishment brings up another flaw in his character, his inability to take the gods seriously. One might argue that had Oedipus taken the gods seriously, he would have remained in Corinth and awaited his fate humbly and courageously. Instead, he takes matters into his own hands, as if he could by his own actions escape the decrees of heaven. This feeling of independence, even defiance of the gods, is

Here, as elsewhere in the essay, the writer not only summarizes the meaning of the evidence presented in the paragraph, but also ties the evidence to the main thesis of the essay.

Transition and topic sentence.

illustrated even more clearly when
he and Iocasta gloat over having
apparently outmaneuvered the gods'
predictions. "Ah!" Oedipus says,

> Why should a man respect the
>   Pythian hearth, or
> Give heed to the birds that jangle
>   above his head?
> They prophesied that I should kill
>   Polybos,
> Kill my own father; but he is dead
>   and buried,
> And I am here--I never touched
>   him, never,
> Unless he died of grief for my
>   departure,
> And thus, in a sense, through me.
>   No. Polybos
> Has packed the oracles off with
>   him underground.
> They are empty words. (3.917-26)

Transition and topic
sentence.

The writer states an
alternative interpretation and
then argues against it. In
other words, he anticipates
the readers' potential
objections and questions.

The most important result of
Oedipus's refusal to take the gods
seriously is his marriage to Iocasta.
It is true that Oedipus would
understandably have had his guard down
when he came to Thebes. He thought he
was far from the land where his father
and mother lived. He came as a hero,
the savior of the city, and was invited
to be king. To seal his status as king,
he married the former queen. But after
all, Iocasta was old enough to be his
mother--obviously. Even if he still
thought that Merope was his mother, he
might have considered the spirit of the
oracle's pronouncement not just the
letter. It is possible to sleep with
one who is <u>like</u> one's mother, even if

that person is not literally so. In such a case, the sin of incest is no less a reality. Iocasta seems to recognize this possibility when she says, "How many men, in dreams, have lain with their mothers!" (3.68). Oedipus's relationship with Iocasta, furthermore, is warm and close. It is more than just a state marriage entered into merely to secure power. And it is clearly sexual, since he has produced at least four children over a long period of time. The result, then, may be that Oedipus has committed incest in his mind long before it becomes a public, legal fact. The fact that Iocasta is his real mother can be seen as purely an accident. The existence of his incest would have been equally real without it.

The conclusion summarizes the points made in the essay and reemphasizes the validity of the thesis.

What I have tried to show in this essay is that although on the surface Oedipus seems a victim of fate, actually he participates in that fate enough to be responsible for it. He is impetuous, proud, violent, unjust, and heedless of the gods. As such, he is to blame for killing his father and committing incest with his mother. He finally and justly recognizes his blame, accepts responsibility for it, and punishes himself.

Work Cited

Sophocles. Oedipus Rex. Trans. Dudley Fitts and Robert Fitzgerald. New York: Harcourt, 1949.

Célimène's Coquetry in Molière's
<u>The Misanthrope</u>

The writer raises specific
questions about the play.

The instructor may prefer
roman numerals for acts
here.

Thesis. The thesis is the
writer's answer to these
questions.

Transition and topic
sentence. Note the logic of
the writer's organization.
Before the essay can show
that Célimène uses coquetry
to defend herself, it must
first show that something
threatens her.

Célimène's coquetry is one of the
mainsprings of action in Molière's
play <u>The Misanthrope</u>. But why is she a
coquette? Does she keep men on a string
with her "most melting and receptive
manner" (II.22) only to flatter her
vanity? Is she merely the "beautiful
woman without kindness"? My view of
Célimène is much more sympathetic than
this. I see her as a potential victim
who must defend herself against a
predatory world with the only weapon at
her disposal, her coquetry.

That Célimène's world is
predatory and that she is vulnerable
seem clear by the time the play is
over. In the first place, her world is
one of constant struggle. Both she and
Alceste are involved in lawsuits before
the play begins, and Alceste becomes
involved in a second (with Oronte)
almost immediately. The causes of the
first two lawsuits remain unidentified,
but if they are anything like the cause
of the lawsuit with Oronte, they are
trivial. It seems as if one could end
up at law over almost anything, even
over words spoken in unguarded moments.
The struggle in Célimène's society,
however, is more than just legal.
People are constantly gossiping with
the sole intention of doing others
harm. Of all the gossips, the most
malicious is Arsinoé, who actually
comes to Célimène's house to engage in
a pitched battle of insult trading.
Célimène herself is daily confronted
with a struggle over her person and,

presumably, her fortune. Her coquetry may exacerbate this struggle, but the struggle would still exist without it. Her suitors vie with one another for first place in her attentions and bombard her with jealousy and possessiveness.

Céliméne's main need is for a protector. Normally, a family would shield a young woman from those who do her harm, particularly suitors who might turn out to be disastrous husbands. But Céliméne has no family to speak of. Her cousin Éliante is the only relative we see, and although Éliante is "honest," she has no power to help Céliméne. No one in her society, furthermore, is a fitting substitute for her parents, a fact that Céliméne seems to recognize. Her gossip session in act II with Acaste and Clitandre may not show her in the best light, but it at least shows that she is clearsighted about her social peers. She describes them as blunderers, bores, social climbers, egomaniacs, paranoid fantasizers, and pretentious fools. She sees that hypocrisy dominates her society, and we see from Alceste's portrait of the man suing him that such hypocrisy can be dangerous:

> Call him knave, liar, scoundrel,
>   and all the rest,
> Each head will nod, and no one
>   will protest. (I. 135–36)

Céliméne could provide herself with a protector by getting married. But her suitors are all a sorry lot.

[Left margin notes:]

Transition and topic sentence. The essay moves to the next logical step in the organization. It must now show that Céliméne has no means of protecting herself other than her coquetry. This paragraph eliminates one traditional means of protection: family.

Transition and topic sentence. This paragraph eliminates a second means of protection: marriage.

Note that even though it is a separate paragraph, it nonetheless continues to develop the major topic introduced in the above paragraph: Célimène's need for a protector.

Acaste, Clitandre, and Oronte are
vain and foppish. Her portraits of
each in the letters revealed in act V
accurately reflect what we see of them
in the rest of the play. This leaves
Alceste. Alceste has good grounds for
criticizing his society, and it may
be that because he does so he is
more admirable than his passive and
fatalistic friend, Philinte. Also, it
may be that Célimène "loves" Alceste.
At the end he is the only suitor to
whom she feels a need to confess:

> I've wronged you, I confess it;
>   and in my shame
> I'll make no effort to escape the
>   blame.
> The anger of those others I could
>   despise;
> My guilt toward you I sadly
>   recognize. (V.304–07)

She even offers to let him marry her
(V.347).

Topic sentences.

But Alceste would not be likely
to give Célimène the protection she
needs, a fact that she seems to sense.
He has many flaws. One flaw is a lack
of moderation. He takes extreme
positions on everything. In the face of
human error, he claims that "all are
corrupt" (I. 89). Rather than flatter
others, he would hang himself (I.28).
Rather than work out his differences
with society, he would remove to a
"wild, trackless place" where he could
"forget the human race" (V.327–29).
Rather than help Célimène, he would
force her to choose between him and
other human society; he would punish
her with total separation from other

people. A second flaw is inconsistency. Even though Alceste states his opinions in the strongest possible language, he cannot act upon them. He claims to love honesty, consistency, and plain dealing, yet he ignores Éliante, who loves him and who fits his ideal. Instead he pursues Célimène, who feigns indifference and seems the opposite of his ideal. He threatens to withdraw his attentions from Célimène, but cannot do so when the crisis comes. Even in trivial things he is inconsistent. In act II (II.iv,v) he says that he will go, but he stays.

Transition sentence. Although this paragraph develops the topic introduced in the preceding paragraph, the writer begins a new paragraph at a logical break in the line of thought in order to provide a visual rest for readers. Otherwise the paragraph would be uncomfortably long.

A third flaw is Alceste's lack of sound judgment. His attack on Oronte's poetry in act I, for example, seems groundless. He produces little evidence to support his opinions, and the poetry he offers as a model of good poetry seems little different from Oronte's. His accusation in act IV that Célimène has betrayed him is based on an unsigned, unaddressed letter that could have been written by someone else and not necessarily to a man. He even believes the person who gives him the letter, Arsinoé, although he knows her to be Célimène's bitterest rival. Overall, his jealousy of Célimène is a self-fulfilling prophecy. He is jealous before there is evidence of betrayal and thus helps to bring about that betrayal. A fourth flaw is his willful and irrational contradictoriness. Célimène says,

> He lives in deadly terror of
>   agreeing,
> 'Twould make him seem an ordinary
>   being.

> Indeed, he's so in love with
>   contradiction,
> He'll turn against his most
>   profound conviction
> And with a furious eloquence
>   deplore it,
> If only someone else is speaking
>   for it. (II.229–34)

Molière verifies the accuracy of this observation by having Philinte, the most moderate and reasonable man in the play, agree with it. A fifth flaw is Alceste's failure to love Célimène truly as a woman would want to be loved. The love he offers only adds to the strife that threatens her. She tells him,

> If all hearts beat according to
>   your measure,
> The dawn of love would be the end
>   of pleasure;
> And love would find its perfect
>   consummation
> In ecstasies of rage and
>   reprobation. (II.261–64)

Rather, Éliante adds, men should "love their ladies even for their flaws" (II.284).

Transition sentence.

The flaw that most seriously undermines Alceste's ability to protect Célimène is his lack of practicality. If she is to have a protector, she needs someone who can win—or avoid—the battles that inevitably occur in this society. Yet Alceste seems to enjoy alienating everyone in sight, even his good friends. Such behavior will make him a magnet for every contentious crackpot who has the time, money, and power to battle and possibly destroy him. Even worse, he does not care about winning these battles. He would willfully and quixotically lose them just to make a point. He refuses, for example, to contest the unfavorable verdict of his lawsuit, no matter what "cruel penalty it may bring" (V.61), just so it can serve

> As a great proof and signal demonstration
> Of the black wickedness of this generation. (V.65–66)

Transition and topic sentence. Having shown that Célimène has no traditional means of defense, the writer now can argue that she must defend herself with her coquetry.

The corruption of her society and the flaws of the one man she cares for leave Célimène little choice about how to conduct herself. She seems unable at this point in her life to give up society:

> What! I renounce the world at my age,
> And die of boredom in some hermitage? (V.334–35)

She is, after all, very young—only twenty—and not fully cognizant of what she wants. "Her heart's a stranger to its own emotion," Éliante says:

> Sometimes it thinks it loves, when no love's there;
> At other times it loves quite unaware. (IV.50–52)

Topic idea completed.

She has no family and no reliable friends to protect her. So her reaction, perhaps instinctual, is to gain power by the only weapon at her

disposal, her coquetry. With this power
she protects herself from those who
would do her harm. She tells Alceste,
for example, that she keeps Clitandre
in tow because he can help her in her
lawsuit (II.45–46), and she encourages
Acaste because he is a gossip who,
though "no great help," could do her
"harm" (II.100–01). Her encounter
with Arsinoé is a tribute to her
power. Arsinoé comes to Célimène
because Célimène has the power to
retain something that both want,
Alceste's devotion. And Célimène's
victory in this scene shows that she
has learned how to maintain her power
with other weapons approved by her
society, her tongue and her wit.
Another tribute to Célimène's power is
paid by Alceste late in the play:

> Yes, I could wish that you were
>   wretchedly poor,
> Unloved, uncherished, utterly
>   obscure;
> That fate had set you down upon
>   the earth
> Without possessions, rank, or
>   gentle birth;
> Then, by the offer of my heart, I
>   might
> Repair the great injustice of your
>   plight;
> I'd raise you from the dust and
>   proudly prove
> The purity and vastness of my
>   love. (IV. 294–301)

In effect, Alceste is admitting that
because Célimène's power is equal to
his, he cannot make her do what he
wants. And although he may regret this

state of affairs, we can see that Célimène's power gives her the option to choose and that her coquetry is a means of testing and thus weeding out undesirable suitors. Were she as weak as Alceste wishes, she would have no options. She would have to marry the first protector who came along, no matter how unsuitable.

Transition sentence. Rather than conclude by summarizing the points of the argument, the writer speculates about what will happen to Célimène in the future. But in order to do this, the writer reminds the reader of the thesis.

What will happen to Célimène in the future? Will her life turn out well or badly? The end of the play does not offer much hope for her. Alceste seems the same as he was at the beginning. And Célimène seems forced to follow the same course she followed up to now. Perhaps as she grows older she will become more mature and will help to stabilize the mercurial Alceste. But if Célimène cannot find a protector, she will ultimately have to discover some means of gaining power other than coquetry, for the strength of her coquetry comes from her beauty, and her beauty will decline as she grows older. Arsinoé is a graphic example of a woman who, because she has lost her youthful beauty, must grasp at power through hypocrisy, subterfuge, and slander. We can only hope that the youthful, charming, and beautiful Célimène will somehow avoid a similar fate.

Work Cited

Molière. The Misanthrope. Trans. Richard Wilbur. New York: Harcourt, 1955.

INDEX OF CONCEPTS AND TERMS

INDEX OF CRITICS, AUTHORS, AND WORKS

C 0
D 1
E 2
F 3
G 4
H 5
I 6
J 7
  8